Helping Counselors Grow Professionally

A CASEBOOK FOR
SCHOOL COUNSELORS,

William Evraiff

ASSOCIATE PROFESSOR OF
GUIDANCE AND COUNSELING
WAYNE STATE UNIVERSITY

Prentice-Hall, Inc., *Englewood Cliffs, New Jersey*

PRENTICE-HALL INTERNATIONAL, INC., *London*
PRENTICE-HALL OF AUSTRALIA, PTY., LTD., *Sydney*
PRENTICE-HALL OF CANADA, LTD., *Toronto*
PRENTICE-HALL FRANCE, S.A.R.L., *Paris*
PRENTICE-HALL OF JAPAN, INC., *Tokyo*
PRENTICE-HALL DE MEXICO, S.A. *Mexico City*

© 1963, by PRENTICE-HALL, INC., Englewood Cliffs, N.J.

Library of Congress Catalog Card No.: 63-16763

Printed in the United States of America   [C]

To Dr. Mac (H. B. McDaniel)
and
Edgar (Edgar G. Johnston)
who helped me grow professionally

IN RECENT YEARS the emphasis in studying counseling has shifted dramatically from techniques to process. There is a good deal of agreement that the heart of the counseling process is the relationship which develops between counselor and client. In this book the importance of the counseling relationship is not overlooked. Rather, an attempt has been made to help counselors benefit from learning how to review the practices which will improve the total relationship.

". . . new counselors, regardless of what school they feel they belong to, are still committing many questionable acts. It may be the security of the counselor in what he does that is under survey rather than the method he uses." (Dugald S. Arbuckle, *Guidance and Counseling in the Classroom.* Boston: Allyn and Bacon, Inc., 1957, p. 127.)

Preface

School counseling has come of age. The impetus of the National Defense Education Act of 1958 literally catapulted the role of the school counselor into national educational prominence. Before long it will be extremely difficult to find a junior or senior high school without someone on the staff with the title, "counselor."

In the past, counselors in junior and senior high schools have had to rely on interview material drawn primarily from college counseling centers or guidance clinics, neither of which deals with the kind of cases ordinarily handled by secondary school counselors. The essential purpose of this book is to provide school counselors with actual interview material covering the range of problems a school counselor might expect. The counselor's analysis of the entire process is included. Each complete case is commented on by three or four well known counselor educators. The readers can thus compare their own ideas, about each case and about how the counselor handled it, with the ideas of experts in the field. Each counselor educator reviewed his case independently.

The counselors who make the referrals to the laboratory are asked to send cases that they feel can be handled by school counselors who have the time and the training. Almost every referral to the laboratory has come about because, initially, the student has volunteered to come to the laboratory to discuss an educational or vocational problem. The majority of cases do not remain purely educational and vocational.

The interviews in this book were conducted by advanced graduate students who were majoring in guidance and counseling. In almost every instance these students were involved in their first supervised practicum experience in counseling. All but one had teaching experience; several were already functioning as counselors; the others were aspiring to become counselors.

The laboratory in which these interviews were held was located in a nursery school. (A new and modern counseling laboratory is now used by the Department of Guidance and Counseling, College of Education, Wayne State University.) The facilities consisted of a waiting room, a small counseling office, and an observation room. A one-way vision mirror and a tape recorder were used for each interview. Every student who came to the counseling laboratory was told that other counselors might observe at times, and that tape recordings would be made. Each student agreed to allow his case material to be used for educational purposes, with the understanding that all identifiable data would be removed from the records.

The laboratory arrangements bothered some boys and girls. In particular, a few appeared to be affected by the large mirror. There is no way of assessing the degree to which the laboratory environment affected the total counseling situation. It seems that the initial reactions of most clients to the laboratory milieu were soon overcome when the students worked with counselors who were able to demonstrate a genuine desire to help them.

Typescripts alone cannot capture the real tone of counseling interviews. Arrangements have been made so that *the tapes from which the typescripts were taken can be secured from the Visual Auditory Utilization Center at Wayne State University.* These tapes when combined with the typescripts and counselor educators' comments should be extremely valuable to high school counselors studying the counseling process both in counseling courses and as part of in-service case discussions. In particular they could provide an important *supplement* to a most important phase of the counselor's education, his practicum experience. "Counseling practicum is defined as actual supervised counseling experience. . . . Such experience includes all functions associated with handling actual counseling cases, e.g., counseling live students, consulting with parents, teachers, administrators, and other specialized pupil-personnel workers, recording interview notes, writing summary reports, staffing cases, listening to taped interviews, reacting to supervisory observations, participating in case conferences, as well as reacting to personal and supervisory evaluation."*

The author wishes to express his appreciation to Faith Bernstein, Alan Canty, John Peterson, Orian Worden, and Marguerite Zuber, the student counselors whose case material made this book possible. Other graduate students who contributed to the development of the book were Dr. Lloyd Meadow, Natividad Dimaya, Bob Dingman, Dr. Peter Fotiu, Leonard Sain, and Bill Wallace.

In the typing of the final manuscript the author is indebted to Mrs. Donna Mazzola, Mrs. Barbara Nichols, Mrs. Vivian Peyovich, and Miss Luann Prahl. Inevitably the final acknowledgment is to my wife, Lois, who allowed this book to intrude on our vacations as well as in our home.

WILLIAM EVRAIFF

---

* Edward C. Roeber, "Supervised Practice," from *Background Position Papers on Standards for Preparation of Secondary School Counselors* (Unpublished papers, presented at the 1962 convention of the American Personnel and Guidance Association, in Chicago), p. 24.

Table of Contents

I THE SCHOOL COUNSELOR

II FIVE COUNSELING CASES

III   ASSESSING COMPETENCY

I

THE
SCHOOL
COUNSELOR

A Review of the Counselor's Role

Before a school counselor deserves the title "counselor" and before a school system can validly claim that it has counselors, two questions must be answered affirmatively: Is the school counselor competent? Does the school situation permit him to function competently? This book may help counselors to answer the first question affirmatively. Neither in the universities nor in the field have we yet learned how to deal adequately with the second. Counselors continually complain: "What good does it do us to learn that real counseling cannot be done in five- and ten-minute, contrived interviews? What good does it do us to know that counseling takes time? We can't operate that way in our schools." Obviously, we must take a close look at the second question if we are to integrate competencies and functions effectively.

The Counselor's Major Functions

A lack of clarity about his functions is one of the major difficulties confronting the school counselor. Many secondary school administrators have embraced the concept of a guidance program with a vengeance.

2

Unfortunately, too many have tended to think of counseling as synonymous with guidance. Everything related to guidance becomes the jurisdiction and responsibility of the counselor. Since any activity which affects the well-being of a student can be construed as guidance, the counselor is soon loaded down with a gargantuan list of jobs. A familiar expression is, "they're important, and someone has to do them." Thus, a clarification of guidance functions and responsibilities is an essential first step in enabling counselors to do some effective counseling.

Understandably, a description of the counselor's major functions will not make sense for all school systems. In a conference on the procedures for identifying and guiding able students, the following outline was suggested as a basis for giving schools, students, and communities some idea of what to expect from their school counselor:

1. Utilization of effective techniques and tools in counseling to assist students: (a) in attaining realistic self-understanding; (b) in evaluating alternatives; (c) in formulating appropriate goals; (d) in making independent decisions about educational and vocational plans and personal adjustments.

2. Consultation with parents, school staff, and specialized personnel staff about student problems and plans. The staff includes teachers, health personnel, social workers, school psychological workers, attendance personnel, and others. The counselor seeks to interpret and to achieve better understanding of student differences and problems, to encourage and maintain optimal conditions for pupil growth and development, and to derive help from these sources in his close work with the students. The team approach that characterizes case-study conferences to aid individual students carries over into staff interrelationships about such aspects of the school program as curriculum, teaching methods, formation of class groups, scheduling, and administrative procedures.

3. Maintenance of liaison relationships with community agencies and referral services. The counselor must have supplementary and supportive welfare, therapeutic, and informational services to meet individual student needs.

4. Identification of individual talents and aptitudes. The counselor conducts the school program of testing and of identifying and appraising talent and organizes the comprehensive cumulative pupil record plan that is essential to such a program. He also is obligated to develop channels and means for full utilization and interpretation of the data, for the purpose of understanding students more fully and helping them gain better self-understanding.

5. Provision of informational services to include the full range of educational and occupational information. The counselor establishes means for utilizing informational material in occupational files, school libraries, and counseling offices; for individual student counseling; for occupational units taught by classroom teachers; and for group approaches designed to acquaint students with appropriate environmental information.

6. Research and service studies. The counselor has responsibility for contributing data that will provide a clearer description of the school popu-

lation being served, normative data for use in interpreting objective
test data, follow-up studies of former students, and evaluation of counseling services and techniques.
7. Job placement of students and counsel on post-high school education.
The counselor has key responsibility for assisting students to take intelligent steps after graduation from high school. In large schools, the actual
placement work may be performed by others in the guidance program,
but the counselor still holds key responsibility.[1]

Gilbert Wrenn, in his significant study of "The Counselor in a Changing World," made this recommendation:

That the professional job description of a school counselor specify that he
perform four major functions: (a) counsel with students; (b) consult with
teachers, administrators, and parents as they in turn deal with students;
(c) study the changing facts about the student population and interpret
what is found to school committees and administrators; (d) coordinate
counseling resources in school and between school and community. From
two-thirds to three-fourths of the counselor's time, in either elementary
or high school, should be committed to the first two of these functions.
Activities that do not fall into one of these four areas neither should
be expected nor encouraged as part of the counselor's regular working
schedule.[2]

These sources indicate that the counselor has essentially five roles:

1. He works with individual students.
2. He works with groups of students.
3. He works with teachers, administrators and other specialists.
4. He works with others in the community.
5. He collects and studies data.

The first role, working with individual students, involves counseling,
giving information, and placement. The second role, working with groups
of students, includes testing, counseling, and giving information to
groups. The third role, working with teachers, administrators and other
specialists is a matter of consultation and referral. In the fourth role,
working with others in the community, the counselor is a liaison between
the school and community. The fifth role, collecting and studying data,
refers to identifying and appraising student characteristics and conducting
research studies. These roles, while obviously not mutually exclusive, are
a starting point from which a counselor can evaluate what he should and
can do.

[1] *Identification and Guidance of Able Students,* Report of Conferences on Testing
and Counseling, American Association for the Advancement of Science, May, 1958,
pp. 22-23.
[2] Gilbert C. Wrenn, *The Counselor in a Changing World,* The Commission on
Guidance in American Schools, American Personnel and Guidance Association, Washington 9, D.C., 1962, p. 137.

No one can arbitrarily determine which of the roles, and which of the specific functions within them, are the most important. This depends entirely on the needs of the students in any particular community. There is general agreement, however, that in most schools the counselor's primary functions should be counseling students and consulting with teachers, parents, and others in the community. These happen to be the "human relations" functions which are the most time-consuming and the most difficult to handle. As a result, they are often neglected.

The functions that usually dominate are record-keeping, testing, and organizing special programs such as career days—in general, the impersonal activities rather than the personal ones. On the whole they tend to be guidance activities which are more closely related to the administrator's functions than to the counselor's.

The Realities of School Counseling

The counselor is limited in his ability to handle his primary functions by certain realities of the school situation. Some of these realities lie outside the counselor. They result from the perceptions and expectations that others in the school and community have of the counselor's role. Some expect the counselor to be a human computer who will automatically solve behavior and attendance problems, or omnipotently select the right courses, careers, and colleges for each student. In the clinic the counselor is free to allow a client to work through his own problems. In the school the counselor has a host of outside experts, each of whom may feel that the counselor must make the student move in predetermined directions, e.g., take college prep instead of commercial courses, get higher grades, or change his attitudes toward education or people.

The expectation that the counselor should be a hortatory expert has been advanced by Dr. James B. Conant in his recent studies of high schools. E. G. Williamson, in a speech at Kansas State College of Pittsburg, said:

> I heard Mr. Conant state his conception of what a high school counselor should do as a societal agent devoted to the conservation of human talent. I suppose he did not intend to be all-inclusive, but he did recently assert that counselors should "urge" academically able students to take the hard course and, presumably, go to college. Possibly Mr. Conant's prestige will ultimately result in this "urging" function's becoming the overriding expectation for the results of counseling.[3]

Conflicts frequently arise when the school counselor is called on to write recommendations for college admissions offices or for prospective

[3] Williamson, E. G., "A Critical Review of the High School Guidance Program Today," in *Current Status and Future Trends in Student Personnel*, Edited by E. G. Kennedy, Kansas State College of Pittsburg, Pittsburg, Kansas, July, 1961, p. 11.

employers. This aspect of the counselor's job places him in an untenable position. Can a counselor write an honest recommendation without violating the confidential nature of the counseling relationship? And, more important, if a student knows that his counselor may write a recommendation, how will this affect their relationship?

Few of the schools built prior to World War II contain adequate facilities for counseling. Most new schools accept the need for adequate counseling offices and provide private conference rooms for counseling and related purposes. There are still quite a few secondary schools where the counselor conducts his affairs in an open office, a classroom, a hallway, or even in former custodial closets with built-in claustrophobic effects.

The time factor is one of the major limitations the school counselors must cope with. Hemmed in by a staggering host of details, pulled in different directions by the varying expectations of the administrator, the teacher, the parent, the student, and the community, burdened with a counseling load of hundreds of students, it is no wonder that so many counselors feel themselves mired in their own version of educational quicksand. The attitude that counseling consists of telling, of "setting the student straight," is still widely held. Those who hold it can never realize that lack of time is a severe limitation to effective counseling.

Selection of school counselors has posed a real challenge to the development of competent counselors in the schools. The vast majority of counselors are secured from the ranks of classroom teachers, and their method of counseling probably depends closely on the degree to which their teaching was teacher- or student-centered. Those who approach their curriculum and teaching from a narrow, subject-matter, teacher-centered point of view cannot easily readjust their procedures when counseling. Administrators tend to select as counselors those teachers who, from their viewpoint, are good teachers. Obviously, if the administrator's conception of a good teacher is that of a dominant, authoritarian personality, the teacher selected will have difficulty operating within a framework acceptable to the professional counseling community.

Some have felt that it would be wise to select school counselors from outside the ranks of classroom teachers. They would give preference to the individual trained in counseling psychology. Those who advocate this procedure probably misunderstand the way teachers must function. They feel that teachers are either authoritarian in their approach or they must of necessity be viewed by their students as judgmental, authoritarian figures. The person holding this attitude is not aware that the teaching process exists on a continuum similar to that of counseling, and that many teachers are able to help their students grow just as counselors are. Perhaps the main problem in hiring a counselor from outside education is that frequently he cannot see the relationship between counseling and the educational process and school program. Thus, barriers are erected between teacher and counselor, and the possibility of an effective team approach is lost.

A way out of the morass of realities which limit the school counselor may lie in his ability and willingness to assess priorities, to decide which functions should come first. Judgments must be made based on professional competency. The school counselor must become professionally competent and assume a larger voice in determining his functions and procedures.

What Is School Counseling?

For a long time school counselors have been influenced by the counseling continuum point of view. They have learned about differences between the client-centered and clinical points of view. Rogers and Williamson have been variously extolled and excoriated. In more recent years psychoanalytic theory has demanded its share of attention from the future counselor.

In a sense, school counselors have developed their procedures from the personality theories underlying the process of psychotherapy. This is perfectly reasonable except that it sometimes leads to confusion by making school counseling synonymous with psychotherapy. Arbuckle has written:

> The Client-centered counselor may differ somewhat from his fellows in that he assumes that counseling and psychotherapy are synonymous. He does not particularly see one as being "deeper" than the other, and the extent to which one can work with disturbed individuals is not measured by whether one is called a counselor or a therapist, but by the more accurate measure of his competence. Nor can the Client-centered counselor see much point in trying to differentiate between counseling and psychotherapy on the basis that one deals primarily with the conscious, the other with the subconscious. There is no easy line of determination between these two, and problems of the so-called "normal" clients are involved with the subconscious just as are the problems of the so-called psychotic patient.[4]

Tyler has stated her ideas on the issue this way:

> Instead of using the term *counseling* as a rough synonym, perhaps in some instances even a euphemism, for *psychotherapy,* we shall make a clear distinction. The aim of therapy is generally considered to be personality *change* of some sort. Let us use *counseling* to refer to a helping process the aim of which is not to change the person but to enable him to utilize the resources he now has for coping with life. The outcome we would then expect from counseling is that the client do something, take some constructive action on his own behalf.[5]

[4] Dugald S. Arbuckle, *Pupil Personnel Services in American Schools* (Boston: Allyn and Bacon, Inc., 1962), p. 170.
[5] Leona E. Tyler, *The Work of the Counselor,* (New York: Appleton-Century-Crofts, Inc., (Second Edition) 1961), p. 12.

It appears to this writer that the argument as to whether or not counseling in the schools is psychotherapy may be primarily one of semantics.[6] It involves us in lengthy discussion over the concepts of psychotherapy.

In spite of the latter difficulty the author does feel that it is important for school counselors to perceive the limits of their role (although it is acknowledged that the expressed limitations are not always easily identified). School counseling does not concern itself with treating individuals who have deep emotional disturbances and who would require long-term help. It does not attempt to provide the professional help needed by individuals whose perceptions of themselves, or the world around them, are removed from reasonable reality.

Over twenty years ago Garrett expressed a point of view that still seems to make sense for school counselors:

> Very often it is unnecessary ever to bring to a client's clear consciousness truths about himself of which the interviewer has become fully aware. It is important to remember that an interviewer's goal is seldom, if ever, to achieve a complete personality change in the client. As a result of changes in little ways and of slight modifications of attitude, people often come to be able to make their own decisions and work out their most pressing problems without having become consciously aware of the many factors that the interviewer may see in the situation.[7]

Every school counselor ought to develop for himself a reasonably consistent frame of reference upon which to hang his counseling hat. The multiple roles required in a school setting almost necessitate an "eclectic" approach. The difficulty for the school counselor is to develop procedures which are not only functional but also defensible theoretically. Whatever procedures he adopts should be his way of answering these questions: "What is it that he attempts to accomplish when he works on an individual basis with students? Is he meeting the school's and the counselor's needs, or the student's needs?" It would seem appropriate then for every counselor to review periodically, and if need be, to revise his concept of counseling or his practices.

Definitions of counseling are very numerous. Some understanding of the differences in counseling definitions may be obtained by a look at those stated by well known counselor educators.

Williamson and Foley:

> Counseling has been defined as a face-to-face situation in which, by reason of training, skill or confidence vested in him by the other, one

---

[6] H. J. Eysenck, "The Effects of Psychotherapy" in *Handbook of Abnormal Psychology*. Basic Books, Inc., New York, 1961, pp. 697-725.

[7] Annette Garrett, *Interviewing, Its Principles and Methods* (New York: Family Service Association of America, 1942), p. 49.

person helps the second person to face, perceive, clarify, solve, and resolve adjustment problems. . . . [It] includes all efforts on the part of both counselor and client to face, clarify, and solve immediate problems.[8]

Rogers:

The process by which the structure of the self is relaxed in the safety of the relationship with the therapist, and previously denied experiences are perceived and then integrated into an altered self.[9]

Tyler:

The process through which individuals are enabled to make good choices and thus improve their relationships to the world and to their fellow men, as they set the pattern for their own unique patterns of development.[10]

McDaniel:

Counseling is a series of direct contacts with the individual aimed at offering him assistance in adjusting more effectively to himself and to his environment.[11]

Arbuckle:

An interaction between two people that enables the disturbed individual to come to the point where he can make choices and decisions that are rational and logical; It is an interaction that is basically verbal, and is emotional in nature; it is an interaction that enables the individual to accept and to use information and advice, and to accept an unchangeable environment without being overcome by it. The complexity of the emotional disturbance requiring counseling must be such that it can be modified only by the experiencing and the feeling on the part of the client, and this results from the interaction between the counselor and the client.[12]

Roeber, Smith, and Erickson:

Counseling has but one major aim: to assist each pupil to make more effective adjustments to the environment in which he lives. For a given individual, maintaining or recovering a proper degree of adjustment may require the solution of problems with which he is confronted, or it may require making a choice or decision of some other kind.[13]

[8] Williamson, E. G. and J. D. Foley, *Counseling and Discipline* (New York: McGraw-Hill Book Co., Inc., 1949), p. 192.

[9] Carl R. Rogers, "Client-Centered Psychotherapy," *Scientific American*, CLXXXVII (November, 1952), 70.

[10] Leona E. Tyler, *op. cit.*, p. 13.

[11] H. B. McDaniel, *Guidance in the Modern School* (New York: Dryden Press, Inc., 1956), p. 120.

[12] Dugald S. Arbuckle, *op. cit.*, p. 165.

[13] Edward C. Roeber, Glenn Smith and Clifford Erickson, *Organization and Administration of Guidance Services*, (New York: McGraw-Hill Book Co., Inc., Second Edition, 1955), p. 8.

Johnson, Stefflre, and Edelfelt:

> Counseling is a process in which a person with special competencies (1) assists other persons toward better understanding of themselves and their environment and (2) encourages them to assume responsibility for making decisions which will lead them to satisfactory adjustment or acceptable resolution of problems being considered.[14]

That so many writers feel the need to create their own definition indicates that the words we are using to convey our concepts are either not understood or not accepted. The variety of definitions also emphasizes the idea that in order for a definition to have meaning it should be an operational one growing out of the counselor's own unique counseling experiences. The definition that follows represents the author's present view of counseling.

> School counseling is an ongoing process in which:
> 1. a student is free to explore his feelings and what he perceives to be his problems;
> 2. the counselor provides an accepting, understanding, nonjudgmental climate;
> 3. a relationship is created which enables the student to become increasingly self-directive and capable of dealing with the world around him.

The core of the counseling process is the relationship, and the essential purpose of counseling is derived from the consequences of the relationship. It may be very important to help a student resolve what he perceives to be his immediate problems. However, the active intervention, or manipulator role, must be reduced and eventually eliminated if the student is to develop the ability to use his own inner resources. The situation is complicated when counselors (and many other adults) are unwilling to relinquish their roles as "influential" and "limit-setting" figures with adolescents. They may have too little faith in the capacity of individuals to become self-directive or they may have a personal need to keep the adolescents they are counseling dependent on them. The test of the lasting effectiveness of the counseling relationship is whether or not it enables an individual to improve his ability to cope with life's problems. To accomplish this the counselor must help the student develop greater respect for himself as a person, and more understanding and acceptance of himself in relationship to society. In this helping process the counselor must view counseling as helping students prepare for the world *they* will live in, not the one the counselor has known. As Margaret Mead has commented, "No one will live all his life in the world into which he was born, and no one will die in the world in which he worked in his maturity."[15]

---

[14] Walter Johnson, Buford Stefflre and Roy Edelfelt, *Pupil Personnel and Guidance Services*, (New York: McGraw-Hill Book Co., Inc., 1961), p. 294.

[15] Margaret Mead, "Thinking Ahead," *Harvard Business Review*, XXXVI, No. 6 (Nov.-Dec., 1958), pp. 164-170.

Wrenn believes it possible to predict the future directions in which counseling will move. He projects only the counselor's work with students. Excerpts from his list and descriptions of functions are as follows:

1. To Contribute to Student Self-Understanding and Self-Acceptance

. . . the stress is upon giving attention to counseling as a prevention rather than as a cure, counseling which stresses growth, self-determination, and self-responsibility. This is a remedy for the "man in the white coat" emphasis whereby the counselor takes over and attempts to cure the ills of the student. Counseling has become a way of assisting at different choice points in the life of the growing child and youth, assisting him in the art and science of making informed decisions.

2. To Be Sensitive to Cultural Changes Which Affect Student Self-Understanding

The counselor must be sensitive, not only to the student's characteristics, but to the characteristics of our culture which will mean most to the student. The dynamics of our society must be as meaningful to the counselor as the dynamics of the student.

3. To Help Students to Make Informed Educational and Vocational Choices

It is now believed that choices made regarding a vocation are an attempt upon the part of the individual to find a vocational environment which will contribute to the kind of person he wishes to become. . . .

The choices to be made are several, not one, hopefully each one in the sequence utilizing more information about the vocational world and about oneself. Perhaps one's vocational choice is never completed—any one choice is an event in a lifelong process. . . .

Youth must be prepared for the inevitability of rapid change and be assisted in developing enough flexibility to meet these changes. Vocational planning should include the very real possibility that the vocation chosen may change materially within the next ten years.

4. To Develop Group Learning Experiences for Students

Group experiences may be utilized by the counselor to orient the student in certain kinds of understandings that will make individual counseling more valuable to him. Beyond this, however, is the opportunity for the student to learn from other students and to see himself reflected in their reactions to him. This is a value not to be found by any other procedure. Leadership in such a group experience calls for an understanding of the dynamics of group interaction that makes it quite different from the supervision of homeroom situations or occupational information classes.

5. To Increase Student Self-Reliance

It becomes a task of assisting a student to learn how to make decisions, rather than the counselor's assuming responsibility for the decisions that must be made. . . .

. . . If the counselor's relationship to the student makes him more dependent, then the counselor has failed. There are times, of course, when the counselor must give support in a time of crisis even though no decision is made and no solution is found. It is more important, however, that the counselor assist the student to become an increasingly self-understanding and self-reliant individual, and that the counselor work to the same end with other adults who influence the student.

6. To Counsel Girls Realistically

Many changes are likely to take place within the next decade or two that will modify the role of women in our culture. . . .

If it is recalled that at least nine out of every ten women are likely to work outside the home during the course of their lives, and that six out of every ten women now working are now married, the relationship of vocational planning to marriage planning is a reality that must be accepted and given careful thought by the counselor. Increasingly, women are entering or re-entering the labor force in their mid-thirties, and many girls will work immediately after leaving school. Vocational planning is as essential for them as it is for boys.

7. To Accept and Encourage Diversity in Talents

It has always been the counselor's responsibility to be aware of individual differences, but the new awareness calls for recognition of an increasing variety of talents that are needed by society—intellectual, social, mechanical, and artistic. Counselors carry a heavier responsibility than ever for knowing how to identify many kinds of human talent and how to interpret their significance to the student possessing them. The counselor must himself be respectful of talents different from those he possesses if he is to deal fairly with them. There is a tendency to be threatened by that which someone else possesses and we do not possess. This is fatal in the counseling relationship.

Beyond this the counselor must be dedicated to the free choice of an individual to use his talents in ways that seem justifiable to him. After the counselor has contributed as much as he can to the student's self-understanding and to his awareness of the culture in which he lives, the moral justification of a student's use of his talents is his own, not the counselor's.[16]

BIBLIOGRAPHY

Arbuckle, Dugald S., *Pupil Personnel Services in American Schools.* Boston: Allyn and Bacon, Inc., 1962.

Garrett, Annette, *Interviewing, Its Principles and Methods.* New York: Family Service Association of America, 1942.

Identification and Guidance of Able Students, Report of Conferences on Testing and Counseling, American Association for the Advancement of Science, May, 1958.

Johnson, Walter and Buford Stefflre and Roy Edelfelt, *Pupil Personnel and Guidance Services.* New York: McGraw-Hill Book Co., Inc., 1961.

McDaniel, H. B., *Guidance in the Modern School.* New York: Dryden Press, Inc., 1956.

[16] Wrenn, *op. cit.,* Selections from pp. 127-133.

Roeber, Edward and Glenn Smith and Clifford Erickson, *Organization and Administration of Guidance Services.* New York: McGraw-Hill Book Co., Inc., Second Edition, 1955.

Rogers, Carl R., "Client-Centered Psychotherapy," *Scientific American,* CLXXXVII (November, 1952), 70.

Tyler, Leona E., *The Work of the Counselor,* New York: Appleton-Century-Crofts, Inc., Second Edition, 1961.

Williamson, E. G., "A Critical Review of the High School Guidance Program Today," in *Current Status and Future Trends in Student Personnel,* edited by E. G. Kennedy. Pittsburg, Kansas: Kansas State College, July, 1961.

Williamson, E. G. and J. D. Foley, *Counseling and Discipline.* New York: McGraw-Hill Book Co., Inc., 1949.

Wrenn, C. Gilbert, *The Counselor in a Changing World,* The Commission on Guidance in American Schools, American Personnel and Guidance Association, Washington 9, D.C., 1962.

II

FIVE
COUNSELING
CASES

The Case of Carl

Purpose of the Interviews

This case was referred to the laboratory by the high school counselor. The client had stated on his personal data sheet that his purposes in coming to the laboratory were to discuss his abilities and "where he would be best fitted." The school counselor's referral indicated that the client wanted to find out about himself—"a sort of self-evaluation," to use the words of the client.

Background Data on the Student

Client is an eighteen-year-old twelfth grade student at Washington Heights High School, Washington Heights, Michigan. He has no brothers or sisters and lives at home with his parents and an aunt. He was born in Birmington and has lived there since birth. Client's father is a retired worker. His mother does not work and his aunt is employed as a cook. Client is presently employed at a supermarket as a stock boy. He has held this part-time job since June, 1958. He earns approximately $25.00 per week.

Client was administered Form C of the Henmon-Nelson mental ability test in September, 1957 by his high school counselors and a score of 45, percentile rank of 37, and I.Q. of 98 was reported. In June of 1957, he was administered the Iowa Tests of Educational Development. His percentiles ranged from a low of 2 in Reading–Natural Sciences, to a high of 60 in Vocabulary. His composite score was at the twentieth percentile.

Client is a low academic achiever, and, from the test results received from his school, he is a low ability under-achiever. His high school grades have ranged from B work in World History (two semesters), Physical Education (one semester), and B (one semester) to D and failing work in his other subjects. English and mathematics are consistently his most difficult subjects, as reported on the high school transcript.

Client indicated that his first choice of occupation was lawyer. Law-enforcement work of some sort was his second choice, and radio and television work was his third choice. His parents would like him to enter the Army. He stated on his personal data sheet that he reads most of the popular men's magazines and that biographical books and articles are also of interest to him.

16

The Interviews

FIRST INTERVIEW	COUNSELOR'S COMMENTS

C1 Carl, I'm Mr. Williams.

S2 Glad to meet you, Mr. Williams.

C3 Nice to know you. I see you had a little trouble last week.

S4 Right.

C5 Mm-hmm. What have you been told about our counseling laboratory?

Probing. To determine the extent of client's knowledge about lab.

S6 I've been told that it is a guiding center where you explore the areas that are— or the job that might best suit you.

C7 Mm-hmm. Well, that's the general idea in part. Were you told anything else about what to expect down here?

S8 Well, nothing else, just more or less. It was, you see, before I got interested or heard about this. It was in my English class in school and we took a Kuder test. This was a measurement of your interest and abilities. And I figured I should know more about myself.

C9 Mm-hmm. I see, well, everything we discuss or talk about down here is confidential in that it is between you and me. And the interviews go for 45 minutes. The 45 minutes is the time that you may use in any way you wish as far as what you can talk about or in which direction the interview will go. The interviews are taped. We use the tape for my purposes in playing back so that I don't have to write or use my attention in other ways when we are talking. And in that way if we have other interviews I can study it to see in which way, or what it might mean. The room is set up so that there is a possibility of our being observed. Sometimes there are people observing the interviews and sometimes there are not people observing. The reason I point that out is that they are not observing you. They are people who are counselors or who are training to be counselors and they are studying techniques that we use in handling our cases. So with that in mind we wanted to tell you this so that you would know for sure what is going on down here.

S10   I see, I understand. (*Long pause*)

C11   Good. Now you mentioned that you had taken the Kuder in your English class.

> Restatement. Wanted to begin with specific information about past test experience. Probably shouldn't use "good." Don't think I would start this way again.

S12   Yes.

C13   I see. When did you take this?

S14   I think it was the second week of October. Yes, that's when it was. I'm sure.

C15   Have you had an interpretation?

S16   We did the interpretation ourselves.

C17   I see.

S18   And it was four fields: the arts, social work, mathematical, and outdoor and indoor work.

C19   Now, do you know the areas in which your profiles were highest?

S20   The profiles were highest in social services, the second was art, third one was literary, and the lowest one was mathematical.

C21   Well, since I know much less about you than you know about you, and these interests, if you'd care to tell me about yourself and your interests in terms of how you are interested in them, and activities which you might

> Probing with idea of structuring somewhat the roles of client and counselor. To give client opportunity to talk about himself.
> (Responses C11, C13, C15, C17, and C19 were for the benefit of the counselor. They

have engaged in, in which this interest might have shown itself.

served no useful purpose at this point in the interview because no use was made of the information secured by these responses. C21 would have been one better way of beginning the interview.)

S22 I work in a supermarket. I enjoy being around people, meeting people, and I've always liked to help people ever since I can remember. And I figured I would score a high score in social services. And, on my career's day thing, I put down law, law enforcement, and radio and TV. That's what I put down for career's day. Out of the three choices I picked for career's day, I'd rather be a lawyer. The second choice would be police enforcement, and the third would be radio and TV.

C23 These areas present an opportunity to be of help to other people.

Restatement with attempt at understanding included.

S24 Yes; and my father, long as I can remember, he's always been helping people, and he's also been a police officer himself. And, uh, he took the responsibility, I think when he was twenty-four, of bringing a family from the South and supporting it.

C25 So your feeling of wanting to help people is something that's been with you for some time.

Understanding. Yet not so much of S24 as of content of S22 and S24 together.

S26 Yes. And, uh, I worked in the school radio station. I put that down. And in my outside interests, I like to express myself in music and art which I'm taking this semester.

C27 You care to tell me about your musical activity?

S28 Well, I use music more or less as a form of expression. And, art the same way, just the idea of expressing, or pastime interest.

C29 Your feelings about a lot of things seem to come out best in music and art.

Understanding. I might have followed S26 with this.

S30 Yes.

C31 Do you play an instrument?   Probing. To determine type
                                                    of musical participation.

S32 Yes. I'm in the band and I've been
     playing flute in the band. I just began
     buckling down to art this semester. I'm
     having a little rough time with this
     water, but I think I can master it if I
     practice, more or less.

C33 So, an artistic interest which you men-   Summation of information
     tioned the Kuder did show seems to at   brought out up to this point.
     least agree with your activities in art.   The goal of this statement
                                                    was to have client begin
                                                    relating his abstract interests
                                                    to concrete examples of ap-
                                                    plication of the interests.

S34 Yes.

C35 Art and music both being in the artistic   Clarification of intent of C33.
     area.

S36 Yes. So I think the only thing that might
     handicap me more or less might be my
     low rating in Math and English. I've
     never "cottoned" to those subjects very
     well.

C37 Mm-hmm, mm-hmm.   Understanding in that at this
                                                    point client began to relax
                                                    and I felt he was aware of
                                                    the relationship and would
                                                    talk.

S38 I feel . . . I have a teacher now, Mr.
     S., at the high school. He's trying to
     build up my interest, but, more or less,
     I just don't seem to grasp on to it.
     When we are in class, I can get the
     theories, more or less, but when I go
     home I forget about them. And Eng-
     lish, my mother is always getting down
     on me about writing and I never re-
     member all the right things or right
     formulas to put out for English. So, I
     haven't scored very high scores in those
     particular areas.

C39 Math and English are courses in which
     you have trouble.

S40 Yes. But, I'd like to go to college myself and to take law, and you have to
have mathematics to get it. To at least
get in there and stay. And you have to
have, a, to be a lawyer, you have to
have a very good knowledge of English.

C41 So, you have mixed feelings about your
abilities in these areas.

S42 Yes. I feel that I'm not too sure of myself in those other fields. Like History,
English, no, not English, well the only
part I like about English is literature.
Well, subjects like sociology, we had
that and I did my best marks in that.
And I really felt a little bit of interest
in those classes.

C43 So you get marks in classes where your
interest is high.

Clarifying, although it is
meaningless because type of
mark not specified, i.e., high
or low.

S44 Yes. That tends to be the case. Like in
history I always scored B's until one
teacher, she just wouldn't let me have
B's, she just gave me a C. But the work
I was doing was B work. And she told
us that to get a B or an A in her class,
we had to read about 30 pages a week of
outside books. Going to work and getting my other homework done, well
that would take too long a time. But on
my tests, I scored on the B average.

C45 You scored high enough on the tests to
get a B.

S46 Yes.

C47 But you couldn't do the other requirements because of outside activities.

Restatement and understanding.

S48 Right. (Pause) And uh, I like tennis as
an outside sport. Oh, I like to try skiing
and skating. I never "cottoned" to too
much sports. I like to watch football.
(Pause) And I guess that's about it.

C49 So, it seems that your feelings are pretty
clear about what your interests are and
uh, what your abilities are to do your

Summation, understanding.
Last part, interpretative.
Leading into what lab can
offer him.

work in. And where your interest is high, you've done work that is acceptable, C and B, certainly acceptable. Perhaps finding out more about you and your abilities would be something you'd want to pursue further.

S50 Yes. I'd like to know definitely what I can do and what I can't do. I feel that it would help me a lot in that it would give me confidence that I could do it.

C51 Mm-hmm. And, some more concrete way of knowing is really what you're interested in.

> Understanding, although more interpretative in that he did not mention a method of finding out what he can or cannot do.

S52 Yes.

C53 Well, part of the experience down here includes the areas of testing that we will tell you about. And, the testing is only just part of the things a person would get out of coming down here. This would be something they would decide, in terms of in what areas they wanted to go and find out more about themselves. I'll show you our guide that we have made up in terms of what tests we have and I'll tell you a little bit about them. And then on the basis of that information you can make a selection, or we can at least find out. (*Pause; counselor gets test guide from shelf*). Now, we'll just move this over here a little bit [mike], so it won't bother us any. This is a test selection guide of the tests we have here in our laboratory. We have tests of aptitude. These are tests of scholastic aptitude and the ability to do school work is indicated in some way by the tests in this area. And then we have tests of interests. Interest inventories as they are called here. And next we have a kind of check list area of testing. Under

> Informational.

> I should have said "you" rather than "they."

that we have two tests a person could take to find out more about personal problems. Not necessarily find out more about them, but at least get an indication as to what might be personal problems they see on these check lists that they might want to talk about. Then the last area is reading. We have a test of reading to give you an idea of how your reading ability would compare with other students' reading abilities. So these are the four big areas. Tests of aptitude, interests, and the check lists, and the reading.

S54 Well, where shall we start?

C55 Well, it would be left up to you in terms of what you would like to find out about yourself.

Placing responsibility in the student's hands.

S56 The more I know about myself, the better for me.

C57 Well, now the uh, did you understand my mentioning these big areas? Like the aptitude test measures your ability to do school work, or the potential to do school work.

S58 Yes.

C59 And, you mentioned you had taken the Kuder. This is one we have here.

S60 Yes, I've taken that one.

C61 All right. Now I'll tell you about these two aptitude tests. This one here is a general aptitude test [CTMM]. And it really is a scholastic aptitude measurement. In other words, this one test would give us an idea of how much ability you would have to, uh, to compete with other boys and girls of your same educational level in doing school work in many areas such as math, verbal reasoning and so forth. That's this one here. This one [DAT] would be seven sub-headings under here and is one that gives somewhat similar in-

Informational.

formation to this one but only it is a little more specific. You see, each area is itemized here.

S62   Like the three R's. Reading, writing and arithmetic.

C63   Yes, that's kind of the idea.   Reassuring.

S64   Uh, when do we start testing?

C65   Well now the testing schedule can be   Informational.
worked this way, Carl. We can use our 45 minutes to talk and get an idea of what all this means to you in terms of what the results are, or we can use part of the 45 minutes for testing and use what's left for interview. Or we can have you come down at another time than the interview time and take the test. Say, earlier than an interview appointment.

S66   Well, I have Mondays and Wednesdays off from work.

C67   I see.

S68   I think I'd rather have 45 minutes of interview or 45 minutes of testing.

C69   I see. Well then, we could do it that   Informational.
way. On Monday, our lab is not open over here. We are only open Tuesday, Wednesday, Thursday and Friday in the afternoon from 4:00 to 6:00. And on Saturdays from 9:00 to 12:00. Of course this is something we can work out in terms of what our other schedule is for the other part of the week. Well, if that's the way you would like to do it, it is fine with me.

S70   Yes, this is the way I would like to do it.

C71   Fine. Well then we can arrange for a   Informational. I should not
test, not this Wednesday, because of   have used *fine*.
Thanksgiving week coming up and you will be out of school. But when we do arrange for you to come in, we'll have you come in for a test say on a Wednesday. And we do have another place for you to take it. Then we could schedule

our interview time which would be different from that and we could talk.

S72 Okay. That's quite all right with me.

C73 Fine. Well, this gives us an idea here of what our testing part of the experience is. Now, this is not all of it, in terms of what we hope you would get out of it, or what you would think you want to get out of it would be what this means, and when we put it together with how you feel about these areas that you are interested in and that you'd like to pursue. So that's the idea there. Gives us a little more concrete idea about it. I'll put your name on this. If you'd like to ask more questions about any of these on here so that you could decide on one that you might like to start off with I could tell you about any that you would have any questions about.

Continued informational, but too redundant and elliptical in phrasing. Use of fine *not necessary.*

S74 Well, I'd like to start off with a general over-all picture of this one.

C75 Which one?

S76 This one, the California—

C77 The California Test of Mental Maturity?

S78 Yes.

C79 All right. This test is one that takes 52 minutes.

S80 52 minutes?

C81 Yes, for the whole thing—so you could plan on an hour.

S82 An hour?

C83 Yes. And in all probability I would be the one who would administer it to you and then in our next interview I would have the results if you wanted to talk about them.

Informational.

S84 OK.

C85 OK, fine. I'll put the date on here. This will always be available and we can bring it out so that if any others on

Informational. No comment was necessary here. Fine *unnecessary.*

there you might think you'd be interested in . . .

S86 I feel that actually, I need to advance quickly. That's what I feel. I need to advance myself as quickly as possible.

C87 You feel that you want to get ahead.

S88 Yes. I figured that law would be the best field that I could advance quickly in, and do the things that I like to do.

C89 And that's helping people.

S90 Helping people, more or less. And that's about all.

C91 Have you talked over your interests with anyone else?

S92 Well, my father and I, we don't talk very much about it, but I told him I'd like to be a cop. And he told me don't be one. So, in my English class, I put down law enforcement and I had a couple of letters I've—I have to write to the Federal Bureau of Investigation, and I have to get those off and into the mails soon. I asked what were the requirements and advancement and what would you have to do.

C93 Mm-hmm. (*Pause*) You haven't gotten those off yet?

Probing. Not sure why though.

S94 No, I am going to get them off this weekend. As soon as I possibly can. Oh yes, I wrote the same one to the customs service. So, that's about it.

C95 You talked with your dad about being a policeman and he feels—

Attempted understanding through restating S92, but S96 reveals my lack of success.

S96 No. But, I don't see anything wrong with being a policeman. But he says they are underpaid. The salary that they get isn't sufficient for the risks that they take. So I agreed. So, he suggested that I should take up law, law as a career maybe. Because it's almost like law enforcement. Only thing you have to do is assemble the facts and present them. And that's about it.

C97   So, law enforcement is your first choice and if this works out not to be the case, then a career as a lawyer would be it.

S98   Yes, that would be about the best bet for me. Ah, I was, I wanted to go . . . I was last Saturday, last Saturday was the 14th. They had a teen-town, where they had people from the various fields. And, I think they had Judge Smith as a guest speaker. I wanted to go there.

C99   Mm-hmm. Were you able to make it?

S100 No. I had to work all day Saturday. And I couldn't get off. A friend of mine, she lives not too far from here, it was her sorority that was giving it. She told me about it. I wanted to go but I couldn't.

C101 Your interests seem to be very strong in the whole area of law, law enforcement, and helping people who are in trouble in this way.

Restatement and understanding.

S102 Right.

C103 Do you know anything about other jobs that are in this whole big area of law enforcement and law?

Probing. Here I intentionally wanted to structure. Wanted him to expand his thinking.

S104 Yes. They have police cadets and they have law librarians for large companies to keep the books. There is the general type. There is, uh, I think the highest degree a person can attain is a juris doctor, or doctorate and there is more or less criminal lawyers, and common pleas lawyers. That's about all that I know about other fields. But there are probably a lot more that branches off into it.

C105 Perhaps there are a lot more jobs that are still connected with it that you don't know about right now.

Suggestive. He gives me a yes and then moves on.

S106 Yes. So that's about it. I never gave radio and TV too much interest. Oh, at one time I did, but, it wasn't too much. Just, more or less, radio and TV, everybody was talking about it. I wanted to see what it was like. Television has a lot of possibilities if you have the technical know-how. However, I'd rather be on a technical crew than to be an actor or have a program of my own.

C107 You'd rather work behind the camera.   I wanted clarification.

S108 Yes.

C109 In terms of keeping the show going.   Interpretative.

S110 Yes, and, I've explored all those three careers that I think I want. I'm not too sure. And my outside interests. No, wait a minute. I'll get to, get right to the point. I can never find nobody at my level to help me. You know. Whenever I need friends, or friends who know the books or like the same things I like, I can't find them. And, when I have homework and need help, my friends, they don't have the same interests as I do. So, it's pretty hard to find a person who has the same, uh, well, the same type of feeling more or less, or the same interest in the same thing. Where he can help me and I can help him. So, that's been my biggest problem, trying to find someone who I think is at my level, or where I can communicate with ease.

C111 Mm-hmm. The lack of having someone to share things with is a real problem.

S112 Yes. My mother and father, they don't seem to take very much interest. But, uh, they do take interest, but, uh, they didn't go very far in education. But anything like talking politics, anything on that, they're great on that. But, when I need help pertaining to school work, anything like that, I can't get any help. And, uh, my sister, more or less, she's a step-sister. Uh, she's out in

California, and that's too far. And, uh, I've got one good friend named Tom Rice, and, uh, he's always gone so it's very hard to find someone to, uh, communicate with. But, when we are together, we do have fun.

C113   Most of the time, it's being alone with these interests and feelings about them.

Understanding. Interpretative in that he does not clearly state in S112 that he is *alone*.

S114   Yes. And, uh, I've noticed a couple of things about myself and interests. I can pick up an interest real quickly and I can drop it real quickly. Like homework, I tend to more or less not buckle down to it like I should. Like uh, in my social studies or literature classes that I had this summer the work was appealing and I did my best grades in them, but my study habits are poor, very poor, because, I think, more or less, it's, uh, not finding the right people to help me with the work. Where, you know, I can share and have the same interests. And I think in order to go to college, I must find some friends of my own level and sort of discipline myself to the same level. And, take to the homework.

C115   You feel that if you were studying with someone of like interest your work would improve.

S116   Yes. I have another good friend, Herman Lang. He's, uh, he has a aptitude of education but, it's just a matter of distance that's so far between us. Uh, when we go out together we also have fun. So, it's awfully hard to find someone within the immediate vicinity where I live at that can help me or I can help them or with the same interests.

C117   It's just hard to do the work alone, by yourself.

S118   Yes. So I guess I'll have to keep on

looking and trying to discipline myself. I haven't actually started yet. I
always keep on saying that I intend to,
but, eventually I'll have to get around
if I want to really pursue these careers.
So I think these tests will see if the
interest is strong enough to pursue, and
if the job I want is the job made for
me. And I feel if the general picture of
the results of the tests will be enough
for me to really buckle down and get
behind it.

C119   If the picture that's presented by the   Summation. Understanding.
       test shows that this is what you're best   Interpretative in that he did
       suited for then you feel you can exert   not mention succeeding, I
                                                     did.
       the amount of discipline needed to
       succeed at it.

S120   Yes. And, uh, other subjects that I
       really didn't like, I would cut the
       classes or not go in because I felt, more
       or less, it was just a waste of time. And
       they have this system where you have
       to go to your classes or you'll get kicked
       out of school. I think that should be
       done away with entirely. I think they
       should have a place where a person who
       is stuck with a class can rechannel his
       interests or something like that. Be-
       cause, I think it isn't necessary to kick
       a person out of class because of this
       one class that he, uh, doesn't like or
       that he can't get along very well in.
       Although, getting back to one class,
       in math, I was having trouble and my
       counselor came up with a special math
       class. It was conducted by Mr. Taylor,
       and first day I took a math ability test
       and second day, when I went back
       there to get the results, they told me
       it was for 9th grade only. So, all
       through going to school, I've never
       passed a math class, so far. That's why
       I've always disliked math. So, but I
       thought I could really get ahead with

that special attention. It was a small class and I felt I could have learned more and the interest would have been stronger toward that particular little field in math. But, it was for 9th grade only. And, last week I took a test, it was a math test. If you don't pass this test—you have to have math to graduate —if you don't pass they will put you in a class called B and I math but I don't think this has the advantages that this small class had to offer. So, I know I scored very lowly on the test because I didn't have a good interest in it at all.

C121   The special attention in the smaller class is something you feel will help you quite a bit.

Understanding.

S122   Yes. Not only in math. A lot of other people have to suffer and be stuck into the class when actually it's a waste of time to be stuck in a class where your interest are very low and the class is very large. The teacher wants to help you but, you can see the other kids progressing at a A and B rate and you just feel discouraged and you just quit. So, I feel that our school system should have this special math class at the various grades for people who have a deficiency in math.

C123   In all grades. Not just the 9th grade.

Interpretative, yet probing for clarification as to the extent he felt classes should be offered.

S124   In all grades, not at the 9th grade, but at all grades. I thought me and the teacher were really going to make progress but they moved me into a study hall so, rather than to be sitting idle all the time, I took drawing, no Commercial Art. And, uh, another class that I really enjoy this semester is contemporary problems. There's no textbook, because the problems of the world change so rapidly that we use *Time* magazine. And I like that class an awful lot. I think I got a C in that one, but, uh, I'm planning to exert more interest into that class. *(Pause)*

C125   Something you're really interested in, you know you can do better.

                            Understanding.

S126   Yes. I know I can get a better mark in there. And, uh, I can't, uh, getting back to my study habits, I can't blame my friends. Most people say well, it's my friends, uh, when I start to get my homework done, they say my friends call me up and we just have to go out somewhere. But it isn't that. I think if I could get with a special group, people with the same interests, I could excel and meet the requirements to pursue my interests.

C127   So, it's not some other fault, someone else's keeping you from your—

                            Understanding attempt that isn't successful.

S128   No, it's not that. It's myself. Actually, I can look at TV, although I don't go for it, but, it seems a nice diversion. And I can always tell myself I can get it later. But, on the days off, I couldn't make up on my homework, because I get off from work about 9:00. They say 9:00 at the job but when I get off it's more or less 9:30 or 9:45. So, when I get home I eat and mess around and I be a little bit too tired to do homework. I just go to bed then. So, on off-days there should be no excuses for me not making up on the homework that I miss on the days that I worked, or should have done.

C129   You feel you should apply yourself—

                            Understanding.

S130   I should apply myself more. But, I feel I can apply myself more with people on the same level, same interest—being more or less to my benefit. And, uh, I could really apply myself.

C131   It's difficult, with all these other things to keep up in a group where it's large and you can't get the help where you really need it.

Understanding. Interpretative in that it includes more than he had actually said in S130. Yet he accepts interpretation and moves on.

S132   Yes. It's not, more or less, the teachers. Some kids say the teachers won't help me, but I think if they just sort of change the school system to where a person could be with people of his own level maybe, the same I.Q., the same common problems, that the group as a whole could raise itself, excel itself, to the interest that they really want. And, that's how I feel about that. (*Pause*) And, uh, what else was I thinking about. (*Pause*) And, that was it, I guess.

C133   Well, Carl, our time is up for today, our forty-five minutes. And, would you like to come back?

Closing.

S134   Oh, yes.

C135   All right. We can go across the hall and I'll check the appointment book to see when you can come back.

Summary of Second Interview

Interview began by client wanting to know his results from CTMM. Results were interpreted to him: within average range on language data score, below the average range on nonlanguage data score when compared with general population. As normative group became more selective, he was told that his language data score fell progressively below the average range as did his low nonlanguage data score. Client accepted interpretation and after a few more questions about the nature of the CTMM, he discussed careers day at his school. He heard speakers on law, radio-television, law enforcement, and dramatics. Law is still his main interest. However, he is now thinking of Junior College to strengthen his verbal abilities and he wanted to know what counselor felt about remedial schools advertised in *New York Times* book supplement section. Client went to High School basketball game last night and attributes his forgetting what he had to discuss today to the excitement of the game. Nothing more to talk about. Test selection guide was brought out and he selected verbal reasoning from DAT. Test was administered during last thirty minutes of interview time. Another interview was scheduled.

THIRD INTERVIEW	COUNSELOR'S COMMENTS

S1   How did I make out on that test I took?

C2   Ah, the verbal reasoning test you took last week?

S3   Yeah.

C4   Well, I did score that and the results were that on this particular aptitude you were below the average that has been found when given to boys and girls in senior high school of your age level.   *Informational.*

S5   I probably took too long on some of them.

C6   Yes. I noticed that you didn't finish it.   *Supportive. An unnecessary response.*

S7   I felt that I could have finished it, but, uh, some of them I had to make sure they were right.

C8   Mm-hmm.

S9   Recheck them. That's probably what took so long.

C10   Mm-hmm.

S11   So . . . Oh, uh, in May I'll be filling out my application for Junior College. And, uh, they have remedial English over there. I think, English . . . I forget what they call it, they have a special number for it. So I think when I get over there I might be able to fill up the weak spots in English . . .

C12   Mm-hmm.

S13   that I had before. And, uh, I think I'll get a couple of outside books on English and try to do it. Oh, yes, uh, I sent off for an art aptitude test from Famous Artists School. And, uh, I'm going to send it in Monday. I've completed the test and everything. I'll send it in Monday and I guess I'll get the results a week after next. It was a, uh, good test. They had, ah, tests concerning imagination, the ability to shade, your ability to draw given characters in different moods, and uh, clothing. And, uh, what was the other, uh, picture composition. That was the main part of it. So, I'm going to send it in Monday after school. I think I'm going to pass. My art teacher says you're a cinch to pass because they need people to subscribe to their course. So I think I'll make it. But it's the money that's so high. I asked a friend. He previously took the test and, uh, he said they want about three hundred dollars. So I'll see what my father says about it before I go on with it. *(Pause)* And that's about it. I still got letters to do in English, and interviews to do. And, uh, that's about it.

C14　You feel that, uh, because on the test you did take here the, uh, taking the time to make sure the ones you did correctly, uh, were the ones you did correctly; in other words, uh, that if you had worked faster perhaps . . .

　　　An attempted understanding response. Counselor is redirecting attention on to test performance.

S15　Yes.

C16　not spent so much time on it . . .

　　　Continuation of C14.

S17　That's the way I am in all my classes. When I take a test I seem to be the last one to finish because I have to re-check to make sure I did it right. And the rest of the kids, they go at a rapid pace. I have to make sure that at least the majority of them are right—and try to correct the ones that are not. And, uh, I made a couple of errors on that test. I put two in one column of numbers, you know, and I had to erase. *(Pause)* That was about the hardest part about it. I had the right idea but I put it in the wrong one and then I had to erase it and that took time off.

C18　Mm-hmm.

S19　So that's about it. *(Pause)* Let's see. What other faults am I having in school? I, uh . . . that math is what really bothers me.

C20   Mm-hmm.

S21   I can get it if I'm situated in a small
       class. And, if I get in . . . I'm trying
       to find a nice small school, or college,
       where I can get a lot of help. And so
       . . . I've been looking through Love-
       joy's College Guide, and uh, looking at
       the small colleges. And, I haven't de-
       cided on which one I wanted yet, so,
       I'll just wait until I get through Junior
       College to, uh, make that decision, which
       one I should go to.

C22   Mm-hmm.

S23   If I go to any. And, uh, I've always had
       this problem of not making enough
       money. I mean, I feel that I should make
       more money for something like that, be-
       cause I figure right by now I should
       have an automobile or car, or some-
       thing like that to, uh, shuffle back to and
       from school, but the way the job situa-
       tion is, it, uh, doesn't even give me a
       stable job to buy a car with. Yesterday
       I went to work and, uh, they told me
       couldn't use me for that day. So, I had
       already made some long-range plans.
       And, I, uh, getting stuff for Christmas,
       you know, for my parents and for my-
       self, and that sort of throws me behind
       schedule in payments, and things like
       that.

C24   Mm-hmm.

S25   So I, so Monday after I send in my test,
       I'll walk around town to see if I can find
       another job, done on a more steady
       basis. Because that little job where I
       work at is not so steady. When I first
       got the job, it took me twice as hard as
       everyone else to, uh, get to, uh, the job
       of stock boy. I worked in the store and
       I worked twice as hard as everyone else
       in the store and, uh, it took about a
       whole year before I got the raise, and,
       uh, whereas people who came in as

packers, I knew their work wasn't done as well as mine, but, uh, they worked in packing positions for say, two or three weeks, or say maybe a month and a half, and they went directly over to stock. And, uh, I thought maybe I was falling behind or something. And the manager didn't say anything, I asked him. I had to pound, and kept on pounding him until finally I got my raise. And now that I have got it, it's nothing what I expected it to be. I expected it to be at least steady and stable where I could, you know, sort of count on the work that I'm doing. At least I wouldn't be laid off; being laid off, that's sort of difficult. And you know you have to tell your creditors, you have to wait, and so forth. So, today doesn't look like a promising day to go to work. Because it's raining. And people don't like to come out in the rain to buy groceries, but I think I might be able to at least work five hours today.

C26 Mm-hmm.

S27 And that's what, that's what really worries me the most of all the other problems—is, uh, finding a place, or a status where I can live comfortably, or how to get there fast as possible.

C28 Mm-hmm.

S29 You have any solutions?

C30 Your feeling is, security is the important thing.   Understanding.

S31 Yes. Now we own the house that we live in. But I'm not satisfied with that one. It's a real nice house, but, uh, the rooms are quite small and everything. But I feel that if I could really find myself a job or a job that I could be happy at, I could improve the old home and sort of leave my parents set to where they can sort of maintain and keep the house. The house is not in jeopardy but it could use some modernization. And, uh, I would leave and find a house of my own.

C32   Mm-hmm.

S33   And, uh, I think that problem is what causes me to be so restless at night. I don't sleep very well. Uh, I know, you know when you're supposed to be asleep your mind is supposed to be working at its lowest point, I think. But mine just seems too active, I mean, I can feel myself moving about. I can, I don't be even dreaming at all.

C34   You really never go to sleep.   Reflection through restating.

S35   I really never go to sleep. My eyes be closed but I'm never asleep. So, I was thinking about going to a doctor. Maybe I might suffer from insomnia or something like that. (*Pause*)

C36   You're not sure just why you don't go to sleep?   Understanding.

S37   Yes. Because I be awfully uncomfortable. My mother says I change positions about five times every minute. (*Pause*) So, I've went through everything that could be bothering me at the time. Sometimes I wake up in the middle of the night and sort of take stock of myself and see what has been bothering me all day long. But I just can't seem to find the root of it. So I just give up.

C38   Mm-hmm. You try real hard to find out what it is that's bothering you?

S39   Yes.

C40   But you can't do it.   Understanding.

S41   No, can't do it. (*Pause*) I think I can make it. My teacher says that if you don't get mathematics, you can't exist because the, uh, whole world is just about mathematically—whatever you do is combined with math. Ever since school I've always hated math. I never enjoyed it. When I do catch on to the problems I be so far behind, I be working maybe at sixth grade level of math, but, uh, when it comes to money, I can add and subtract real fast. That's the whole evolution of math, is adding and subtracting. And, uh, when it comes to problems, like story problems or problems, like algebra, I, in math, that's supposed to be, I mean it gives you an introduction to algebra and, uh, things that I don't see that's not there I can't work with them. I, the teacher, says that X equals the unknown, but if you don't have anything to work with the unknown, I just don't understand it, that confuses me. And, uh, my interest drops in that class and I don't do my homework like I should.

C42 The problem is there and, uh, if it's something that you don't get right away and you know you aren't going to get it right away, the interest just kind of leaves.

Restatement and understanding.

S43 Yes. And, uh, if, uh, and, uh, I think one thing that I really lack is self-confidence, because sometimes in art if things don't go up, or, I seem to blow up real quick, uh, a little real short patience. And, uh, sometimes I start an art project and be almost through and, uh, somewhere in my mind I feel it's not right that something is wrong with it, I tear it up and destroy it, or do away with, but just won't finish it (*pause*). I have the ability to start, but finishing, that's what gets me. It seems so long and drawn out. Especially in math. If I get the first, maybe formula, in school I can learn it. But when I go home I forget the formula and uh, I tried to, uh, look at the formulas, then when I'm looking at the formulas, I forget the terms that's supposed to go with it and, uh, it's hard to do, if you don't know both. So, uh, I've tried it, to remember it I've started taking notes down in class, and it helps a little bit to, uh, keep me right on the problem. But, I think math and English are the most two difficult things, obstacles that I have against me.

C44   Mm-hmm.

S45   And they make me feel uneasy when I have to do them because I know that I'm not up to the potential that I'm supposed to be, or the average that I am supposed to be working at.

C46   Mm-hmm.

S47   And, uh, I get mad. Because, I forget the terms and I don't understand the homework. And, uh, sometimes, well, uh, in math class I just want to get away from it all, and sit in the back of the room where nobody can bother me and I don't get a chance to bother them. In English, English wouldn't be so difficult if I could only master the simple mechanics of—I know the basic meanings of the nouns but the other things. Like, I think I could get—I can spell the words and I can pronounce the words but when it comes to writing a theme or something like that, I forget about it. I forget about the spelling of the words and I only go by the sound only.

C48   Mm-hmm.

S49   And, uh, if I got a book to really concentrate on it, and uh, the atmosphere at home, it isn't one, it isn't one that you can really work at. Or, there is no one in the household to help me. So, if I could just find the place with people more or less my own ability and somebody who has the patience and the time, I think I can rebuild my self-confidence.

C50   Mm-hmm.

S51   And uh, master writing and the things that are really holding me back from attaining my goals. (*Long pause*)

C52 It's, uh, rebuilding your self-confidence   Understanding.
     that's important.

S53 Yes. (*Short pause*) My uncle suggested
     that I go into service. That might do
     the . . . , rebuild confidence. But, I
     think I can do it without service, or,
     military service. I have put out a large
     . . . ninety per cent of this effort myself
     to find what's wrong with me and the
     best way to, uh, build up this confidence.

C54 Mm-hmm.

S55 I had the same trouble with manual
     dexterity, in wood shop and grade school.
     I knew the plans the job has laid out
     and everything, but every time I would
     do it right I would take pains and care,
     and the job would turn out all wrong
     somewhere. Only one thing I made, and
     it's not too perfect. It was a plastic
     piano, and that wasn't too perfect. It
     stood up. But all the other jobs were
     a waste of money, because we had to
     buy the boards, nails and glue, and all
     that. The nails wouldn't seem to go
     right, nothing would go right when I
     would take a course like that. (*Long
     pause*) So I've been looking through
     careers and saw some of the things, like
     —I'm still set on law. If I can only get
     that English, if I can't get the English
     I won't be able to take law, because you
     have to know English very well, almost,
     you might say for a person to be a lawyer
     he must master the English language
     very well. If you don't master it you
     can be a very good lawyer at reasoning.
     They prefer you not so much to study
     on the sciences, but the humanities, and
     all the other courses like History and
     Sociology I've gotten along just fine.
     That Math and English are the only
     ones that might stop me from entering
     a college (*Short pause*) or might stop
     me from getting a job.

C56 Mm-hmm.

S57   So I've been looking, ah, to try and find
      someone to help me. It's almost theo-
      retically impossible for me to stay after
      school because I have to work, and some
      of the time when I go there my teachers
      are not there. If I could just get some
      sort of outside push or shove in the right
      way I could make it. (*Pause*) Sometime
      I feel lost, you know, just really lost.
      Everybody's just going on by real fast,
      working at a high level. I seem to be
      stranded—an outcast. (*Pause*) So, I'm
      trying to find the right course or the
      right formula to put me on the right
      path, or something.

C58   You feel that you're just kind of out.   Understanding.

S59   Yes.

C60   Everyone else is going in some direction,   Understanding.
      at least.

S61   Yes. The only trouble is, I know that
      I'm out, but I just can't find the right
      direction to go. (*Pause*) That's about it.

C62   The feeling is, "I really want to go, I   Understanding.
      really want to move, but just where is
      causing me a lot of problems."

S63   Yes. I think if I could find where, I
      could work twice as hard to get there,
    • because my father, he's very old and I,
      ah, he wants to see some sign of achieve-
      ment, or something, and I feel that I
      have to show it to him that I can do it,
      and I have to do it as fast as possible,
      because I think now he's seventy-five and,
      ah, he keeps on telling me that he's not
      long for this world and, ah, I feel I
      have to show him something.

C64   And there's pressure to do something.   Understanding.

S65   Yes. It's not played up so much but I
      feel within myself that I must achieve
      something, not only for his sake but
      for my sake; what can I do? My uncle
      asked me a couple of nights ago, "what
      can you do?" I was stunned. I didn't
      know what to say, except go to school.

(*Laugh*) So mostly I've been thinking what could I do very well. I went through all my academic subjects, and found that the only thing I really enjoyed was the Humanities, or Social Science and History. I got fairly well in Science, and Biology.

C66 Mm-hmm.

S67 (*Pause*) So I guess I'll have to find some way to fit it in, there must be a pattern that I can fit in without too much Math or too much English.

C68 Ideas are interesting to you and you seem to handle them in your Humanities.   Restatement.

S69 Yes. (*Pause*) And that's about it, I think money is, no, there's not too much trouble with money, it's just that I don't save it away. Sometimes I just spend it recklessly, I don't manage it right like I should, and I feel that, like clothes, I should get all my clothes at once, or attain everything all at once. And my mother says this isn't good for me, uh, my daddy, he doesn't, ah, he gets a check from the government and he works down at the Church and, anyhow, he gets about twenty dollars, and the check of, I guess, about one hundred dollars, and he seems to manage this pretty well. But I make almost, I used to make about the same amount, but I have trouble managing it right, because, if I don't get it all at once it just doesn't seem to fit. I have to have, because, I guess that's why I'm so short patient. At one time my mother says, "I need this, you need that." I knew I needed all those things myself, and, uh, I went and put things up in the layaway, and I tried to get them all out at once, but the working conditions at the store fell down, and I got laid off, and you had to get the things out within thirty days, plus I had to contribute something, five dollars to my mother because she's not working and, ah, so, ah, it sort of cut down on what I can do. But when I was making a small income I knew, I didn't have that much trouble, but now I'm making a larger amount, and it's not too large, it's about eighteen dollars a week now and it's possibly going to go lower because of the winter months, because people are baking things, too, at home. I mean, they're not buying expensive foods, they buy enough food to, uh, with enough vitamins to keep them going, and, uh, that's one of my other problems; it's how to attain everything at once.

C70 You're just impatient for waiting for things to come about.   Understanding.

S71 Yes. (*Pause*) And one of my other classes, the teacher says you just can't wait, is Music Appreciation. I love the class, but some of the records I've heard before and the teacher, he loves music almost to a fanatical point. I think, ah, he seems to dominate everybody else's opinion. If, uh, you hear a record or a concert you might have the sound of a train, but he says, "No, it's not a train"—he'll prove it to you on the album. He seems to dominate everybody's thought and everybody says, "Yes, yes, that's right— it's a train," or something like that. It sounds like grade school. The teacher points up at a picture of a cow. It's a cow. And the whole class (*Pause*). I like to enjoy music by myself because, I mean, you can listen and get your own concepts. I like to enjoy music by myself, but whereas you're listening to a record and being interfered and somebody is putting in his own ideas, you don't get a good picture of music, and you don't like it so well.

C72   And you feel that what you think about   Understanding.
      it is as important as what someone else
      might think about it.

S73   Yes. (*Pause*) And that's about it. I've
      said that about five times. (*Laughs*)
      (*Pause*) That's all I can think of right
      now, that bothers me, is how to get there
      fast, as fast as possible, and the right
      direction. Is this wrong thinking? Is this
      objective thinking?

C74   The feeling you have is mixed about   Understanding.
      where you want to go, and just how you
      should think about that.

S75   Ah, I'm trying to find the direction, but
      how fast. Some people say it's wrong to
      try to accelerate, although I am working
      at a low level to get there fast, you might
      say would be almost impossible. But I
      think there must be ways that a person
      can get there and to achieve something
      at a fast rate, or find what he's looking
      for.

C76   You want to make it seem as though it's
      moving along fast.

S77   Yes. (*Pause*) That's about (*Pause*) so I
      think Law might be, they say it's a slow
      process, Law, but I think if a person
      can exert enough drive he, ah, might
      be able to make it. Because they say
      lawyers are just maturing and reaching
      the height of their careers at thirty-five.

C78   Mm-hmm.

S79   And, uh, other people tell me, ah, that
      you might find security, some people
      say at a later age, and uh, some people
      say you might never find it. Because a
      couple of friends of mine say they've
      been working at the same job for years.
      They're not happy with it but it can
      keep them going, and, uh, sometimes I
      think I might fall into that type of en-
      vironment, and do something I don't
      like. I used to have those terrible dreams
      of being something lower than I am. I

always dream I'm down on skid row or somewhere (*pause*). So that's what really bothers me. I tell my mother all this and she says it's nightmares or something like that. But the dreams they just happen too many times to be nightmares. (*Pause*)

C80   You feel they happen more often than they should just to be nightmares.   Reflection and restatement.

S81   Yes. Seems like I never dream about anything good. (*Laughs*) (*Pause*) The house is, ah, where I come from the block is, it's OK. It's not the best block in the world, but I always find that I'm somewhere I shouldn't be, like somewhere, you know, people in the same class but I don't feel that I belong there. Sometimes I dream I'm among drunks.

C82   You feel you're somewhere you really don't belong.   Understanding.

S83   Yes. (*Long pause*) So I really don't know how to go about it. The problem is there, but I've been searching, trying to find a way but I just haven't found the way.

C84   No matter how you think about it or feel about it, or try and talk about it, it seems to still be there.   Understanding.

S85   Yes, it still seems to be there. Sometimes when I go downtown, ah, to a show somewhere, I forget about it, I feel that I'm accepted more or less, these people don't notice me so much. But after that the problem is still there.

C86   For a short period of time you feel that you are acceptable. People are not noticing you.   Reflective and restatement.

S87   Yes. I feel that achievement, you really want to achieve something, but what it is I don't know. My mother always cite about friends, people who started out at the same age—"So and so's in the Army now," and, uh, "So and so's doing this and something better," and I'm still stuck in school, but if I hadn't flunked a couple times—it really took me a long time to figure out if I should stay in High School. And, uh, when I finally found out I could stay in High School, and if I applied myself I could graduate, but one time I thought about quitting. I think I mature slowly or something. I don't mature fast. My folks don't (*Pause*) when I was smaller and it was nothing but big kids and I couldn't go out because my father was afraid that I might get hurt or something like that, and when I moved over here I found out that kids who were my own age and still I just couldn't be accepted by them. I had to play with smaller kids until I was about twelve—until I really found a friend my own age, and uh, he's moved. Sometimes when I do my homework it'll be awfully lonely on that block. It's a big ol' house, your parents are there— sometimes my mother, she's—goes to a friend's house, and my father's home all the time, and he's getting older and he has his set patterns. Sometimes he'll walk in the house completely mad. I don't know what he's mad about; sometimes I wonder if he does, and it's hard to find, you know, something to please him, and at the same time please myself.

C88   So, even being accepted now and getting away from this feeling of being alone is a problem.   Understanding.

S89   Yes. I have a lot of friends that I joke around in school with, but, I mean, a real good friend is hard to find. I have one, but he lives so far and since he's moved, I have two—a couple of good friends that are really a lot of fun to be around, but it's just the idea of time, space—sometimes when I'm working they're off, and sometimes we do work

together, but when we get off work it's
nine or ten o'clock, and sometimes if I
go over to their house I can only stay
a short time. My father, he worries. I
got stuck over in the elevator, over here
at Jeffries' Project and a friend of mine
called my father. He magnified the accident and thought I was hurt and everything, and he really got upset, so, and
uh, you know, he makes snap decisions
before he thinks. He might accuse me of
doing something that I really hadn't
done, or make a false analogy, or something like that about me. It's pretty hard
for me and my father to get along.
Some of the time we get along, I mean,
like if we don't say very much to each
other, and then some days we're both in
a good mood, and sometimes I find
myself unconsciously snapping at my
mother, or something like that.

C90 You feel that there might be a lack of   Understanding.
understanding between you and your
father.

S91 Yes. (*Pause*) So, we don't say much to each
other, we don't get along. I mean, we
get along very well, sometimes play together. Other than that, our opinions,
conflict. I think in his mind he still
thinks I'm small. Sometimes I feel that
I just want to cut loose from my parents,
find it somewhere on my own. (*Pause*)

C92 You feel that you really aren't small.   Understanding.

S93 That's right. I feel that I'm really not
small. Uh, my mother, if she had her
way, she would let me go out more
often, but I can go out often sometimes
if I really want to, but finding the right
crowd acceptance, but the few friends
that I have is awfully difficult.

C94 Even if you did go out more often you   Understanding.
would still have the problem of finding
the group you would like to be with and
being accepted.

S95 Yes. My mother always tells us you might want to be with the Joneses, or something, but I feel that most of the Joneses in the world are average—I just have to work twice as hard to get there. But what am I going to work with, the resources are very weak, so I have to find some way that I can build up English and Math and the right group, and I think I can achieve something. (*Pause*) But other than that, going along right now I'm very unhappy because it's terrible, you know, just wondering, sometimes I think this job is the best job in the world, although it is small. (*Knock on door*)

C96 That indicates that our time is up for the day. We can arrange an appointment for you to come back next week. Is that all right with you?   Closing.

S97 OK.

**FOURTH
INTERVIEW**

S1 Nice day outside.

C2 Yes, it's beautiful out.

S3 (*Pause*) I've been working on my Math. My teacher says I'm beginning to show signs of progress in the class, and I think I can make it now. I've been doing my homework the best that I could, and he's giving me a little bit of help every now and then in class, so I think I can pass this card marking. It may be the first Math class that I've passed. So I'm going to continue to work on it. And uh, in English I'm going to try and, ah, to, ah, get my English all caught up. So I think I'll buy me a book and start practicing and correcting writing habits that I need to improve. And, ah, it's ah, (*Pause*) and that's about it.

3.1   I think I can make it, uh, when I start even though the problems that I did get right and I felt a little bit of self-confidence coming back and, ah, so I'm going to really crack down on my Math, and, ah, try and get someone to help me with my English. There's a distant relative in our family. She's teaching in the Detroit system. I think I'll tell my father to give me her address where she lives and, ah, I think with her help and help in school I should be able to, ah, make, ah, college, and, ah, in May I'll be taking examinations for Junior College and, ah, the only problem that's worrying me now is trying to clear up my debts as soon as possible. And start saving money and putting it away, and I'll have to start getting used to a new budget for '60, so I can save some money for the things I really need, so I'm going to try and cut down on some of the unnecessary expenses so I can get myself prepared to go. I think, ah, let's see, what else was I going to tell you. You see, on Friday nights I have everything planned out what I'm going to say, but when I get here I forget it.

3.2   (*Pause*) So, that's about it. I seem to be getting a little self-confidence in my Math class a little bit, and I'm going to exert extra effort and see what I can do. I think one of my problems is when I sleep and toss and turn at night is, must be some wrong type of something, I don't know, it happened, but for the last couple of nights I have been sleeping generally well, I don't toss and turn as much, but I'm still a terrible sleeper. I think it's due to the little bit of self-confidence coming back and, ah (*Pause*) English is not so hard, only thing I need is some type of remedial English to, ah, really crack down, and I think they have

Client talked for such a long time that his response is subdivided.

a course over in the Junior College that I can take and bring my grades up. And generally, I'm going to buy a 1960 and ah, I'm going to stick to a new study plan where I can really concentrate on my work, so I'm going to see if I can get a cut off next semester where I can get out of school early and, ah, say, leave about 12:00 and I could, ah, the library isn't very far from the school I go to, so I can go there from, say from 12:00 to maybe 3:00—and get two hours of study before I go to work. And that would give me extra time to, ah, really get to the problems that's going to hold me back from this college education, and that way I think I can come out better ahead and I think I'll talk to my boss to see if I can, ah, work all day Saturday and maybe, ah, a little bit more hours on Friday so I can have most of the week days off and, ah, catch up and raise myself up to an average level. (*Pause*)

3.3　So that's about the new plans for '60 that I'm going to forecast for myself. I have some problems at home and as soon as I get off from work tonight, and if I'm not too tired, I guess I'll tackle them. And that's about generally the picture. I don't seem to be as worried about that other problem of getting there first, I mean fast, making some type of achievement real fast. I guess the most important thing for me is to get confidence in myself, to try and change my short-temperedness, and ah, maybe have longer patience, so that I can generally do the work better, so I'm going to try to be less snappy than usual and take time and reason things out like I should. I think I can do it, and I'm going to look around and see if I can get all the self-help I can, and if necessary, get someone to help me. (*Pause*)

3.4 I hope it works, it probably will work. I honestly and sincerely think it will work, if I can really do it. Ah, yesterday we had problems in Math. I felt very good because of three problems, they were not difficult problems, but they cover the basic essentials a person must have in Math before you can do anything else, and I got two out of the three on my own, so, I felt very proud about that little achievement, although it is small. (*Pause*) And, I'm just quitting this idea of getting there fast and the best way I can because I might miss something that I might need, so I'll get there in time, I believe. If I can take more tests, so far I've got a general picture of myself and the basic things that I really must have, and the things I really want. I know that if I can master the things I need I can get the things that I really need. (*Pause*)

3.5 I know this is going to be sort of difficult, especially this self-help program that I'm going to lodge in my spare time, because it's going to be a little difficult, because there won't be anyone over my shoulder all the time telling me what to do. I think that's where I'll need the patience. I'm going to try and not rely on people so much—I want to sort of do this on my own because that's where I really need the confidence, doing something on my own, and having people, you know, not criticizing me, and telling me, "You should be on so and so's level," or "You should keep up with the Joneses." I think the Joneses are fine people because they "got it," but I can get there in my own time, so I'm just going to, not relax, but going to think along, I figure that if it's at a

snail's pace I think I can get there in
time. Ah, my father was telling me it's
not how fast you get there, it's, ah, once
you get there can you stay there? So,
I'm going to take it at a snail's pace—a
pace I can generally work at, and I
think I can really get there, because I
think it would hurt me more if I skipped
around and, ah, messed around and
have people take me out of pity, not
for what I really am, what I'm really
worth. And, ah, I thought about grade
school; how all the grade school teachers used to pass me because all my friends
were passing and, ah, and ah, my marks
would be low in Math, and ah, that
might stop me from passing anyhow,
but I think that that really ruined me—
it didn't help me at all because I should
have been kept back and really taught
and the teachers should have exerted
some extra help. I think most teachers
in grade school, ah, I know teaching is
a hard job and it's a difficult one, I
mean when you have a class of generally
all, say, ah, at least 85 per cent of your
class at a normal level, you're bound to
have a few stragglers, behind, and it
takes time because when you really know
something, when a kid really knows
something, I think he's more apt to respond and be there first. And if you take
time with the people that's catering, the
stragglers, they would, ah it takes time.
Some kids get this complex, well, the
teacher is not recognizing me and are
such. I think teachers should, ah, have a
little room, you might call it progress
house where the stragglers can receive special attention, so they can work at a nice
pace where they can really work and not
be concerned about the rest of the class,
because you have to be around more
people of the same thoughts and the

same needs. You can work together as a group and catch up to the level at your own pace. So, that would be it. The regular class can go on but I know, I admit there's a need for trained people in this field of special teachers and, ah, most people, most people look on the job as, different schools, they might call it Special 103 and people get the mis-concept of it, they call it preparatory training, another school, the people who belong in that class, they are working, they have one in my school, they are working at, ah, you know, a pace, but people, the other people around them seem to make this, ah, destroy the work the teachers are doing because they say it's for dummies or this is for delinquents or special people and they overemphasize the people as special and they forget that they're just people who need help. It would be nice if they, if I could find a school like that where people my own age, my own level, with the same thoughts as mine, we could work to-gether and catch up at our own pace and time. (*Pause*) That's the way I really feel about the problem and that's what has happened to me. (*Pause*)

3.6 So, I've been looking again through the small colleges. I've been reading infor-mation on small colleges, and what they can offer me, and I think they can offer me a lot, generally if I, in a large col-lege with a professor and all your classes, he has hundreds of people to work with and if you fall behind his time is so valuable because he has to do other civic events. He has his own family life, whereas in a small college you're among people, ah, who, you know, might not be termed so bright but they're people working hard to attain their goals in life, and ah, it could offer me a lot, but the training might not be as accelerated, but it would be helpful, with self-help I think I could retain a lot and use a lot from a small college, and I'm still set on being a lawyer. My English, it looks like a hard road to climb, but I think if I take my time I can master it considerably. I was looking through several schools and you have to be above average. I think it's a nice thing for this, ah, I think it's the American Bar Association, to have. But basically a man doesn't have to be above average to know his law. I think law should be taught to those who really need it and who can really work at it. So, that might be one obstacle is, ah, if I'm working at a C level and I eventually pushing myself up to a B, I think it can be done but from the information inside some of those law schools it seems pretty hard to do. It's a lot of time and a lot of money, but I guess basically it's just patience in the long run that gets people where they are going, it's your patience, your ability to reason and ability to work. So I'm beginning to accept myself not as a fast worker but I think I can be an honest and sincere worker to myself and really get there. (*Pause*)

3.7 So, so far your tests gave me a general picture of basically where I fall down and where my basic faults lie at, and, ah, where I really need to work on. It's, ah, really helped me a lot. In this case of Math, it's ah, given me a push that's seldom exerted before, and ah, I look at my age, I'm nineteen, and actually I'm supposed to have been out, but I disqualified the rule of age because I've read in the high school paper, and I see evidence in my own high school, where there's older people. I don't know they had the time to, ah, pass high school or whatever their basic problems were, but I think they are working toward a diploma, so, ah, age, it doesn't count in education any more. I think if you really want an education you have to disqualify that factor, age, so that's what I'm trying to convince myself now. I'm not so old and, uh, if I work at a snail's pace I can do it because, I mean, I'm bound to make a lot more mistakes now, so I feel I won't make more mistakes than I did back then because people were just passing me out of pity or out of my plea, "I've got to pass," and all this. So I don't think, I think if I really work at it I think I'll get the things I really deserve to have. (*Pause*)

3.8   So, that's about it. So, oh yeah, I want to wish you a Merry Christmas, and I'd like to thank you for your services, and I will come back in the New Year and continue to take these tests.

C4   Well, thank you very much, Carl, on the Season's Greetings. I certainly wish you the same. The Lab is going to be open during the holidays.   Informational.

S5   It will?

C6   Yes. If your schedule of work allows you to come down we could check ours and see what time you might continue. We are not closing for the holidays except for the day of Christmas and that weekend and the day of New Years and that weekend.   Informational.

S7   Okay. Oh yes, I was supposed to take a test Wednesday. I completely forgot it. I had Christmas spirit on my mind, and I forgot I was supposed to take a test down here so, ah, when can we schedule the test I was supposed to take?

C8   I'd have to check the calendar, and we could arrange it for you.   Informational.

S9   Well, OK.

C10   Anything else you'd like to talk about?   Probing.

S11   Well, that's about it. My time is running
short and I have to be going to work.

C12   All right, we can go check our calendar
now.

Case Summary and Counselor's Comments

Case Summary

Client was a conscientious, serious individual who was genuinely interested in finding out about himself. He was comfortable in the counseling
relationship and talked easily about himself and what he felt to be his
major problems. Inability to do satisfactory school work in Mathematics
and English was of great concern to him because of his career goals. He
wants to be a lawyer and he realizes that success in these areas is necessary
for successful completion of the training. He felt that he does his best
school work in courses in which his interest is high. Client feels that his
biggest problem is finding people of similar interests and abilities. He
would like to have more individual attention in school, smaller classes
where individual differences are provided for. He expressed feelings of
failure and of being rejected because he has not been able to succeed in
his school work. He would like to please his parents by succeeding at something. There has been pressure from home to join the Army but he resists, feeling it wiser to finish high school. His father discourages the idea
of police work so client wants to be a lawyer although police work is his
first area of interest. He wants to help people, whatever job he performs.

Client was administered the California Test of Mental Maturity
(CTMM) and the Verbal Reasoning (VR) of the DAT. CTMM results
were:

	Language Data	Nonlanguage Data	Total Data
I.Q.	102	83	93
Intell. (M.A.) G.P.	9.8	8.0	8.9

Client scored at the 20th percentile on the VR test.

Test results were interpreted to the client by the Counselor. He felt
his low performance on the VR test was due, in part, to his failure to
complete the test. The impact of the meaning of all test results was not
accepted fully by the client. At the end of the last interview he had altered
his views about the rate of speed at which he would attain his goals. He
stated that the interviews had helped him crystallize his thinking about a
lot of things and that he had more self-confidence now that he could accept himself with his slow rate of achievement. Client wants to attend
college and will continue his efforts to gain additional information about

requirements. He did not keep three subsequent appointments, although his counselor reported an attempt was made by client to contact the laboratory.

Counselor's Comments

Throughout this case, client resisted the idea that his difficulty in school subjects was due primarily to his lack of ability. Instead, he stated in the first interview that his low level of performance was due to his inability to "buckle down," lack of self-discipline, and lack of interest. These rationalizations were used most frequently by the client and only very briefly in the first interview did he perceive the difficulty in terms of his lack of scholastic ability. His ambition to become a lawyer indicated an unrealistically high aspirational level. This is shown by his poor scholastic achievement record, low level of scholastic aptitude as indicated by the test results, and his own feelings of inadequacy in the important areas of English and Mathematics. Client projected his own inadequacies onto the school situation and intellectualized at length in his area of school performance. He ascribed responsibility for his lack of "interest" onto the structure of the school. To him, it appeared that the school situation failed to provide for his level and type of interest. Client's theory that the school system should be changed to one in which people of similar interests would be together is a recurring substitute for the non-acceptance of his inability to perform in the usual class situation. Identification with his father is implied in his choice of vocational area and the reasons given for the choice. His father had worked in a law enforcement capacity and the father's past activities of extending aid to others influenced client's perception of himself as a helping person.

The third interview was significant in that feelings of failure, rejection, loneliness, and of unhappiness in general were expressed and without the protection of any clearly defined defense mechanisms. Earlier in this interview, client felt that his lack of achievement in school subjects was caused primarily by too large classes, insufficient personal attention in Mathematics and English, and the absence of people of his own interest and ability level with whom he could work. He continued to feel that factors other than his lack of ability were contributing to his poor academic performance, i.e., lack of self-confidence, impatience in general, forgetfulness, insufficient mastery of simple mechanics of Mathematics and English, poor home atmosphere for study, and the need to be with people at his ability level and interest. Again, in this interview, client was unable to accept completely the idea that he lacked the ability to do acceptable school work at the level required if he was to achieve his goal of becoming a lawyer. And as a result, he resorted to the above rationalizations.

In the third interview, client began to express mixed feelings about

attending a four-year college and there was even some doubt expressed
about his attending any college. But, it was pointed out by client that
money, not lack of ability, was the deciding factor. This, of course, made it
easier for him to accept the thought of not attending college. Yet, client
maintained throughout the interview that law was the only career for him
and that he must "get there fast," both unrealistic aspirations.

Despite his continued use of rationalization and intellectualization
as defense mechanisms, in the third interview client moved toward a
greater understanding of himself and his problems. He was able to face
his feelings of rejection, defeat, and loneliness even though at times their
bleakness made acceptance of these feelings, as reflected by the counselor,
very difficult. Also, he began to feel that other factors outside of the
educational framework were contributing to his self-concept of being a
failure, i.e., an atmosphere of disappointment in him at home, a lack of
feeling of success with people, and a sense of financial insecurity.

The fourth interview was a distinctly different interview from the
third. The client's emotional tone had changed from a pessimistic, negative one to a decidedly more optimistic and positive approach to himself
and his problems. He expressed the feeling that the success or failure of
his projected plans for self-improvement depended primarily on his
personal efforts. He felt he was more willing to accept his slower rate of
achievement and that he was not so concerned about "getting there fast."
In this interview, client stated that there had occurred some growth in
his self-confidence concerning school achievement. He appeared to be
much more comfortable throughout the interview. Although he maintained his feeling of serious concern about his difficulties in school and
elsewhere, there were many more expressions of confidence and cautious
optimism about the possible success of his plans for the future.

At the conclusion of this interview, growth was evident in client's
general attitude of renewed belief in his ability to do something. As a
result of his experiences at the laboratory, it was felt that client was
helped in that the atmosphere of the interviews allowed for crystallization
and verbalization of thoughts and feelings about self in relation to school,
to others, and to self.

Client will continue to need the opportunity to explore his thinking in
an acceptant, non-judgmental atmosphere. He realizes his need to function
in situations where pressures to excel are absent. Smaller classes would be
beneficial because of the individual attention he would receive. His
aspirational level is totally unrealistic in light of his poor scholastic
aptitude, and achievement records. He does have insight into his difficulties in school and if he can get into situations in which some feelings of
success will be found, the drive to become a lawyer may no longer be
needed and he will feel worthy and comfortable in some other area
requiring less academic training.

Counselor's Self-Evaluation

Every possible effort was made by the Counselor not to consciously influence the process in these interviews. However, in the first interview a conscious attempt was made to increase client's awareness of the diversity of the field of law and law enforcement. This was done because it was felt that any lowering of client's unrealistic aspirational level would occur more easily if he, himself, began to think of jobs other than that of lawyer as acceptable in this area. Perhaps values and attitudes cannot be prevented from influencing the manner in which all reflections are phrased. Whatever influencing of the process that did occur in these interviews I attribute to my firm conviction that a non-judgmental approach was my. goal and that this approach would be most likely to create a true helping relationship in the process. Lack of success in realizing my goal as fully as I would have desired was caused by inexperience in the technique needed to do so.

My ability to establish a good relationship with this client and maintain it was important to what degree of success the client and I felt over the effect of the interviews. Use of a non-directive approach in a fairly comfortable, yet somewhat effective manner, was also felt to be a strong point. Test interpretations were done in full awareness of the limitations of the results and yet in a way that client's low performances were clear to him as being just that, low performances.

My most apparent weakness was my wanting to make it easier for the client to recognize his low academic aptitude, accept this fact, and change his goals accordingly. My test interpretations were difficult for me because of this. Perhaps I was empathizing too much. I realize now how painful it can be if one's feelings for the client enter too actively into the process, especially when low abilities and high aspirations are involved. Excessive verbalizing was another weakness that I am now aware of. Unnecessary and meaningless phrases in explaining test selection guide, and in describing specific tests were glaring examples of this tendency. However, it was in the first interview that this was most clearly noticeable.

Case Reviews

DUGALD ARBUCKLE

I am writing this after having listened to the three interviews, as I followed them on the typescripts. Let me react to each session specifically, and then generally to the entire counseling experience, and the counselor's reactions to it.

My immediate reaction to the background data was, "What do we need all this for? Is the counselor now going to operate on the basis of the data he has on Carl, and thus possibly reject Carl as he presents himself to the Counselor?" I realize that data of this sort are often considered quite necessary in high school guidance centers, but in counseling, at least, I wonder if it really does anything other than hinder the counseling session by giving the counselor a biased and distorted concept of the client.

Session 1. The first picture presented to the client is one of counselor dominance. He is told in C3 that he has had " a little trouble," and then he is told that he might be heard and observed by others without really being given a chance to say that he doesn't like this arrangement. Did the long pause after S10 indicate this feeling of uneasiness?

In such a "test oriented" situation it is difficult, if not impossible, for the counselor to avoid being dominant and directive, even if he didn't want to. Thus, although in the beginning comments in this session the tone of the counselor is pleasant and acceptant and unhurried, and although the counselor does give the client plenty of time to come in if he wants to, still, the very nature of the approach is such that the counselor is being set up as a directing and manipulative agent.

The counselor's comment after C37 indicates the dilemma that often confronts the school counselor. Doubtful and uncertain about the ability of the client, the counselor may resort to verbalizing, with or without direction, to help the client to relax. The difficulty here, however, is that right at the beginning of the session the client is learning that the counselor is a fellow who does things for you. The Client-centered counselor would feel that it is important that the feeling the client develops is that the counselor is one who understands and accepts, one who does not direct or manipulate, one, rather, who is with him as he talks and feels his difficulties and problems.

In C53, the counselor is placed in the position of being a center of information. To what extent could this sort of information, and that supplied in C61, be presented via the written word, or even possibly explained, if necessary, by a secretary? Having given information, the counselor finds it difficult to get out of this role, and thus the counselor would appear to have either missed or ignored the feeling expressed in S56. Many of the comments that follow would seem to illustrate the difficulty of trying to combine a counseling function with an information giving function. The counselor says it is up to the client, and yet as the source of information surely the counselor is saying to the client, "*I* am the dominant figure."

Such comments as C91-93-95-101-103 would be saying to this reviewer, "I don't want to stay with you on this, but why don't you come along with me and look at this point. . . ." The counselor's comment in C107, "I wanted clarification," raises an interesting question. Does the counselor want clarification so that he can more adequately guide and direct the client, or does he want clarification because his lack of understanding threatens him and causes some uneasiness?

Eventually, however, the client does get rolling, and when this happens, after some fits and starts, every counselor must ask himself, "Is this now happening because of me or in spite of me?" It would seem here that the client wants to express himself, and despite the obstacles that have been thrown up, he eventually succeeds.

Session 2.   This again may illustrate the "shutting off" effect of testing. Does the client really have "nothing more to talk about," or does he find it difficult to talk because of the atmosphere?

Session 3.   The counselor still shows the effects of his test interpretation experiences, but the client moves along, expressing his deep and personal feelings. The counselor almost seems to gradually become more acceptant, and have less need to direct and manipulate and control. I have often wondered if the "eclectic" counselor who directs and manipulates at first, and then "becomes non-directive," is not slowly developing a feeling of some security and comfort, and then, when this is achieved, can afford to become "non-directive." He is not, of course, actually Client-centered in anything other than name, since he does not, apparently, have confidence in the capacities and strengths of either the client or himself!

Session 4.   It would appear that the client has made real progress toward a better self-understanding and self-acceptance, but it is interesting to note how he refers to the tests as having "really helped me a lot." This might be another adverse effect of the use of tests—they give the client the impression that what has happened is because of the tests, rather than because of his own effort. The counselor manages to slip in one last bit of direction in C10, but by this time the client is secure enough so that he can easily reject the suggestion.

Case Summary and Counselor's Comments

Again, in the Case Summary, I have a feeling of some scepticism as to the value of the information which is presented about Carl. The comment is made that, "the impact of the meaning of all test results was not fully accepted by the client." But how can any of us accept test results that sharply contradict our slowly developed self concept? Does the presentation of information, which is so often perceived as a major counselor function, really have any effect? Or is it rather the counseling, the human relationship in which one can talk about this information, that carries some hope of growth and change? There are various media for the presentation of information—but there is no substitute for the human relationship. It may be that the counselor's, "Lack of success in realizing my goal" was not so much because of his inexperience in "technique," but rather because he was still thinking of "client-centered" as a technique of manipulation. Possibly as he moved along he began to feel more trust in the capacity of his client; this in turn increased his own feeling of security and his "comfort level," so that he has less need to manipulate and direct and control. Did the counselor possibly feel at the beginning that somehow the client must be helped to see the unrealism (from the counselor's frame of reference) of his vocational planning, and did the counselor thus deeply reject the aspirations of the client, and thus the client as well? If the counselor is to be *Client*-centered, then all of the client, including his aspirations, are accepted. Realism, or the lack of it, is no problem for the Client-centered counselor. The person is as he is, and he is accepted as he is. If realism is a problem for the client, then it is the client who will work it out. Since the counselor is neither judgmental nor manipulative, he has no uneasy inner concerns about the degree of realism of client choice.

EDWARD ROEBER

In any analysis of *The Case of Carl* one is struck by the persistent attempts of this young man to express his feelings. A few self-references give the tone of the first and third interviews:

> "I can never find nobody at my level to help me."

> ". . . the job would turn out all wrong somewhere . . . nothing would go right."

> "Sometimes I feel lost . . . just really lost. Everybody's going on by real fast. . . . I seem to be stranded—an outcast."

". . . there must be a pattern I can fit in. . . ."

". . . still I couldn't be accepted by them (other kids)."

"I can't blame my friends." (inference that he has none to interfere with his school work.)

"I feel I have to show him (father) something."

From such self-references it is easy to understand the young man's frustrations when faced with failure on every hand and yet filled with a desire to amount to something, to be somebody. Whichever way he turns (work, school, home), he feels his performance always puts him in a bad light. He has a strong desire to express his own individuality—it would help so much if he could simply find some direction or means of expressing himself in a favorable light.

Coming from a home where there is nearly sixty years between father and son, one can sense the psychological distance between the two, ". . . mother and father, they don't seem to take very much interest." Carl wants to show his father that he can do something big and prove himself before his father dies. His relationships with his peers are probably marked by cutting adolescent indifference and/or hostilities, such as those given to the "ugly duckling" type. No matter what he does, Carl sees others achieving and becoming the kind of person he would like to be. He cannot seem to find anyone who understands and accepts him, or who can really help him at his level. On the other hand, he is not too bitter toward those who do not understand or help him—"They would help me if they were patient with me and had the time."

In terms of the counselor's behavior, there are a few pertinent considerations. First, in the first interview, the counselor tries to understand and to convey understanding. But the early tone of voice and the pace of his responses betrayed his inexperience. His responses indicated that he followed the "words but not the melody"—he wanted to follow the examples in the textbook but was fumbling and not in tune with the feelings expressed by Carl. In defense of the counselor it should be said that beginning with C111 he began to understand and reflect his understandings —the change in tone of voice reinforces this conclusion. Second, the third interview, although momentarily derailed by the test results, soon returned to the pattern set in the first interview. It reinforced the trend of understanding and acceptance. It represents some of the counselor's "best efforts." Third, the final interview, although it would rate high on a criterion, such as client-counselor talk ratio, does not measure up to earlier standards. This conclusion is based upon the counselor's unwillingness at strategic times to participate or in any way enter into Carl's monologue. Whereas the counselor participates and gives expressions of understanding in earlier interviews, he suddenly becomes a silent partner. What conclusion would Carl draw from this type of counselor behavior?

Would he need the support of minimal reflection or clarification? Did the counselor behave in this manner because of some prior resolution to be silent? Or, was he afraid to break a silence because of prior supervisory experiences? Or, did he not know how to reply to the stimuli presented in one of Carl's complex responses? There are, of course, no clues to the answers. But the free association which characterized Carl's behavior leads to a serious consideration of what the counselor had in mind and whether the interview accomplished what the counselor thought it did.

The total interaction between Carl and his counselor suggests one or two other observations. Take, for example, Carl's defense in terms of the perceived relationship between interest and effort: "I can pick up an interest real quickly and I can drop it real quickly," in contrast to ". . . you can see the other kids progressing at a A or B rate and you just feel discouraged and you just quit." Carl's use of the word "interest" is different from the usual definition of the term. At times, he seems to use it as a synonym for ability. There is a reluctance to admit that he might lack a capacity for realizing his aspirations. In this connection the counselor is also faced with a dilemma.

How far does the counselor go in helping (or leading) Carl to accept reality, i.e., his lack of ability? Has the counselor been ineffectual if Carl does not accept such a reality? Aspiration-ability conflicts, at least conflicts in the eyes of the counselor, are not rare occurrences. In a sense, until a person gives up and settles for the status quo, or less, there is some of this conflict in everyone. It could be argued that Carl's gap between ambitions and ability is abnormal and more serious than the ordinary case. If the counselor perceives his role as that of narrowing his gap, he will direct his behavior toward this end. His behavior repertoire can vary among forms of coercion, persuasion, suggestion, interpretation, or clarification. He can force the issue until, figuratively, Carl admits he lacks ability. Or, at the other extreme, he can present information in the hope that further talking will clarify his aspirations and abilities and help to narrow the gap. It could also be argued that, if Carl can settle for less when necessary, this gap is not serious. In this latter situation, the counselor may still discuss aspirations and abilities but more in terms of how Carl can find further tryout experiences. The counselor does not wish to prejudge Carl's potentialities. He believes that human potentialities are indescribably difficult to assess, that an individual has the privilege of making a mistake, that he has the right to choose the "hard" way of accomplishing his goals, and that the "good" decision is one which Carl can accept and is willing to follow through.

Another observation was the change from negative and ambivalent self-references in the first and third interviews to ambivalent and more positive self-references in the last interview. This change might indicate some movement. Whether this change in verbal responses transferred and affected overt behavior only follow-up activities could ascertain. There is always the danger that what appears to be a change in attitude is actually Carl's feeling that, "This is what the counselor expects me to say," with no actual change in behavior.

Still another consideration might be Carl's speech patterns, slow reactions, and lack of coordination. The physical status of Carl might have some relationship to his lack of achievement and even attitudes toward self. With no data this concern about the general state of Carl's health is purely conjecture—a hunch.

BUFORD STEFFLRE

My primary reaction to this case is one of compassion. I am uncertain, however, as to who is most deserving of this feeling—Carl, the counselor, the school, or the reviewer. There is much here to concern us and few blessings for us to count.

Carl, by his Southernisms ("my eyes be closed," "I don't be even dreaming," "I've never 'cottoned' to those subjects very well"), his bewilderment, and his deep feelings of inadequacy, seems to be reacting to a delayed cultural shock related to the differences between the big city North and his family's previous home. But not all of this cultural anxiety is occasioned by geographic or rural-urban differences. His father's work as a policeman seems to have represented upward socio-economic mobility for the family and Carl fears that he may slide down the ladder again and lose his tenuous hold on the lower middle class rung. His repeatedly stated vocational objective of lawyer, his Pyrrhic victories over the forces in school tending to eliminate him, and his open statements of naked mobility fear (III, S65, S79, S81) suggest that the family's social and psychological trip has taken more than a generation and has made Carl a displaced person with many of the problems connoted by that term.

A young man in Steinbeck's *Grapes of Wrath* in the depths of defeat and confusion sees an ad in a cheap magazine for a course in radio repair. He daydreams about sending for the course and living happily ever after—the fantasy serves to dull briefly the pain of the present but it also turns his attention from the reality that demands his full energy.

In a parallel situation, Carl sends in an "art aptitude" test to a learn-by-mail art school (III, S14). Carl, however, is living in a more sophisticated world than the Okie and is not even permitted a temporary opiate—his friend and a teacher explain the high cost and questionable motivation of the school, his counselor laughs. (It speaks well for the counselor's integrity that he resisted what must have been a terrible temptation to erase that laugh from the tape. He didn't, however, resist omitting it from the typescript!)

Not only cultural but familial and individual factors result in Carl's being "out" of it. There is a suggestion of parental over-protection (III, S87), the unexplained absence of his mother and the presence of a step-mother, an interest in art and music which is probably not common in his group, no mention of dating or girls, a voice marked by hesitation and immaturity. It is not surprising that he experiences a deep loneliness always near the surface (III, S57)—a loneliness which may be manifesting itself in symptoms of insomnia (III, S35) and which may be contributed to by his apparent failure at taking a masculine role common in his sub-culture (this last is sheer guess work—I mean, "clinical intuition").

Not surprising either are the aggressive impulses which he lets bubble to the surface but which are never responded to by the counselor. First, in a small voice (I, S44, S100), then in a phrase (III, S47, first sentence, and in S69, "I'm so short patient," finally more clearly (III, S71, S89, IV S3.3, 3.6) he tells us that he is angry at people in his world— very angry. His several missed appointments coupled with his avowed enthusiasm for testing suggests that he may also be, at some level of awareness, angry with the counselor.

The counselor appears to be a zealous new convert who doesn't yet understand his catechism but believes implicitly that he believes it implicitly. He tells us that, "Every possible effort was made by the counselor not to consciously influence the process in these interviews." Such a goal seems neither desirable nor possible and, in any event, we cannot judge its attainment because we have little knowledge of the extent to which the counselor's behavior was "consciously" motivated. If the counselor would rephrase his purpose by substituting "unconsciously" for "consciously," he might take the first step toward needed changes. As it stands, he seems to be trying too hard to be something which he shouldn't be anyway—distant, correct, uninvolved. The tape, even more than the typescript, conveys this aura of emotional virginity.

He at once establishes that Carl is no better at giving right answers at the counseling center than he is in the classroom (I, C5, C6) and then emphasizes the test-centeredness which comforts him (I, C11 and following). Carl's plea for reassurance (I, S50) is understandably difficult for the counselor but it probably should not have occasioned such a precipitous flight into psychometrics (I, C53 to C85) in view of the fact that Carl seems anxious to share himself with the counselor (I, S85 and on). For the rest of the first interview the counselor responds to content but not so clumsily as to deter Carl, and their relationship continues to be good. His test assignment procedure with his insistence that Carl do the selecting would seem to illustrate his somewhat doctrinaire approach to counseling—it is as though he felt guilty at mixing tests with his creed of "not consciously influencing," and was trying to rid himself of the guilt through the stylized ritual of client selection of the specific instrument. (There is a western state in which a prisoner condemned to death may choose between two methods of execution. Presumably, the good people of the state feel much relieved at this official expression of respect for the individual.)

In the third interview the counselor, beginning with III, C58 and continuing to the end, shows genuine attention and sensitivity. The fact that he starts nearly every response with "you feel" is a minor point and the cliché doesn't seem to bother Carl who probably hasn't read the same texts as the counselor—he sounds not disapproving so much as disengaged. He knows the words but not the music. Carl, though, has tasted counseling.

In the fourth interview, which I gather pleased the counselor and goes down in the record as a great victory for "the method," progress and counseling stop. Carl becomes the "good" client as he has been the "good" son; he abandons his search for realism and embraces Couéism. Counselor and Carl give up and by conspiratorial double-think agree to call losing "winning" and confusion "clarity." The counselor masks his fear of a relationship with the kind of hostility he believes will bewilder Carl and bewitch his peers and supervisors—silence. See how he leaps at the opportunity to restructure the counseling on a more conventionally social and psychometric basis—IV, C4 to end. The counselor has told Carl, in effect, "I'd rather not be this close to such an untidy personality," and Carl for all his limitations got the message.

Taken as a whole, this is better counseling than Carl would get in 95% of our schools or training laboratories. The counselor does some things well and seems intelligent in this case analysis. (It occurs to me that being both bright and cold it would be a good bet that within ten years he will be working as a counselor-educator.) My concern is that the usual education for a counselor is designed to emphasize his intellectual skills even more but does little to overcome the psychological distance toward the client which he now evidences. The assignment which resulted in his analyzing the typescript might very well increase his defensive correctness. Certainly, when he criticizes himself for an occasional rather meaningless word (I, C71, C73, C85) but overlooks more major mistakes (most of interview IV; I, C49, C53) he is straining what he should easily swallow while swallowing more than he should. I don't think his counseling will improve until he tries consciously to use himself with humanity and without reserve to increase the client's self-awareness and clear perception of his world, and to convey to the client that he is "received." To do this he will need to make contact, not hold himself so tightly in check.

Now, most dangerously of all, I submit one way of looking at the case of Carl—*one* way, not *the* way. Carl might be seen as suffering from what the semanticists call the IFD condition. "I" for idealization and its impossible demands on the self and the world. Carl wants a car now with no waiting and no interference with other goals; he wants marks although he has little ability and invests little time in study; he wants to be a "good" son and a free man; he wants the school to play by his, not society's rules; he wants the right to be a lawyer whether or not he has necessary skills; he wants to be passed without question or pity. These impossible demands lead to Frustration, and its accompanying anger and confusion. Frustration in turn results in defeat, despair, disorganization. So, in Carl we see loneliness, hostility, confusion, and immaturity. It is not the counselor's prerogative to reset Carl's feet on a preconceived path, but he might help Carl to assess the cost and worth of his mutually exclusive goals. Sunday morning quarterbacks always know what play should have been called and in this case the counselor might have tested less and played more by heart. Carl seemed ripe for counseling and while I think he was fortunate in not getting a worse counselor, I was sorry to see stylized "insight" replace a deeper experience. Finally, wouldn't it be illuminating to know Carl's present perception of "counseling"?

WILLIS DUGAN AND DONALD BLOCHER

Overview

The case of Carl provides an excellent example of the problem which is posed by a student with unrealistic aspirations. In this case, the situation is complicated by the strong feelings of rejection and inadequacy felt by the client. The combination of client feelings and unrealistic aspirations provides a case which would be challenging to any counselor.

In dealing with Carl the counselor made excellent use of the techniques of simple acceptance and understanding. He created a warm, permissive relationship in which Carl was able to bring out his feelings about himself and to verbalize his many frustrations. As a result of this relationship, Carl was able in the final interview to talk in a more positive way about himself and his future possibilities.

Progress

Unfortunately, however, the crucial elements in Carl's problem were relatively unchanged at the conclusion of the final interview. He still clung to his aspiration for a career in law; an ambition which seemed almost completely unrealistic in terms of his total background. Although he could verbalize more positive self feelings, he still needed the many rationaliza-tions for his performance which were present in the opening interview. One wonders how much permanent value Carl will receive from this counseling as he continues to test his unrealistic aspirations against the world of reality.

Use of Test Data

As one analyzes this case, a number of alternative courses of action come to mind. Carl approached the counseling center in terms of its value in helping him learn what he could do and could not do. When the results of testing did not support his aspirations, however, he rationalized them away. One wonders whether, if the results of the tests had been more skillfully integrated into the first three interviews and if they had been interpreted in a way which Carl might have found easier to accept, if his reaction to them might have been more positive.

The choice of the tests themselves was left entirely to the client. Two scholastic aptitude tests were taken. These, of course, did not support the client's aspirations and did not help identify any alternatives which might have supplanted the unrealistic ambition of law.

Consideration of Alternatives

The whole area of raising alternative possibilities was pretty well neglected in this case. The boy's attraction to police work, which might have had some possible element of reality in it, was never thoroughly explored. The distribution of responsibility for the interview and the talk ratio were commendably weighted in the direction of the client. Perhaps just a bit more counselor responsibility would have opened up some new avenues for discussion which would have been productive.

Client Defenses

Another question is raised in terms of Carl's defense system. He presented a number of strong rationalizations which he apparently needed to protect himself from anxiety aroused by a realistic appraisal of his ability and achievements. The counselor did not tamper with these defenses. In fact, to a slight extent he supported and strengthened them! At the beginning of counseling, Carl's defenses were not working well. His poor sleep, nightmares, and free-floating anxiety were evidence of this. The counselor very wisely did not attempt to break down these defenses further. The nature of the defenses, however, may have made realistic vocational planning impossible for Carl. If the counselor judged that Carl could not function without these defenses, a referral for psychotherapy might have been desirable. Perhaps Carl's vocational problem could not be worked out until underlying emotional problems had been resolved.

Maximal Roles

The case of Carl thus seems to illustrate the values inherent in an accepting, permissive counseling relationship. It may, however, also illustrate the need for sophistication in the use of tests and knowledge of occupational information which would enable a counselor to use his relationship with a client in a maximally effective way.

SIGNIFICANT QUESTIONS FOR DISCUSSION

1. In the first interview Carl says (S50), "I'd like to know definitely what I can do and what I can't do." Do you have some ways of responding to this typical client desire other than that given by Mr. Williams, Carl's counselor?
2. Is Carl realistic in his vocational choices? How does a counselor determine what are realistic choices of a client?
3. How would you analyze the material developed in the third interview? How important would it be for a counselor to be able to analyze the feelings revealed by Carl while the counseling was in process?
4. If you had been the counselor in what ways might you have handled this client differently?
5. If you had a chance to talk with the counselor, what would you have wanted to discuss with him after each interview?
6. Where do the reviewers agree and disagree in their review of *The Case of Carl?* What are your reactions to the reviews?

The Case of Jane

Purpose of the Interviews

When the appointment to the laboratory was made, Jane had indicated that she would like to come and discuss some of the problems she had regarding her plans to attend college.

Background Data on the Student

The counselor knew nothing about the client's background prior to the first interview. The high school counselor had suggested the girl's name to the counseling laboratory, and the laboratory counselor arranged an appointment by telephoning Jane at home.

The Interviews

<table>
<tr><td colspan="2" align="center">FIRST
INTERVIEW</td><td align="center">COUNSELOR'S
COMMENTS</td></tr>
<tr><td>S1</td><td>It's nice in here.</td><td></td></tr>
<tr><td>C2</td><td>We've got the fan going. We're trying to make it more comfortable.</td><td></td></tr>
<tr><td>S3</td><td>Mm-hmm.</td><td></td></tr>
<tr><td>C4</td><td>On the sheet, as I mentioned before, you can take that home and finish it, and, uh, if you do come back you can bring it back or mail it back, whichever you prefer.</td><td></td></tr>
<tr><td>S5</td><td>Mm-hmm.</td><td></td></tr>
<tr><td>C6</td><td>Tell me, did you have a rough time getting down here?</td><td>Better to let client start interview.</td></tr>
<tr><td>S7</td><td>Not rough but, whenever I ride the bus I just get all excited about whether I'm going to get off on time and . . .</td><td></td></tr>
<tr><td>C8</td><td>Oh, and you just made the mistake of going up on the third floor.</td><td></td></tr>
<tr><td>S9</td><td>Yes. Couldn't find it after I got off the bus, too. I couldn't find it.</td><td></td></tr>
</table>

C10 Tell me, did Mrs. Fischer tell you any-
     thing about our laboratory setup here?

S11 No she didn't. Uh . . . she didn't say
     too much about it at all but I did
     know that there was counseling here at
     Wayne.

C12 Well let me explain this to you first.
     Number one, that is a microphone for
     a tape recorder and what we are saying
     is being taped, but the purpose is for
     me so that during our conversations we
     can spend our time talking about what
     you would like, and then afterwards I
     can listen to the tape to see if there is
     something important that we should
     take up again.

S13 Mm-hmm.

C14 And whatever we do say between us is
     strictly confidential and will go no
     further. I want you to understand that.

S15 Mm-hmm.

C16 Secondly, that funny looking mirror is   Perhaps I'm being too defen-
     an observation, one-way, mirror it is   sive.
     called, and from time to time there
     might be some people behind there,
     professional counselors who will be ob-
     serving me. Not you, but me—so I
     should be the one that should be nerv-
     ous, not you. And, as I said, there are
     professional people and what they do
     here will go no further than that room.
     So what we say is strictly in confidence.
     Um . . . we have 45 minutes and the
     amount of time you would like to use
     on that time is up to you. You can use
     the full time, half the time or get up
     and leave any time you like, and you
     are not under obligation to come back
     unless you want to.

S17 Mm-hmm.

C18 OK?

S19 I'm quite used to a tape recorder at any
     rate, not a window where people can

      look, but it makes no difference to me,
      I guess.

C20 Good.

S21 One way or another.

C22 Well, tell me Jane, why did you come
      down here? What would you like to
      talk about?

S23 I'm kind of sick of talking about my-
      self, first of all, because I've had, I
      don't know what I should say, trouble,
      I guess, is the closest thing to it. Not
      with the police, not with anyone like
      that, but with my own self and maybe
      with my family.

C24 You found that you have been a little   Should have left out "a
      bit confused and mixed up in your   little bit."
      feelings and with your family up to
      this point.

S25 Not really only just a little bit either,
      quite a bit. Uh . . . I don't know. I
      think I'm quite a lucky person, so
      lucky that I just can't understand that
      I've done so many things that I've ever
      wanted. I've always got them. And one
      was to go to Europe last summer. Mrs.
      Fischer, she helped me do that. When
      I came back everything seemed so dif-
      ferent. I question everything and I
      don't like the discipline I find at home
      and I don't like the restrictions and I
      find . . .

C26 You found that you have changed your
      attitudes after you returned from this
      trip to Europe?

S27 Very much, and I think that if I hadn't
      gone to Europe I wouldn't have changed
      quite that much because now I can
      see that. I have a twin sister first of all,
      and if it's not I that overshadows her
      then she overshadows me, at one time
      or another. We always would grow in
      spurts and one is always ahead of the
      other.

C28 You feel there's always a competition

going on with one leading at various times.

S29   And at this point right now I think she is, because I'm so mixed up I just don't know which way to turn. I don't know what I want to do. I know I've got a scholarship now to go to college, but the college I am going to is expensive anyway and I don't want to take any money from my parents, yet I am going to because I want to get away from home, and I know if I stayed home it would be cheaper, but they are willing to give me the money so I am going to go.

C30   In other words, you have got a scholarship to go away to college but you are still going to have to take money from your parents. You feel somewhat mixed up about this but you are going to go ahead because you want to go away badly enough.

Might have also reflected statement, re sister.

S31   Yeah. And as mercenary as that sounds it is the way I feel.

C32   Well you have mixed feelings about it. You feel it may not be the right thing but you feel it is what you need to help you.

S33   Yeah. That's another word I'm sick of too because I take so darn much help and I can't help myself much. I had a special counselor in high school just last year. Mrs. Fischer. I told her that I had quite a bit of trouble and she referred immediately to Mrs. Meadow at our school, and so . . . I, she's helped me somewhat, but I want to know what I'm going to study for and whether it's going to be worth it. I know I can get through school. I'm quite sure I can anyway, if I keep up my work, but it seems like I keep sliding and sliding and sliding.

C34   In other words, right now there are

three questions, what you are going to do in college, what you are going to study, and you are worried if you are going to be a success at it or not.

S35　Mm-hmm. Mostly, that's it I guess. Whether it is just going to be worth it, whether it . . . It seems like nothing is worth it any more. I don't go to church and that's another heated point at our house. My parents have always forced us to go to church and yet they never do and so—I don't go any more. Maybe they think I do but I don't.

C36　You feel somewhat guilty about not going when you did before.

I'm putting words into client's mouth.

S37　I don't know if I've ever felt guilty about it. I've always felt rebellious against going to church. I've always rebelled against it. It seemed like every Sunday we had a big fight, always did, even if all of us kids really wanted to go, or just were going to go without any argument. It was either—well, it was either that, or if we didn't want to go, the argument was about that, but if we were going to go my mother was always up in the air about what we were to wear.

C38　There's always been some kind of argument associated with going to church on Sunday.

S39　Mm-hmm.

C40　You find that you can't accept many of your church teachings at this point, whereas before you did without question.

Again I'm introjecting a thought which client did not state.

S41　Sure. I didn't question it at all. I just never . . . It was just something that had to be done and I never did question it too much at all. I never knew too much about it although I did go to Catechism. I never knew too much about it, and now I don't, and so I made it my summer project to read the

Bible which I am going to do. I always tried to get my hands on religious articles to find what everybody thinks about it, and what's what, but it seems all of them have something that I don't agree with.

C42 You can't find one religion that holds everything you would agree with, but you have decided to start towards that way anyway by reading the Bible this summer.

S43 Mm-hmm. As far as I know now, nobody in my family has read it anyway. Uh, maybe my dad has. I think he has, but he is one of the persons that always, oh, we'd sit you know, kids used to sit around my dad's chair. When he'd talk to us every once in a while, he was always tired, but he would always talk about how he had to go to a Catholic school. He hated it, and he would never go again, and how awful it was and, well, he never goes to church anyway. He never did, he said. As far as I know he never has. Once or twice he goes, as far as I can remember, and he is the one that has always said that he never wanted to go and that he couldn't get it. He was just through with it, period, and yet, he is the one that says that while you're living with us you're going to go to church now.

C44 You can't quite understand his insisting on your going, but yet saying at the same time that he would never go to it again, and he doesn't go but yet he insists upon your going.

Good summary of what client said. May draw her out further.

S45 This is what I feel now after a lot of thinking about it. I do think about it a lot. I think that my dad can see that. This is what my dad thinks, that in the future, some time or other, I am going to want to go to church, and I am going to want to follow this religion that

I have been brought up to, and that he doesn't want me to give it up now because then if I don't, well, then I'll lose it. That's how I think he feels about it, I suppose. I don't know how else he can feel about it because he knows that I don't want to go, and we can't discuss it because he just—one little thing I might say like, oh, silly things like the one thing, the biggest thing right now, is that I can't see them spending all that money on the things that they do when they could take it and use it for something better it seems to me.

C46 You find yourself confused, or you can't agree with your parents spending money for something now?

S47 No, the church.

C48 Oh, giving money to the church now when they could be using the money to benefit themselves?

S49 No, no, no. I mean the church. The church in the Catholic Church. Have you ever been inside one or . . .

C50 Yes, I have. I didn't understand. Perhaps you can clarify this for me, if you want?

I couldn't follow client at this point, so question seems in order.

S51 The church spends this money on goon chalices, and the big beautiful buildings that they do, and they do have big beautiful buildings. A lot of other churches do, too, and it seems like they spend a lot of their money just to keep the church going and to keep the social things up and all that other, I always say, baloney. Probably that's why my dad gets mad, because I treat it completely without respect, because I don't feel much respect for it.

C52 You feel a definite lack of identification with the church because they are spending . . .

S53 Definitely.

C54 A great deal of, well a great sum of money, on immaterial kinds of things?

S55 Mm-hmm.

C56 The building and different items that are used.

S57 It seems a futile thing to talk about. It's just something that can go on and on I suppose but . . .

C58 You get pretty discouraged talking about it and thinking about it.

S59 That's one thing with my parents, and another thing is that they run, been growing more strict, and my mother is rather a nervous person, and I think she is going through the change of life anyway, and besides, she is working. I think she feels she has to work to put us through college. There's always a lot of financial strain at our home. I spend so darn much money. My parents are always talking about we haven't got any money, yet the things we own. We've got so many things. If they would only just either stop talking about it or stop spending it, one or the other, they could relieve all that tension, yet they don't. Both of them work. There's a lot of money at our house. There's six people to support, too. We've got a house here, we've got a house up north, we've got a motor boat, skis, a house trailer, a tractor, a motor scooter, a racing boat for my brother, and now they're going to have to spend money to send us to school. That's the biggest thing I can think of, that they are going to have to spend all that great sum of money for us to go to school and I feel like I am just a big burden.

C60 In other words, you feel pretty upset about accepting this money at a time when apparently you do have all the material luxuries you need, plus more,

The client sees both the church and her parents as extravagant.

yet, your parents always talk about, "We don't have enough and we have to cut down"?

S61 Mm-hmm. It seems like it is, but on top of that, even if it wasn't for that it's just that I don't seem to get along with my parents too much any more, and I feel like if I can't give them the respect and the honor that they deserve, well, then they shouldn't give me the money either. I feel guilty about accepting the money, I guess. That's the biggest thing.

C62 And you feel badly about accepting the money when you don't hold the same values or respect for them that at one time you did, and this is a little upsetting.

Leave out the word "little."

S63 Mm-hmm. Even if I . . . I don't know exactly what values and respect I ever did give to them but whatever it was I think maybe I respect them a little more now, but whatever I do feel, I feel that I get it out of my system. I just tell them what I think. I respect them even more now, I think, because I see that they have to put up with us, and they do. They put up with each other and they put up with us all the time because we are a bunch of big loud mouths. That's all there is to it, I think, and I don't know why it is, but I have grown up seeing my parents yell at each other all the time. They do yell at each other an awful lot and it never seemed to me that they showed each other too much respect in front of us, and whatever it is now I don't know, but I don't show them the respect that I feel, probably, and I do feel quite a bit of respect for them—just for being able to hang on with us, being able to stick together with us.

C64 Surely deserve some credit for maintaining the home despite their own
feelings and the four or five children
you have in the family.

I might have reflected on client's inability to express her feelings towards her parents.

S65 Mm-hmm. Four. It seems like they give
us so much I really feel very guilty
about it, because I know that my
mother is under a strain and so is my
dad because he is worried about losing
his job. My mother is under this other
physical change. I am quite sure that's
what it is. She goes to the doctor every
once in a while for it and yet what do
they do but . . . The house seems to
get messed up quite easily. It seems like
we're the messiest kids there are. I don't
know what it is. It just gets messed up
quite easily. Mother gets up late in the
morning because she goes to work late
in the evening, works until 2:00 and
comes home at 3:00 so it just is inevitably a mess. It's always a mess and the
wash is never caught up on, no matter
if Judy and I both work on it, or if she
does. She just gets carried away, I suppose. Whatever it is. She lets these
things get under her skin. These little
things bother her. Little things!

C66 You find your mother gets upset when
the house is a mess and the clothes
aren't caught up.

S67 Hum. The same as I do. My mother
and I are quite alike I suppose. As
much as I fight it. I don't want to be
as nervous as she is and I don't want
to be caught up in things like she does.

C68 You feel . . . You don't want to have
the same emotional state of being nervous and upset about things, and yet
you feel that you might be and think
about this.

Might have clarified her problems in identifying with her mother.

S69 Hum. I'm closer to her than my dad,
although, you know, we both pick up

different things from both of them, but Judy and I are not alike at all. She's more calm than I am.

C70 So Judy, you feel, is more relaxed and at ease than you are.

S71 Mm-hmm. Uh, if you could meet her you could see what I mean. I can't explain it because we're alike in some things and in some things we're not. I don't know exactly what it is but I do know that when I spent a summer away from my family I changed quite a bit and maybe if I hadn't gone away from them I wouldn't have. I might still be under the same things, under the same . . . I don't know. I never looked at it quite this way but I might never have changed quite a bit, quite as much, because I wasn't out away from them and wasn't able to develop.

C72 You feel that being away from them changed your thinking and made you look at things a little differently.

S73 Mm-hmm. Maybe it wasn't that I didn't go to Germany, and start thinking, "Well I won't go to church because I don't have to, and I don't believe in God, anyway," and all that. But I had to do more things on my own. I made my own decisions. I don't mean I started. I continued doing that. And they don't like it.

C74 You found you met a brick wall when you continued to make your own decisions at home as you had been doing when you were in Europe.

S75 Not that I did so darn many things on my own. As a matter of fact, I did. I had three sisters there, and usually it is an exchange program, but they were older than me. Usually they are younger, or the same age, and my sisters were thirty and twenty-three and twenty-one and, too, my parents were older. They were, I think, wealthy for Germany, and they were used to letting these girls make their own decisions, and so they let me make my own, but was I surprised at first, but then it was kind of nice to have to do these things on my own and not have to report to somebody because I was going to do something. I didn't do anything wrong. I never did anything wrong.

C76 You liked your freedom.

S77 Yes I did, very much. I did exactly what I felt like doing. If I wanted to go for a long walk all day, well then I did, and if I wanted to see Munich I went to see it, and if I wanted to see something that I wanted to see, well I went to see it, and if I wanted to see somebody that I wanted to see, well I went to see them, and I didn't have to report to anyone and, yet, I even surprised myself in the responsibility that I took on, and the right way that I did things. I didn't do anything wrong.

C78 You found that you liked the independence, and yet, along with the independence you assumed greater responsibility.

S79 Mm-hmm. This is something I think my parents won't accept. I couldn't drive a car there, true, but I rode trains which I had never done before, and I rode trolleys which I wasn't used to, and I did everything else like that, and I didn't have the car to go gallivanting around, but whatever I wanted to do I did it, and it's different here. I do want to take the car quite a bit. I'll admit that.

C80 You realize that your desire for the car may be more than what you really should be getting in your situation.

S81   Mm-hmm. Because the transportation here isn't the same there, and I did have the transportation there. I did have it somehow if I wanted it. But if I wanted to take a bus here—humph— you have to walk a mile just to get to the bus stop and then it takes all year to get you there and its not comfortable, and so I want the car, but they don't seem to think it's quite safe for me to go out on a weekend like on a day trip because the traffic is so bad. Things like that.

C82   In other words your parents still are treating you like a little girl.

S83   Somewhat. I'll have to be fair with them and admit that they give me an awful lot of things that I want, but those things that they do give me are in the order of material things and no, well, like for instance if I want to bake a cake or make a pie my mother wants to be there to show me how, and I want to do it on my own, even if I make a mistake. I want to do it on my own. Some things like that. She'll give me all the things to do it, and she'll clear everyone out of the kitchen for me to do it, and everything, but she wants to be there too to help me do it. That's just a small thing but it's one thing that really gets me, gets under my skin because I want to do it myself. I'm seventeen years old and I should be able to make a cake.

C84   You feel that when you decide that you want to do some minor task like this in the house or something, for your own good, you want to do it by yourself and if you make a mistake then you will profit by your own mistake . . .

S85   Mm-hmm.

C86   Rather than have someone else, your

mother, there telling you not to do it this way.

S87   Mm-hmm, which is something that I can honestly say that I haven't been able to do. My mother has always wanted to show me how to do things. I don't know why it is, but Judy's escaped a little bit of that. I think she has.

C88   You feel that your mother is kind of, been even more overlooked, or spent more time looking after you in a sense of making sure that she was always there when you were doing things. In other words, kept you down more than Judy.

S89   I think so. Even looking at it quite objectively, I really do think so. Why I don't know.

C90   You don't know the reason but you feel she has been more strict with you.

S91   Mm-hmm. Maybe it's because I've been behind Judy for quite a while. I was always above Judy in scholastic abilities but when it came to maturing socially and getting along with other people, well I was usually behind her.

C92   You estimate that you were ahead scholastically, but Judy, socially, you felt or you feel was ahead of you.

S93   Mm hmm.

C94   For a time being. You think this might have some bearing on why your mother chose to be more strict with you.

S95   Mm-hmm. More protective. Let's put it that way. I think it's better. Just protective. Maybe another reason is because she saw me, saw herself in me. She wants me to have the things she didn't have.

Client has considerable insight, re her mother.

C96   You feel . . .

S97   She wants me to do the things she didn't have and she doesn't say that to Judy.

C98   You feel she identifies with you more and this might be one explanation for her overprotectiveness towards you.

S99   Mm-hmm.

C100   And she has told you so in so many words.

S101   Mm-hmm. And then that's, uh, these kind of problems seem to be the kind that will iron themselves out but I am kind of worried about what I am going to do in college, too, because I wanted to be a writer for a long time and yet this whole situation is making me quite nervous. I feel like quite a nervous person even just sitting here talking with you. I don't know which —what to say next and yet I just keep rambling on. It's how I feel, I guess, like a disconnected ninny and so I can't sit down and put my thoughts down like I once could maybe a year ago.

C102   You feel the home situation is upsetting you to the point that what you would like to do as a career, uh, the two just don't go together. You're too upset really to sit down and give your full effort and concentration to writing your thoughts coherently and slowly.

S103   Mm-hmm. I'm not even . . . I'd like them to be coherent, yes, I'd like them to be—anyway if I could only sit down and write something, and there were times when I could. I like to write letters to my sisters in Germany and I found that difficult to do even now because I just can't sit down.

C104   Just can't sit in any one place for any length of time.

S105   Mm-hmm. I just can't unless I am reading something and I read an awful lot lately, more than I ever have. I read anything I can get my hands on, every

Client is expressing real anxiety and deep fears at this point and I should have reflected these feelings more intensively.

magazine that comes in. I read it almost from cover to cover and any book that we have got and I go to the library and get more books. It seems like the only thing I can do, unless I do ironing or something like that which takes a little thought. It seems dangerous to me because I don't want to turn into a nut. A nut. Why do I use these phrases. I don't want to have a nervous breakdown and I feel like I might. I really am afraid of it.

C106 Well, you're somewhat concerned about feeling and thinking about these home problems so much and not being able to sit still and the only thing you can do is to read and then you are a little concerned about this.

S107 Quite a bit. (*Long pause*) And the problem grows bigger than I realize and just think that I always have to have an extra counselor.

C108 It's kind of upsetting, too. You feel it's kind of upsetting to always have to lean on someone.

S109 Mm-hmm. Quite. (*Pause*) The only time I didn't have to is when I was on my own. And then Mrs. Meadow at Lincoln said that for myself to really consider myself adjusted I am going to have to adjust to these things at home, and yet I just can't. No matter how much I try I just can't. If it's not one person arguing with another it's another one.

C110 Presently you just can't resolve that situation at home.

S111 No, I can't. I just want to get away.

C112 You feel you want to go away.

S113 Quite a bit. Even if I—(*Pause*) just to get away from one part of them—to go up north maybe. Sometimes it helps quite a bit just to get away from my mother or just to get away from Charles. If one person is missing from this picture it helps sometimes.

C114   If you could just go away with one part of the picture missing.

S115   But I can't do that for the rest of my life, just keep . . . oh, and that's another thing. I don't like to have many friends either, and that sounds funny, but I just don't like to feel obligated to a bunch of people.

C116   You don't want the obligations and responsibility of friends.

S117   Yes. I like to pick my own friends. That's what I mean and my mother likes to pick my friends for me.

C118   Your mother makes choices of your friends rather than you making your own choices.

S119   Well, if there's somebody that I like very much and I want to bring him over and she doesn't like him, well, I just can't. The only person that I considered a good friend in high school was one girl that I met in the tenth grade and my mother doesn't like her at all, and so I couldn't bring her over. It's not so much that she said don't bring her over, but when you do bring her over, and my mother happens to be home, picture this, and your mother happens to be home, she will ignore this girl, just ignore her, and be surly and stomp around and yell at everyone else, just make it impossible, just make it embarrassing to have the girl over. I can't have her over and we're not such good friends any more because we just kind of—it's too much of a tension for me to keep her as a friend.

C120   The only friend you had in high school your mother didn't like and as a result, now the friendship is kind of broken off.

S121   Definitely. I haven't seen her since school let out. I can't mention her name because my mother, you can just feel her get upset about it, and there's no sense in mentioning her name. I don't mean I didn't. . . . A friend is someone that I consider an intimate friend, someone you can talk to, someone you feel understands you, someone you feel might have the same kind of problems you do and someone . . . I also feel that a good friend of mine has to have some sort of intelligence because I'm not a stupid person myself.

Client may really be talking about me now. Asking whether she can really confide in me.

C122   A mutual friend should be able to have compassion and understanding for your problems as well as being an intelligent person.

S123   A mutual friend, yes. It should be a mutual friendship, someone that I can understand and someone who can talk to me, and someone to whom I can also talk.

C124   There can be a give and take in the relationship.

S125   Yes. And I had a—I knew almost everyone in school and I held a lot of offices and I had all that other stuff, but those were acquaintances and they were, you know, high school friends but not, how can I say it? I don't know how to differentiate. They were the popular kind of success. They were part of this popular success that I think someone else looking at me might feel that I enjoyed in high school, because I did enjoy popular success in high school.

C126   Outwardly you appear to be a very popular successful girl but inwardly you were very upset and didn't have any close friends.

S127   Yes. I don't mean to sound bragging

about it, but I feel that is the only way I can tell you about it, that I was rather, you know, part of the social world and sometimes I enjoyed it, but if I should ever feel alone, well, I could never feel that there were too many people that I could turn to— only this one girl who my mother did not like.

C128   In your loneliness you only had one person to turn to, and your mother prevented that.

S129   There were two girls, I should tell you also, in the seventh and eighth grade, who were good friends of mine and good friends of Judy. My mother liked those girls very, very much and they are nice sweet individuals. Quite nice, but there is something that I think, I don't know. I don't feel that I want either of these girls to be my best friends and we were best friends in the seventh and eighth grades but when high school started I—I don't know. I will have to say that I always envied one or both, one I know for sure, and I still do because she seems to be the epitomy of femininity and I want to be so feminine. I don't, maybe that is part of my problem. That is another thing. I want to be a feminine person and this girl seems to be ideal in my mother's eyes, too, and I don't like to be around her, especially if my mother is there.

C130   This was one girl who you were friendly with and your mother approved of, and you don't want to be around her when your mother is there. She also epitomizes what you would like to be.

S131   Yes.

C132   In your mother's eyes.

S133   One quality that I really would like to have and that is to be feminine. Her type of femininity, and I know there are a lot of types, but this girl is a soft, white-skinned blonde. And now I don't know if I want that quality that she has because I know her quite well now, and I wouldn't want to be her, and I don't know if I want to be a fair-skinned blonde but this . . . I think the problem is that my mother loves this girl so very much I always feel like she would rather have her for a daughter than she would for me.

C134   You feel somewhat envious of this girl because your mother seems to lavish so much attention and love on her in comparison to you.

S135   She would like to have her over, and anything that I wanted to do, if I was doing it with Barbara, it was OK, but any other friend, well, I just couldn't do it.

C136   She always conceded to your wishes when it included this girl, but not any others.

S137   Mm-hmm, and there is another problem that all ties in with this Lois. Lois is the good friend. Mary is the bad friend, and Lois is an intelligent person, someone who I enjoy being with. She won the Ford scholarship, things like that and it's not that—she's not rich or anything. I don't consider our family rich but we did have quite a bit more than Lois did and that didn't tie in at all, I don't think, as far as my mother was concerned, but she is an outspoken person and (*Pause*) not only outspoken, but we were both rather silly with each other, you know, saying silly things and making up crazy things to say and we always understood each other, but probably no one else would understand because we just had a funny way of talking to each other and we could understand.

C138   You enjoyed a lot of foolishness together.

S139   Together, yes, but with other people
both of us are rather reserved and . . .

C140   You both withdraw from other people.

S141   Mm-hmm. Shy, I don't know. It just
seemed no one else could understand
our thoughts. She reads a lot too. I
don't know whether that has anything
to do with it but . . .

C142   The two of you just seem to understand each other.

S143   Yes.

C144   Whereas no one else seemed to understand you two.

S145   Yes. Now that—another thing I will
have to say is that this breaking off of
our friendship isn't necessarily a direct
result of my mother's forbidding it,
forbidding my friendship with her. It
just seems to be a drawing away because there is some quality, this quality
of sharpness in Lois, is more and more
repelling me because I don't know. She
is making friendships with other people, too, and people that I didn't too
well approve of.

C146   You feel this quality of sharpness and
moving out to other people that you
wouldn't associate with is really the
reason for your breaking off rather
than your mother forbidding you to
see her.

S147   It's more that, because no matter what
my mother thinks, even if she didn't
want me to have Lois for a friend, well,
I would anyway.

C148   You feel you would go ahead and retain her as a friend even if your mother
didn't want you to.

S149   I would try to, yes. I would try to because I need a friend. I mean, well,

By continuing to talk about
her friend Lois, client sees
that it is not just her mother

you just can't say, "Well my mother doesn't want me to have you for a friend, so I won't see you any more, and I'll do everything I can, even though I would like to have you for a friend, I will do everything I can not to have you for a friend." I could never do that because I needed her and so this growing away is more probably my wish than my mother's. However, this is a tension still, and I will probably never have Lois as a close friend again unless —until I move away. I'll have to see what develops then. We will probably write to each other but . . .

that interferes with the friendship.

C150   You feel there is a possibility in the future but only if you are away from home.

S151   Mm-hmm. Only if I feel free to make my own friends, which I never have, except when we lived in Detroit, before we moved. Everybody was friends with everybody on this block that we lived on in Detroit. It seemed like kids don't do that any more but the whole block was one big gang, it seemed like. But then when we moved my mother became so choosey about who we were going to associate with.

C152   You felt that you did have friends and found it easy to relate to people when you lived in Detroit. Everyone just seemed to get along together, but when you did move, your parents tended to select friends, became very selective.

S153   There weren't any kids on our block and there still aren't—our age. There is no one in our neighborhood our own age except these two girls. Probably that's why—that's another reason we were friends. They were the only ones around and yet they were good girls, too. They were nice people to know. It was lucky for us, I suppose, that

Client may be expressing a wish to confide in me further.

they were in our neighborhood, somewhat anyway, and it's such a complex
picture. There are so many things that
probably you should know and yet . . .

C154   It's a pretty confusing picture.

S155   It is confusing. I know it is. Everyone's   Another remark that may
life is confusing. I know I always say   relate to me.
that I will never understand anyone
completely, because I can't even understand myself, and I will never expect
anyone to understand me.

C156   Well, you feel it is a confusing picture
at this point.

S157   Yes. Maybe you can see it more clearly   When I don't respond to
than I can. (*Very long pause*) What   what client is trying to say
my abilities are and everything, right   she changes the subject ab-
now, I just don't know. My grades went   ruptly and gets back to safer
down in high school this last year.   ground by talking of her
They have never been as bad. I've held   school problems.
an A average all the way through since
maybe the third or fourth grade in
grade school. Maybe, you know, I
would drop down a little bit but it
was still either B or A, and in high
school it was more difficult than ever.
I expected it and I—it always seemed
if I wanted to do well I could but all
of a sudden this twelfth grade it just
became impossible for me to settle
down enough to do this work that I
have to bring home and do. I couldn't
do it at home.

C158   No matter how much you tried you
just couldn't do the work at home in
the twelfth grade.

S159   No. I had the ability to do it, yes, but
I couldn't sit down and do it.

C160   You realize you could do it.

S161   I feel that I could.

C162   You had the ability but it was just
something at home. You couldn't do it.

S163   Mm-hmm, so my average is more high
C, or maybe it's a B or low B. It's
probably closer to that. B minus instead

of the A minus that I had. That doesn't bother me so much as what it points to, bothers me. That I couldn't do it, couldn't do the work.

C164   You're worried about the cause of the drop.

S165   Yes. I don't know. Do I worry more about these little things . . . I—than other people do? I don't know.

C166   You're wondering if you worry more about these things than other people do.

S167   Yes. And if I would stop worrying then maybe these would straighten out easily, more easily.

C168   You feel possibly if you stopped worrying about it they might straighten themselves out.

S169   Not completely stop worrying about it, but do things about it instead of just worrying about it.

C170   You feel you should do things about this, do something for it instead of worrying about it all the time.

S171   Yes. Like now, I should have a job I think. I should have a job, and I did have a job last year, last semester, while I was in school.

C172   You feel you should be working now.

S173   I should be getting some money but, uh, there again, I get too picky about where I want to work. And at our house there is also the problem of transportation, because we have got two cars, but my mother takes one to work, my dad takes the other to work, and unless I work in the neighborhood, well, there's no good transportation. There's no bus system that I could use.

C174   You feel you should be working but you're a little too selective about the kind of job and . . .

S175   I'll have to admit that, yes.

C176   Then there is the transportation.

S177 That's an excuse, but the selectivity is really in me. I wanted to be a camp counselor.

C178 You feel the transportation was an excuse.

S179 It's rationalizing for one thing, but it also is a real excuse. There is no other way. There is no transportation out where we live, by Roosevelt and Wilson, except the local bus, but which just goes down Wilson to Roosevelt and turns, so transportation is a problem. It is, but I feel like if I wanted a job I could go out and get something.

C180 If you want a job enough you could overcome the transportation problem.

S181 Mm-hmm. I really do think I could.

C182 I tell you Jane . . . I see that our time is running out for this afternoon. Would you be interested in coming back and talking some more?

S183 Yes. Uh, would it be possible for me to have an earlier appointment?

C184 I tell you what, I think so. Let's go outside and look at the appointment calendar.

**SECOND
INTERVIEW**

**COUNSELOR'S
COMMENTS**

S1 That's the same kind, you know.

C2 Oh.

S3 Same kind of case.

C4 Same kind of case. Nineteen-cent bargain?

S5 I don't know. It's my dad's. He'll probably get me when I get home.

C6 Oh. Well tell me, how have you been?   Poor way to begin interview. Should have allowed client to start.

S7 Well, vacation was a lot of fun for me, so I feel better.

C8 Oh, you look real nice. You got a beautiful tan.

Irrelevant and tends to personalize interview, which is dangerous.

S9 I did. I'd feel cheated if I didn't get a tan in the summer.

C10 That's a very pretty skirt.

S11 Thank you. Well, am I going to have a chance to have another interview after this one, or are you closing up or . . .

C12 Well, let me explain this and perhaps this will help you decide what you would like to do with this session and, as I say, the choice is up to you.

S13 Mm hmm.

C14 Uh, there is a possibility we're going to be open one more week. That is next week. Uh, if you would like to come back and see me next week and do some talking, or whatever you would like, we can make time ourselves. I'm in the midst of moving, myself, so it's a little hectic, but if you would like we can make arrangements and you would be able to come in once, perhaps twice, next week if you felt you would like to.

My personal problems should not be injected into interview. I tend to overemphasize the choice is up to you. It may be my own anxiety as to whether client will continue.

S15 Mm-hmm.

C16 We could make this arrangement, but at the end of next week the lab will be closed, and that will be it as far as the lab goes. Now in the future, and this is something we'll talk about more later on, as far as your going away to school and if you would like to do something up there, but in the event you do remain in Detroit, or would be back and would like to come back down to our lab here, I can give you the number and the person who will be in charge and you can contact him at any time if you are ever interested in coming back. We're always glad to have you come back, and you certainly should feel free to call this number and the person. I'll give it to you at the end.

S17   Mm-hmm.

C18   So, considering this, that this could be the last time we see each other, if you like, or there is a possibility of once or twice more next week, but next week will be the conclusion.

S19   Mm-hmm.

C20   So considering this, what would you like to talk about today?

S21   It seems like I spent a lot of time last week talking about a lot of things that have been troubling me in these last two weeks. I know I'm weary of the panacea of going away and coming back. Everything is all cleared up, but it seems to have happened that way. I was very troubled about religion, extremely troubled, and now I even said my prayers the other night. But I have just decided that if I can't believe in it, I am just going to leave it alone, and so that's not too much trouble any more. I met some pretty nice people while I was up north and maybe that restored a little more confidence in myself, which I was losing. I wasn't seeing any kids all summer. I just wasn't making many contacts and I was disappointed because I wanted to get a job. I didn't. I actually don't want to work. I don't want to have someone bossing me around, which seems to be what happens to me. Probably, everybody else does too, but I don't like it and I have a twin sister, as I said. When she gets a job she takes it in her stride. She doesn't mind these people. You know you've got to have someone bossing, a boss, period, but she can take it. And when she comes home and talks about her job it's different than when I come home and talk about my job. God almighty! What a difference, and so I didn't get the job and I felt badly about it, but now it doesn't bother me quite as much. Most of the summer's gone anyway, and I had a good time on my vacation, and I didn't feel like I was wasting so much time.

C22 In other words, the vacation, being away, kind of being time to get your feet on the ground, do some thinking, and the meeting of people your own age, kind of gave you back the confidence you had lost at the present time when we spoke the last time.

Might have related being bossed on a job similar to being bossed by mother.

S23 I couldn't have seen this, as I was talking to you, as a loss of confidence, but it was kind of a loss of something anyway. Maybe it was graduation fatigue.

C24 Kind of an empty feeling.

S25 Mm-hmm. Kind of like that. Not like I was losing three hundred friends, because I wasn't. Like I told you, I wasn't that close with those people, but just like something was gone anyway. Now what, I don't know. I still can't put my finger on it.

C26 Not quite certain what it was, but you felt the loss of something.

S27 Mm-hmm.

C28 After you graduated from high school.

S29 It felt kind of like running around and not doing anything.

C30 You felt like just completely forgetting everything and just running, without any ties or anything.

S31 I wanted to get away. I still want to get away, but I find that if I keep myself busy at home and keep a little more organization, well, then I don't feel so much like I should get out, because I'm at least doing something. Before, I was wasting so darn much time not doing anything, and getting frantic, and trying to do something, but actually doing so many tiny little things it wasn't anything after it was all scraped together. It wasn't nothing left done.

C32 The wasting of time bothered you.

S33 Mm-hmm. I don't like to waste time. Probably, I don't like to waste time too much, and therefore I waste a lot. That's how it seemed anyway. More, uh . . . huh, did you think that was distracting me, you playing with that? Oh. More planning. I find that if I plan my time well enough that I get something done, then I don't feel so bad if I waste a little time, but wasting all the time, all the time, is not good. I don't like it at all.

Client very observant as to what I'm doing. She probably was distracted.

C34 Who does?

S35 I don't know what to talk about. I just ramble on.

C36 It's OK. There's no set pattern of talking. Uh, when someone comes in here it's a choice of what they want to talk about. If they want to sit and think, or just sit quietly, this is up to them.

Instead of reassuring client I might have interpreted her concern as to what she was liable to say.

S37 Do people do that when they come in? Just sit.

C38 Sometimes. Whatever you feel comfortable in doing.

S39 Something I do want to do is tell you how glad I am that you turned out to be the way you are, because, I don't know, I, did I tell you how suspicious of people, wary of people, sometimes I am? I feel this is not a good trait, but I am.

C40 You realize you do feel suspicious of people and you don't like this, but you can't help yourself.

Client is talking of our relationship, and I ignore it instead of drawing her feelings about me out into the open.

S41 Mm-hmm, and I've tried to overcome that. Gee, for the longest time I've tried to do that, and that gets on my nerves sometimes. Trying to do something.

Then you're walking down the street and I think, "Why Jane, why should you try to change it? If that's the way you are, you're just going to make yourself worse trying to be something you're not. And so then, I feel real suspicious and walk down the street and be like I really feel, scared to meet people and, yet, I . . . This must be after I saw you. Did I tell you I was getting a job, I was going to work? Well I was—at the same place my sister was working as a waitress, and she kind of got me the job. She was seeing her beauty at the beauty parlor next door when the guy came in and said, "Would you like to work for me?" And I went to pick her up and she said, "Come here, Jane. I want to introduce you to Bob," and on and on and on. At first, I thought this is just what I need. I'll be able to work with Judy, and really be able to do the job well, and then I went in and talked to this fellow and we don't get along well. He wants, he talks about his philosophy and he thinks that all there is in life is sex and food and sweets, or something. I don't know, so I decided I wasn't going to work for him and I told him I wasn't going to, and went on vacation. But the thing that really made me decide I didn't want to work for him is he compared me with my sister. The first day I went in he just observed. I wasn't being paid or anything. I went to observe for a few hours. Actually, it was really my own time, and I don't care, but I decided I wasn't going to work there because he compared me with my sister. And not only did he compare me, I mean you can tell people compare twins. Why shouldn't they? But, he didn't have to tell me about it.

He said that, well the other woman in there, we happen to know her, and her son goes to school with us, or did, and she was saying something about . . . she's a goof anyway. And she was talking about, when I came back, everyone was expecting, back from Europe, everyone didn't know whether I was going to be snobbish or whether I was going to be stuck up, and she said she was so glad I turned out not to do that and things like that, and then Bob said, and she said, something about, "You're friendly," or something. I don't know. I was making an effort which is what really hurt me because that is what he said, "That Jane has to make an effort to make friends and Judy doesn't." And he said that I try to be some things that I am not and Judy doesn't, and all that baloney, and whether I do or not, maybe I do. I'll say one thing though, that I'm trying to improve my mind. Maybe that's what he means. I don't know, but that's what he said and so I don't want to work there.

C42   It bothered you that he compared you to Judy and said that she makes friends very naturally and that he felt you had to make an effort. This is why you didn't want to work in that situation.

S43   I felt that people feel that way anyway because you can hardly get around that. I do have to make an effort to make friends. That's another problem I've got because I've decided now that I won't make that effort unless it's somebody that I really like, and that I want to have as friends, have a friendship with, but he went . . . He's the first one that has ever been so blunt about it, and I think he was absolutely tactless about it.

C44 It kind of hurt that he just blurted it right out like that.

S45 Yes. They were discussing me when I was sitting there, like a little girl, and I didn't go there for him to be my father either. I don't really mind the thought so much, but I don't want another father. Cripe, that's what I get out of the house for.

C46 He reminded you of your father, the way he was comparing you, and you felt like a child there.

S47 Yes and I felt like . . . I like my father very much. He's a personality that I like, but I didn't like him treating me as such a little child, not that I was his daughter, but that I was some child, any child. I guess that's all part of adolescence, not wanting to be a little kid any more, but that's why I didn't want to work for him.

C48 Well, you feel you, that you understand you don't want to be a little growing boy.

S49 Mm-hmm. (Pause) So Judy's still working there. She works seven days a week. She works her little head off, and he's all right. She'll get out of it pretty soon though, and go to school, and so will I. My dad said he's only paying for out of school, out of town, or out of state schooling for one year, and after that I'll just be on my own. The awakening.

C50 Your father will pay your expenses for one year.

S51 Mm-hmm. I'll be working, too, and I've got a scholarship, too, but then he said that, uh, if he can't swing it then I will have to be on my own. I don't mind too much because all through high school, even before then, from the seventh grade on, or sixth grade, I've always understood, as far as I can remember, that I would go to college, and I've always wanted to. It's been a drive and now all of a sudden I've decided that maybe I don't care if I go to school. I'd rather travel, and so I'll go to school because it's always been in me.

C52　You feel somewhat of a conflict. Your expectation has always been to go to college, but now you find that you want to but at the same time you would like to travel and get away.

S53　Mm-hmm. I really want to get away and go travel. That's one thing I think I'll do while I'm in school because I can travel on a little bit of money. I've got used to it. That's one thing I'm glad of and so—I like to camp. Traveling to me doesn't mean going to the biggest hotel, it means just seeing things and it won't cost much money. Well, I don't know, when I get in school I'll probably have to study a lot more than I ever did. When I come to the bridge I'll cross it, but anyway I'll be away from home and I hope I like school. I'm pretty sure I will because I've missed studying. Even now, I had to type up a resume for my dad and I enjoyed doing it. It took me a long time but I enjoyed doing it, and so I know I'll like school again.

C54　You're looking forward to school with a little bit of anxiety about . . .

S55　Mm-hmm.

C56　About college.

S57　But my experience has shown that things like that iron themselves out if I am only willing to work at it, and I am.

C58　You feel, given a chance, you will be able to work it out.

S59　Mm-hmm, for myself, too, without my mother and dad.

C60 I know.

S61 Yes, without anybody, even with Judy.
It's funny because since school, since
I can remember, Judy has always been
struggling to get away from me, and I
always thought why is she struggling
to get away? I don't hang onto her. I
was always ahead of her in school, in
the elementary school that we went to.
It wasn't that I was double promoted
or anything, but they had to split up
the rooms and they put, as far as I can
understand it, they put the faster, or
the brighter, or something, students in
the grade ahead, a half a grade ahead,
to study with the group ahead of them
selves, or what I don't know. But, I
was always ahead of Judy and so I
wasn't hanging on to her that way,
academically anyway. Socially for a
while, but it seems now that socially
she is always ahead of me. I'll catch up
to her and then suddenly there I am
again, I, she's ahead of me again. I'm
getting used to that, too. That's frustrating but, so now all of a sudden it's
hit me that I am depending upon Judy
more and more than I ever was before
because we've grown together, we've
grown against my parents together,
kind of like, it's not like we hate our
parents, but we're both independent
people.

C62 Well, you feel in your attempt to become independent it's been kind of a
unifying force putting you and Judy
closer together than you have been in
many years.

S63 Mm-hmm, because there was the jealousy, too, for a long time, especially
between friends. I don't know whether
especially between friends, but it sure
was strong for a long long time. There
is a little jealousy concerning our

physical looks, too. Judy's a little heavier than I am and things like that. One thing that fumes me about her, she tints her hair, or she bleaches her hair, and my mother does it for her. If she hadn't done it in the first place, if my mother hadn't done it, Judy maybe would have left her hair alone. Now she's got the ugly head of hair, blond, and she's got to do it all the time. My mother does it for her because she doesn't want to take her to a beauty place. She can do it herself. She used to be a beauty operator, whatever they call it, but she's got to do it when my mother wants it done and that is havoc. That is a mess. My mother cuts my hair, too, so when I go away to school I'll learn how to do that. Judy went to a school, too, to try and gather her charm and, I don't know, I think there is something there. I've never mentioned it to her because it's silly, but it's something that catches inside almost. And I'm slimmer than she is and she always wants to be slim but she can't lose weight. I'm catching up to her I'll admit but . . .

C64   You realize the fact that you've been almost competing over the years together.

S65   Mm-hmm, a lot of competition.

C66   And you feel that these two areas, particularly, are the ones that you've had the assets in, that Judy is kind of jealous of this.

S67   Mm-hmm, in those two areas. But then there is art, and Judy is ahead of me and—what else. It might appear, as Bob said, this guy, he said it something like this, oh, I don't know, "I think Jane can probably make many friends more than Judy because she tries," or, "she has to try," or something like that, and that is probably—that's what it was—the truth hurts. I do have to try. I'm more nervous than Judy, but she is at home, and, yet, I can see her in a group and sometimes she's completely ill at ease, just nervous, and she just wants to leave where I'll stick it out and stay and decide that I'm just as good as them and, you know, and all that baloney, or going into an expensive restaurant which gives me thrills upon thrills. I love to go in places like that, not because I'm with rich people. I think it's because, I think it's their, they've got atmosphere or something, and Judy is ill at ease there and I'm not. I just figure that anybody can go, so it's things like that. She can make a warm kind of friendship much faster than I can. It's more like paper with me.

C68 You feel that in the intimate ones who want contact, that she does it more easily.

S69 No not that either because she doesn't have the intimate friendships that I have. I don't know how to put it.

C70 Initially she makes . . .

S71 Super . . .

C72 Superficially?

S73 No. They really are sincere friendships, but they're more funness, yeah, fun, and Judy never discusses, well, for instance, I don't think she ever discussed her heart throbs in high school with her girl friends. I'm positive she didn't. I'm almost positive. I don't know, but I don't think she did, where I would with my closest friend. That's what I mean. It's not superficial. It's warm, but it's not intimate. That's the difference and I can hold a friendship like that and it can last and last and last and always would. I'm mad at

Lois now, the girl I told you about.
My mother has always opposed her, but
I'll always be her friend. I'll always
be loyal to her because I understand
her, I think. If I don't understand her,
I'm still sympathetic with her, and I've
got another close friend. Her name is
Betty and a few more friends up north.
They're still nice. It was nice. After
two years I saw them again and it was
nice to know that I still have these
people as friends, and I didn't have to
be anything but myself, and that made
me feel good. And the girl that drove
me down here knows exactly what I'm
like, too, and knows what I feel, and
Judy's got a couple of goofy girl friends.
That's what they are. They love to
goof off. That's the kind of friendship
they are, yet, she is sincere and she is
loyal to her friends. That's the difference. I don't know but there is a
difference in our friendships. Then
there's the confidence that comes in a
large group, where I don't feel. I know
what it is. She can make the contacts
with the people in a large group if she
feels a little confidence, but in a large
group I probably will just snub everybody and feel like I belong there as
much as everybody else. It happened
at a wedding we went to, a big affair.
A daughter got married to one of our
different relatives and we went to that
at the Riverview Inn, which I liked
quite a bit, and I wanted to have a
good time. Yet, I went and decided—
I wore a dress I shouldn't have worn
anyway. It was a dress that was low cut
and I felt conspicuous in it, so I decided
that I had as much right as anybody
else there, that I didn't. I had a crummy
time and Judy had a real good time.
Of course she drank and I won't lean

on that because I'm afraid I could turn into an alcoholic quite easy by using a crutch like that.

C74 You feel you don't want to rely on some other element other than being just yourself to relate to people.

S75 Mm-hmm. If I'm with my friends then I don't mind drinking. It sounds like I go to booze parties all the time but I don't. It's just that while I was in Europe I drank with my family. Yet with a group I'd rather not have drinks, because who knows what could happen. You can't lean on that. I had a great time. I don't know why I'm talking about her so much.

C76 You find it odd talking about Judy so much.

S77 Unusual. Never done it before in conference with my counselor at school. Maybe it's because I realize that pretty soon I am going to be leaving her, and not only just for school, but maybe I'll stop seeing her, maybe summer vacations and stuff like that. But from now on we're out of high school and we won't be going to the same school together. It will be kind of like parting of the ways.

C78 You feel that you're thinking and talking about her partially because you're not going to be seeing her that much, because you are going to be parting your ways.

S79 Mm-hmm. When we went into high school Judy has always had, both of us have had, an aptitude for art all through grade school and it kind of got like, well, one of us was going to be it and one wasn't. And, I don't know, maybe because I fell in academic subjects, more academic subjects than art, which I don't consider really academic, in grade school anyway, or high school, maybe that's why Judy pulled ahead of me, but anyway she's going into that and I'm not. I'm going into literature. That was the determining factor there, I guess. She's going into that. I don't envy her. In fact, I'm very proud of her being able to go into that. I think it's a nice thing to go into.

C80   You feel proud of her going into this specialty field of art.

S81   Mm-hmm.

C82   Whereas you made your choice to go into literature.

S83   In high school we both had art classes all the way up, and then I don't know what happened but I pulled out in my junior year, bottom, last part of my junior year, out of the art class, which was a lot of fun. I had a good time. Our teacher was a real goof. All the kids were. . . .

C84   You don't know why. You enjoyed art but . . .

S85   I felt the conflict of the teacher. Judy got along with him very well and I didn't, so maybe that's why I pulled out. It was one of the determining factors. I know that. I discussed it with my teacher, uh, my counselor.

C86   You feel that one of the reasons was the conflict between the teacher and the two of you. Judy got along and you didn't. This was one of the main factors why you pulled out of the art curriculum.

S87   Mm-hmm. I decided that when I do my art I would rather do it by myself, without anybody pointing. Kids get silly. Some kids get into the art class that don't belong there. Maybe they're just doing it for the kicks, therefore, or credit. And they used to do silly things which I don't like them to do—

ask me what I'm doing, or what's that, or things like that. I'd rather do my art by myself and Judy, I guess, doesn't mind having people around her, or would rather have someone help her, like the art teacher. They did a lot of projects together and Judy entered some things in a show which she won. They're good buddies, great buddies. That's why, this guy that Judy was going with, not going with but sort of like going with, was a good buddy, too, so they were all good buddies and I was the not-so-good buddy. I mean, uh . . .

C88 You felt kind of left out. Judy and the teacher and the boys she was dating all were pretty chummy and you felt like kind of an odd-ball, kind of out of that group.

S89 Mm-hmm. I didn't mind it so much, but I just felt like I had to get along with them. I had to be part of the group, which maybe I shouldn't have, but it was not the situation. So, I think the best thing I could have done is get out, so I did, and after that our relationship was much better, the teachers and mine.

C90 You felt that once you removed yourself from the situation, relations with him improved. You weren't in that same awkward position.

S91 It definitely did. I could see him in the hall and joke around with him and everything. I didn't feel like it would influence . . . maybe that's what I was afraid of . . . I don't know, or like being obligated, sort of like. I don't like to have. Personally, I don't think teachers should be so personal and so intimate with the students, because then how can he mark your work? And I didn't like the feeling that if I, that

Probably talking about her own feelings toward men and particularly her feelings towards her own father. Also probably expressing fear about our counseling situation.

even if I could get chummy with the teacher, then especially, I wouldn't like it because then he would just give me the mark or something like that. I don't know. I didn't like the situation at all. I didn't like the teacher-student relationship.

C92   You felt uncomfortable in the student-teacher relationship when it became more a personal one than a purely academic student-teacher relationship. You felt the evaluation wouldn't be an accurate one.

S93   It wasn't 'cause he gave us A's all the way through until I got out, but then Judy deserved them.

C94   You feel Judy deserves her A's.

S95   Oh, yeah. She worked much harder than I did. I kind of laid around. I did do quite a bit of creative stuff but not hard work like Judy did.

C96   You did a lot of creative work.

S97   Yeah.

C98   Where you enjoyed your freedom and didn't want to put the effort into mechanical kinds of things.

S99   In fact, I find I do that all of the time. My writing is almost impossible to read. My mother and father are after me about that, too. I got so mad at my mother and father I . . . when I get really mad at my mother, I know that irritates her and is the most childish thing I do almost, I go into my room and type, and she knows that I am typing about what I am feeling right that very minute, and she knows that I know it irritates her. Maybe she doesn't know that I know that it irritates her, but I know that it does, whether she knows it or not, so I do it, and I am just feeling so . . . maybe it's a good outlet. It's an outlet anyway. Even a small thing like that. It made me irritated. It made me really mad because even a small thing like my handwriting . . . they won't leave me alone about it. "You've got to change your handwriting Jane, because how are you going to get a job. People won't hire you with handwriting like that," and all that baloney. I know I've got to change it, and if I get a job it does get clearer because I know it's got to be clear, but when I am writing something I can't take a long time to write it, because I want to be a writer and so when I write things I don't take a long time. I can read it easily. In fact I don't even write hardly. I use symbols and stuff like that now, and when I write letters I type them so people can read them. But a little thing like that they decide I've got to change. The same thing with my hairdo; the same thing with the things I wear. My mother doesn't like the way I dress no matter what. (*Sigh*)

C100 You find that there seems to be a multitude of things now that your parents don't accept that you are doing.

S101 Mm-hmm.

C102 In order to kind of get back and vent your feelings, you will go and do something that you know is going to irritate them.

S103 Nothing destructive. In fact I save everything I write for reference and for notes, but something that I know is childish, and what else . . .

C104 You realize this is a juvenile thing you do, but it kind of satisfies you.

S105 Mm-hmm. It does. I can even have a bursting headache, and then I will go and write then, too. Or, if I feel real frustration, it's better for me to write. I just can't do anything else. There's nothing else I can do unless I do the dishes, or unless I go for a walk, and that gets boring. We have a park right down at the end of our street, but you can only walk along that river so many times.

C106   You find that writing seems to satisfy your feelings and emotions at a time when you are completely frustrated or upset about something.

S107   That's another thing. My parents are, I honestly do think that they are, trying not to let go. They are still trying to pick out our clothes. They're still trying to do this. My mother's happy when I wear things she has picked out for me but I don't know what I'm going to do when I have to buy my college wardrobe. I don't even care if I get any more new clothes. I'll wear all the old ones I've got. I'd rather do that than go through what I go through with her when she buys my clothes. She goes to every store in the whole Detroit area, has me try on almost every dress. I feel like a wreck, and I don't like to put clothes over my head anyway. I don't know why. I'd rather slip into them. She doesn't like that. In a dressing room, or if it's not my dress and I should put it over my head, I do. But if it's my own clothes I step into it, because I'd rather step in. I even try to slip into my nightgown if I can, through the neck. I just can't stand to have something over my head because it's, I don't know.

Can this be some kind of sexual anxiety?

C108   It feels uncomfortable.

S109   Mm-hmm. Like claustrophobia a little bit. She doesn't like that. I've got to be careful that I slip things over my head when I go shopping with her, and then I can like something very much and she'll say we'll get whatever you want, and then she just can't bear to spend her money on something she's not going to like on me, so I don't get it, or get something that I don't really like because I'm desperate for a dress, or a skirt, or something. Then I don't wear it. Then she gets mad about it.

C110 You've reached a point where rather than go through this ordeal that you've been going through, you just prefer to wear what you have instead of going through it again.

S111 Mm-hmm. Actually, as I've said before, I think that I feel guilty about taking money from them, anyway, because I've taken so darn much, and yet for graduation, my mother was willing to spend all kinds of money for graduation, which I think—the trend, I'm pretty sure, is for students to consider graduation from high school a small thing, less than they used to. I don't know how they used to feel about it, but from the way my parents talk it's the biggest thing in the world, and for Judy and I it was nothing, almost, because we were looking forward to college. They wanted to spend thirty dollars on pictures; I wanted a prom gown and they got that. That cost me about twenty-five dollars. I didn't mind that because I wanted the gown. I'd never had one, but the pictures, and the cards, and the announcements, and stuff like that, they wanted all that and we didn't want it. They were willing to spend that money, and when I go to college my mother's going to want to buy me clothes, too. I know it. She has already said that we were going to have certain amounts of clothes and things. I'd rather take that money and save it, maybe, and put it down as tuition, than spend it on clothes, because I have enough clothes to get by on right now. I always used to look forward to being a well-dressed girl on campus, but now clothes are clothes.

C112   You feel rather than use the money and go through what you have, you would put it toward tuition. You know your parents are going to disagree with you.

S113   Mm-hmm. My mother. My father, I believe he would let me take the clothes I've got and scram, go to college, rather. But my mother, well, one thing, I think my mother sees in me more than Judy what she wants to be, and she wants me to have the things she didn't have, and all this.

C114   You feel your mother kind of identifies herself with you more than with Judy, and is almost living her life through you by giving you the things that she didn't have, but wanted.

S115   Mm-hmm. This might be wrong, but through this other counselor that I had, I think I told you that I had a special counselor in high school, well, that's one point that we came to, that probably that was it. She had talked to my mother a few times, too, and even my dad once or twice, once I think, and that was the conclusion, one conclusion, that she came to. A small thing, yet important to me, because it made me decide that I had better be more tolerant toward my mom, which I have been. I don't blow up at her as much as I used to, and try to take a few more things that she does.

C116   With this understanding now you feel that it helped you become more tolerant, more understanding of the situation, and you find you can perhaps accept it more easily, although it's still bothersome.

S117 It's a lot of trouble, but understanding that I think if I had, if someone hadn't really just come out—she didn't just come out only because I saw her every day when I was a senior—but it finally did come out clear one thing, that my mother does see herself in me. I might be wrong, but it's at least something that makes me more tolerant toward my mother.

C118 Well, you don't know, actually, the reason, but it makes some sense to you, and it helps you to assume that in your present situation.

S119 That's kind of what I feel, whether it's the truth or not, that it is helping me, so I like it. It's something that I feel, that people never really can understand each other, because you can't get in someone else's mind, but you can at least try and sympathize, and so I do. I'll sympathize for as long as I have to, and then I'll go.

C120 You feel you'll take it to a point and then . . .

S121 Mm-hmm. Like those clothes. I know even Betty, my best girl friend now, says that, yeah, she's looking forward to college and the few weeks before, because her mother's going to want to go out and buy her clothes, too, and she would just rather skip it.

C122 So your girl friend has the same problem about clothes, and her mother wanting to buy, as you do.

S123 Yeah, although she says that she likes her mother's taste, and she usually likes the things her mother gets her, but she doesn't like the bother of going out, either. I don't like to buy a whole bunch of clothes at once because I—like when I bought this, I fell in love with it and so I bought it, but I'd rather. . . . I like to buy underwear, too, why I don't know. Then there's no choice. You just buy some and wear it, but going out and looking for something when I have no idea what I want is too frustrating. I'd rather not do it. I don't like to be in crowds either, elbowing through Hudson's, anything like that.

C124   You find it pretty uncomfortable, going through big crowds when there seems to be no point. You're not certain what you want. You'd rather wait when you have a specific object in mind and then go and pick it out.

S125   I suppose quite a few people feel like that. I'm not alone.

C126   You feel other people feel this way, too.

S127   Sure, some must. But then there's my mother. She feels that I've got to go out and get those clothes. I'll go with her.

C128   You'll go to satisfy her.

S129   Mm-hmm, although I'll only compromise so far. I won't get anything I don't want. Yet I'll be more tactful than I usually am, used to be last year, anyway. Maybe if I'd gone out to buy clothes with her, I'd be sarcastic, which I have a particular talent for, I think. Why I don't know, but I am sarcastic or a witch at times. I'll admit it.

C130   You feel now that you're willing to go along to a certain point and then when you disagree you can become more tactful, more sophisticated about it.

S131   I can do that, and I'll get more satisfaction out of it, I think, than just being—pout about it. One reason I think I'm more sarcastic than maybe Judy is, is because she yells when she's mad, and I don't like to yell, so I do it the other way, not throwing my doll on the wall but writing in my room.

My mother doesn't like it I guess. I don't like violence too much, but Judy doesn't mind it so much.

C132 You've chosen to kind of keep it in, and let it out in writing or a different way, whereas Judy would choose a more active outlet kind of way.

S133 At least yelling. She doesn't mind yelling and I do. I don't like it.

C134 You don't like yelling.

S135 When I'm having a lot of fun I don't mind. I guess it's the same as with drinking. When I feel sure of myself, and when I'm sure I'm not going to hurt somebody, then I don't mind, but Judy doesn't know how she can hurt me when she yells sometimes. The same with my dad. He yells, too, when he gets mad.

C136 When Judy or your dad shout at you, you are easily hurt by it.

S137 Mm-hmm, because I feel like I have no defense. When people start yelling they are getting, not hysterical, but they are using a, as far as I'm concerned, it's kind of a basic kind of thing, and they are not going to be willing to listen to anything I've got to say, and so there is no defense. Judy yells at me for anything, almost any thing. When she yells, she yells, and I don't want to yell back, and so I can't say anything to her. I'd rather keep quiet and go in my room.

C138 You feel defenseless. You don't want to resort to the, just anything, yelling and shouting, and you feel defenseless. You can't do anything when you're yelled at so you just withdraw from the situation, to yourself.

S139 Mm-hmm. It might be running away, but at least it's not, I don't know . . . I don't know what at least it's not, but it's my way of doing it so.

C140   You feel more comfortable doing this than shouting back.

S141   Mm-hmm. Oh, gee, I can't remember having a really bad scene with my mother lately. Maybe last year. Let me see whether it was before I went to Europe or after. Probably it was both. More before, I think. It's that my mother, maybe she isn't through the worst of this menopause thing, but she usually gets so upset and screams so darn much, and says such awful things, that it got me so much I couldn't do anything. I could just stand at my dresser, and not do anything else but just stand there for maybe a half hour on end. I couldn't do anything else. She got me so upset. I don't know what point I'm trying to make now, I forgot.

Client seems to be quite upset about her mother's menopause and has referred to it on several occasions.

C142   You felt completely shaken up, very upset.

S143   Yeah. I don't know whether other kids did that, but that, she really could get me that way. Now, I don't feel quite as upset. Maybe I'm getting used to it. Either that, or it just plain doesn't bother me as much. Maybe I'm not quite as sensitive as I used to be. That's another thing Judy used to do that really got me. She called me sensitive. When she really wanted to get me mad, or hurt me, she would say I was sensitive. When I was in the eighth grade she would call me stuck up, too. That got me, too. Now I make a joke about it. Maybe a few kids that know, knew what the situation was then, it is kind of humorous to me because I would actually rather have that to contend with, that label, than wear myself to a frazzle smiling at everyone walking down the hall.

C144   You would rather be labeled stuck up, or whatever it might be, but at least remain true to yourself, just being comfortable the way you are, the way you act.

S145 Mm-hmm. Myself, and the few friends I do have. Whether I have a bunch of them, I don't care. The people like me OK, but you can't love everybody, which I tried to do for a while. Maybe that's another part of the reason I had to have that special counselor. It seems like everything started at the end of the seventh grade, when we moved from Detroit out to the suburbs. Life was completely different, and maybe it's because if we had stayed in that old neighborhood we would have grown up with the same kids, and there wouldn't have been that drastic change, because it was right at the beginning of adolescence. Anyway, seventh grade, and the—I—gee, when we walked into this new little school and all the kids there had grown up, well most of them had grown up together, and the boys nearly mobbed us. Why I don't know. I was really scared because all the boys on the street I just moved from, I used to play football with, and hockey, and these boys were looking at me like they didn't want to play hockey.

C146 (Laugh) You found they were looking at you a little bit differently from little neighborhood boys.

I should not show my own reaction by laughing.

S147 Yeah. Well they were goofs, but anyway they scared me. I can look back on it now, maybe even feel embarrassed, and laugh at it. I can laugh at it, yeah, but it's been a sore spot in my whole life.

C148 It was a pretty upsetting thing that happened at that time.

S149 I was so scared that I didn't know what to do with them, so I ignored them and it was real—I was stuck up in a way. I tried not to have anything to do with them, so they thought that I was stuck up and that bothered me then, and so I wondered, I was wondering what was wrong with me and all kinds of stuff, and started to overeat. It was a mess.

C150   It was a pretty trying time then. You started wondering about the whole situation, why you weren't liked, why you didn't have friends, and even, too, to overeating.

S151   Mm-hmm, which I still have to overcome.

C152   You feel you still have to cope with overeating.

S153   I feel like I'm not the only one, because I know, just as one example, they say boys that go away in the Army or Navy, or something like that, get so lonesome or so frustrated that they overeat, too.

C154   It's a normal reaction to the problem. Other people do it, too.   My opinion is not called for.

S155   It might be, but it sure is awful. I don't like it at all because it's a real, it's hard for me to stop eating, even now, when I made these decisions. I haven't tried them out yet. I haven't been away to college, and I haven't seen if they are going to work. I've got a lot of faith in them, but I don't know. Yet I'm still home, and there's still that frustration, and when I get really frustrated, well, when I, like I said, when I am getting frazzled, not doing anything, junky little things, but nothing much at all, then I would rather just sit down and eat than even watch television, because I can't watch television anyway, because I have to get about this far away, even with my glasses, to see it.

C156   You find that you still have to contend

with this problem of overeating, and become frustrated at this point and concerned about it.

S157 Mm-hmm. Yeah, and I don't want to get fat because I don't want to become unattractive, really unattractive, unnecessarily, which overweight would be, unnecessary unattractiveness.

C158 You worry about becoming obese because it would make you unattractive, and this you don't want.

S159 I've tried to get around saying that I am attractive, implying that I am attractive, but I mean that I don't want to take away anything that I've got, that I might have. Maybe I need it for confidence. I don't know.

C160 Well you want to keep status quo.

S161 Mm hmm.

C162 The way you look now, figure, looks, your complexion.

S163 I don't want to be sloppy, that's all.

C164 You don't want to be . . .

S165 Mm-hmm. That's about it. What time is it? My watch doesn't work. I lost my watch.

C166 Oh. I lost track of the time. I didn't bring one in. I imagine we have about fifteen more minutes.

Client probably getting uncomfortable at this point. Might have asked why?

S167 Oh, good. I have to meet somebody. He'll be late. He always is. It's funny about these guys that I'm going with now. I thing he's completely [550]. About the only thing we have in common is a sense of humor, but we went to the art museum today. Does Casals play that cello, or however you say it?

C168 Cello.

S169 Does he? I don't know, but we went to the art museum, and I said, "Casals," and he said, "Oh, he's that cellist, isn't he?"

C170 I believe he's the artist, Pablo Casals.

S171 Yeah, he is, but maybe he is because

he [557] me. He said the guy was quite old, eighty-four or—I don't know—and that he had played at the UN and for the international set, and so it might be the [559]. I don't know, but anyway, I still like the guy even if he is kind of goofy that way. He really doesn't know.

C172   You find him enjoyable although he may not be the most intelligent.

Peculiar would be more appropriate than intelligent.

S173   I don't know how intelligent he is. I've never . . . another thing I try not to do is judge people's intelligence, because you really can't. I can't anyway.

C174   You feel you don't want to.

S175   Yeah. Maybe I don't want to. That's all, because he's so enjoyable anyway.

C176   You find spending time with him enjoyable.

S177   Mm-hmm. He's quite good with people, too, and so I feel quite secure with him in a group, that he can carry us both if he has to.

C178   You feel secure with him because he can kind of carry both of you in a group, and you don't have to worry about your relationship.

S179   Mm-hmm, if he has to. I mean if a thing comes up that he has to. Like when we go out, he is quite poised, especially when he's in a nice place, like I said I get a kick out of going to, and, yet, he's just at ease someplace else. Like at the museum. He was still at ease and we had a good time picking out the things we like, and stuff like that. I got a kick out of telling him things that I thought are pretty basic, like. I'm not too interested in things like that, but I mastered it so that he wouldn't know that, and so on. But actually it's just things that we've picked up, just that I pick up, not even from an Art class, just from reading. We still had a good time together because there's a lot of things I know that he knows more about than I do, golf and stuff like that, which isn't intellectual or anything, but still is something.

C180   You find companionship with him very comfortable and very enjoyable.

S181   Mm-hmm, comfortable.

C182   He's, well, at ease with people, too.

S183   Mm-hmm, he is very much. My dad likes him which is another good thing. Maybe if I had a friend that they like, I won't. My mom and dad like him very much.

C184   You find that makes it very pleasant at home.

S185   More pleasant.

C186   Because both your parents like him, too.

S187   Mm-hmm. And then there's the other thing, where my mother's not home— she works in the evening now. My dad will sit down with almost anybody, and so that's better now, too, because he likes Frank. There were two guys over last night that ride a motorcycle, and the thing is so loud I can't stand it, and they come over and talk to my dad, and so it's better that way. They never leave. They're the kind of guys that want to stay all night, and that is OK with me as long as they talk to my dad, but I don't have too much in common with them except that we can both talk a leg off each other. This guy has been in the, the one I know the most, has been in Hawaii and places like that. Anyway he's got this big motorcycle and my dad will accept him. He's kind of like, not a beatnik but kind of like a, not a juvenile either. It's just . . . I don't know what's the matter with him to tell you the truth. And my dad also accepted Joe. My dad accepted them until my mother got on this, "going to have this disrupting influence, or thing, in the house," and that's where it ended. He likes Carol. He likes all my friends. He'll accept anybody. It's better now because I can bring almost anybody home.

C188 You find it easier for your father to accept your friends than your mother.

S189 Mm-hmm. I'm afraid that my mother thinks anybody that I'm going to meet, who knows, I might marry them, and so she doesn't want, I don't know what. Maybe she thinks nobody is good enough for me. I don't know. As far as I can see, this is what I think. It might be a bitter attitude but I think Frank can put on a good show, not pretentious either, but it's just he looks good in the clothes he wears and he wears clothes that are in fashion. He also wears expensive clothes, not billion dollar clothes, but more expensive than even my dad wears, who is a businessman and should have good clothes, but that's all he's got to spend his money on, and so he can get them. He looks good, and also that he gets along so well with people. My mother likes him and I feel it's kind of superficial, because she doesn't know anything too much else about him, except that he can joke around a lot and feels completely at ease with both of them. That's why she likes him. She doesn't like quiet boys because she doesn't trust them, and she doesn't like short men because her father was short and gave my grandmother a hard time, and they're divorced, and things like that, small little things that I know for sure because she's said them. She won't give people a chance, but my dad will accept them until they do something that he doesn't like, that he feels is wrong.

C190 You feel she makes a quick snap judgment based on her feelings.

S191 Mm-hmm.

C192 Whereas your dad will be accepting until they have proved otherwise.

S193 Mm-hmm. She's very sensitive, too. That's why, another reason she didn't like Lois, because Lois is also sensitive. A lot of people wouldn't think so. In fact most people wouldn't, because she's such a hard, oh domineering and ambitious and kind of hard. It's a word that would describe her—red hair, flashing. She's also sensitive, though. No one else will admit it. A few people might, kids she grew up with, a couple of kids. She's sensitive also, and so she might walk in the house and wait for my mother to say hello to her before she'll say hello to my mother, and my mother feels that she should say hello first, so nobody says hello, and there I am trying to do something, and there's nothing I can do except leave the house with Lois, and then after a while not have her over at all, and then after a while not see her, and that's the way it is now. I don't see her at all, and the things that I do hear are about the way that I [699] her. She came over to the house and irritated Judy, and so I am irritated with her for that reason, and I know if I could see her it would be smoothed over. An agreement that Lois made with me, or that we kind of made together, is that there was no need for an apology or a thank you for things we did together, which I don't completely go along with. However, she doesn't apologize for so many things. Since she has known me she has started apologizing. I feel like I helped her a little bit. Maybe that's another reason that I wanted to be her friend, but that was a silly agreement. I didn't keep it. I still said "thank you" and things like that. It seems like a funny thing to say. Maybe you don't. How do little kids say it. I forget what we used to do, real stupid little things. "I'm going to tell your mom," and things like that, but I mean little things like that, but ones which I think could be important, trivial anyway.

C194   I tell you Jane. I don't have an idea of the time but I kind of feel we've, uh . . .

S195   I kind of feel like there's a lot of time gone by.

C196   Yeah, I think we have used up our time. Would you like to come back and talk next week?

S197   Yes I would if you wouldn't mind. Actually, if you're moving you're going to be awfully busy.

C198   That's OK with me. Perhaps, let's go outside. Let me check the schedule and make an early appointment in the week.

Counselor's comment (C194): I should have had a watch —not a good way of ending.

	THIRD INTERVIEW	COUNSELOR'S COMMENTS

C1   It's kind of noisy.

S2   Do you mind if I smoke?

C3   No. Fine. Let's see, I don't think we have an ash tray. You're not hiding one behind your purse.

S4   I don't carry them in there, either.

C5   Let me see if I can get one. (*Long pause*) Well, finally. How are you today?

Counselor's comment (C5): Better to let client start. Most of chitchat up through S20 irrelevant.

S6   OK. I walked through the library today. I saw Mrs. Fischer today.

C7   Oh, the counselor from Lincoln. Good. Have a pleasant time talking with her?

S8   Just a few minutes as I was walking over from the library.

C9   How was your swimming last week?

S10   It was OK. We stayed out quite late but, well, not late, but for being out all day we did.

C11   Have a good time?

S12   Mm-hmm.

C13   Uh, if I remember correctly it was a pretty nice day, real warm.

S14   Mm-hmm, the sun came out.

C15   It stayed that way the whole day.

S16   Mm-hmm.

C17   Well, if it gets too cool you can let me know.

S18   Mm-hmm, OK. Your dress is so nice and cool looking, and all of a sudden it got real hot, and I wore this crazy warm thing.

C19   It's a very, very attractive blouse as a matter of fact.

S20   Thank you.

C21   Well, what would you like to talk about today?

S22   I don't know. I just don't feel like talking too much today. Nothing too much happened since I saw you last. Maybe that's why. Except my parents, my mother, did I tell you last time I was here that my mother said something about that I'd have to be going away, and I couldn't go to Arbor College. Well, she did. She got explosively mad again, and said that I couldn't go to Arbor. Oh, probably it happened over the week end. That's why I didn't tell you. Judy's working and she, I don't understand her at all. She decides that all the money, she's going to spend it on a sailing boat, and I just don't understand her at all. If I was making money it would

all go for school. I don't even want to
buy any clothes, as I told you before.
And my mother all of a sudden decided she just wasn't going to take it
any more. She thought Judy was getting her own way a little too much,
which she does quite a bit, and decided that, well, she was going to show
Judy. She'd buy Judy all her clothes
and be sure Judy goes away, and that
way show her. And I was going to
stay home, and so she told me that.
Judy went to work and she decided
she was going to take it all out on
Judy that way, by giving her everything
she wanted and not giving me anything. I don't know. I don't know what
she was going to do by that.

C23   Well, you're pretty confused that your
mother suddenly decided to show Judy
a lesson regarding clothes and money.
She was going to send her away, pay
for all her clothing. As a result there
wouldn't be enough money, you'd have
to stay home and go to Warren University.

S24   It really is quite confusing, but I am
quite used to my mother, anyway, doing
things like that. I know she'll go back,
and she did. She said that we'll have
to see, because I decided that I'd talk
to her adultly and explain to her after
a period of time passed when I knew
that she'd be more calm about it,
that, "Mother, it's kind of late for,
to apply for another scholarship," and
things like that, and "I've kind of
worked for it and five hundred dollars
is something I don't want to throw
away," and things like that. It's not a
big scholarship, but it's a point, and
so she said, "Well, we'll just have to
see," and stuff like that, so I suppose
I'll go. But I didn't tell her this be-

cause I know it'll just make us all more trouble, but I decided that if I have to stay home and go to Warren, I love Warren University, and I really would go there, but I won't stay home. And if I have to go there I won't stay home. I'll go away. I'd just as soon, I don't want to live at home.

C25 You feel then that if you're forced to come to Warren, you'll go to Warren, but you'll leave home and live somewhere else.

S26 No. I won't even do that, I don't think. It's not the idea of going to Warren. If I was going to JC or if I was going to anyplace around here . . . the point is that I'll have to stay home. I'll get a job or something. Maybe I'll never go to school, but I don't want to stay home. If my going away means Judy's going to stay home, I won't do that either, because I've taken too much. I went to Europe last summer and that was always on Judy's mind, it seems. Though she doesn't mention it to me, my mother says she brings it up to her all the time.

C27 In other words, you feel that you don't want Judy to have to stay home on your account, from school.

S28 Mm-hmm.

C29 But if you're not allowed to go away to Arbor then, if I'm understanding you correctly, then you just, you won't stay home. It's just too much. You just can't take it any longer. You'll leave home or you'll go away.

S30 That's kind of dramatic and it's selfish. I understand that and that's why I haven't said it to my mother, and it's even selfish as I say it to you, but then that's what I'm here for, to tell you the things that are on my mind. And, chances are, I wouldn't do it anyway, unless I really decided after really calm deliberation, not just a stupid running away, pack your things in a bag and go. I'm almost positive, and one thing that would keep me at home is that it would hurt my parents' feelings an awful lot, and also they want a lot for us and they want us to be good. I think part of it is because we're so, we're the first girls from the whole family that are going to college. My dad's family has ten kids and my mother's has three, and it's supposed to be a pretty big thing, grandchildren anyway. A lot of the other relatives have gone to it, but we're the first grandchildren and they want us to show. I suppose they want us to make a good showing and I think if we didn't go, if I did back out, it would be kind of running away. That would really hurt my mother very very much. I know it would. But then there's the other thing, where my mother still feels that she wants to pick out my clothes, and she wants to do this for me, and that, and everything else, and didn't want me to wear this blouse and another skirt and heels, and I couldn't see it and so I went anyway. I didn't make a big fuss about it, but I went anyway. I didn't make a big fuss and neither did she, and so that was that, but it's things like that. I don't want her to keep on treating me like a little kid.

C31   In other words, it is just the constant small things that, the selection of your clothes to go to church, to buy your clothes, all these things keep adding up to a point where you just can't take it any more. You just don't want to be treated like that.

S32   Yeah, that's kind of like it. Oh, it seems

kind of stupid talking about it because
I'm pretty sure I'll be going anyhow.
I'm pretty sure. My parents will do
anything to give us what we want. I
know that unless they get into the
thing where everything gets so mixed
up and things become so, uh, well,
there's so darn many people in my
family. We haven't got a huge family,
but there's six of us and two dogs, and
I don't say that to be silly, because
these dogs, I'm telling you, they get
treated like one of the family, both
the poodle and the pomeranian, and
they have to be treated well and they
are. They're one of the family and so
that makes for a lot of chaos at our
house. And if everybody doesn't really
try to get along well then one little
thing can throw everything off, especially in our house. Why I don't know.
I know it's not like that in a lot of
houses. I'm pretty sure anyway. And
one little thing like this, Judy throwing her weight around because she's
got some money, can just mix it up
for everybody, like for me.

C33 In other words you're kind of a little   She is more than a little bit
bit perturbed with Judy at this point   perturbed with Judy.
because things were going along
smoothly and now this business with
college and clothes and money may
upset the calm at the house at this
time.

S34 I'm kind of expecting it to get all
mixed up again, anyway toward college, because for as long as we've been
talking about college and for as long
as I have, especially, been warning my
parents about the cost . . . I know
they realize it themselves, but they
haven't developed a husband and wife
team that sits down together and decides certain things that are going to

happen, be sure that they'll be ready
for it. They don't do that. I can't remember them ever doing that. They
do things as they come instead. And
then everybody gets all nervous, especially my mother, and then if my
mother gets nervous, she gets everybody all excited, and my dad can only
take it for so long. He is extremely
patient but he'll take it not forever and
ever, and then he blows up and everything gets all mixed up and then there's
not much to do because it's beyond
repair, the whole situation, and then
even if I did go away. I don't want to.
I'd go of course, and all I can say is I
just don't like . . . it's just like when
I was a little kid going to birthday
parties. It never failed. Both of us
went and there was always a big crying
and pulling of hair and jerking around
because there were two of us to get
ready and she waited until the last
minute to get us all ready and we went
to the party crying. I was always crying when I went someplace because we
were always late and I never wanted to
be late and on top of that there was
always such a big rush. Everything was
all. . . . Mother wouldn't want to get
up and we were screaming around and
trying to get our things together. I
could never find my shoes and neither
could she, and that's how it was. Well,
that's how it would be with college,
and I don't want to do that because I
have grown to be punctual myself.
Maybe because when we were little
kids we were always late, and I didn't
like it, and so I always want to be on
time myself and it's like that going
away to college. I'll go, and it won't
ruin my life to go in an upset state,
but why should I when it's senseless.

C35　In other words, this conflicting pattern of chaos and disorder at the last moment before going to something big, you kind of fear like this is going to happen again, and you don't look forward to it. You'd prefer not to have it just before you go away to college.

S36　Mm-hmm. I think that it will happen because there will be two of us, but even though, even if I went out of my way to stop this from happening when I go, Judy won't. I'm pretty sure because there are certain things that she wants, and I want the same things, but she'll do more to get them. She'll work harder at it and she'll be a little more aggressive. There are some things that I want that I'll give up in order to make things easier at home but she won't, and she decided that she wants to live off campus. She's got some girlfriends up there that have an apartment, and this girlfriend of Judy has an older sister who goes there who has the apartment and she could live with her. Well, if she decides she wants to do that she'll work on it and work on it and work on it until she gets it. In fact, that's one thing Judy has been telling me lately, that, uh, she just can't understand why I always ask. Why don't I just tell them that I'm going to do something? And I tell her that sometimes it's better to ask and not demand because Dad doesn't like it, and stuff like that. She's beginning to make me wonder if I do ask too much because I am eighteen, seventeen. But then I decided that if I feel I should ask, then I'm going to ask, and baloney with her, because sometimes I don't like it when she demands things from me, and so I imagine that's how my dad feels, too, and my mother. So whatever it is, that's what I mean about Judy. She'll demand and chances are nothing will go wrong because, well, she does demand because there are a lot of things that are . . . She doesn't do it too often, not all the time, and so it just might happen there is nothing she wants to demand at the time and she'll go without making a fuss, but I feel a disaster coming, as I told her.

C37   You kind of feel that a storm is brewing.

S38   Mm-hmm. I feel like I feel it coming, and this is the beginning of August and I won't be going until September 20, but I'll need my stuff that whole week before September 20, be getting ready and to be sure I can get there on time, but who knows, I might not be going.

C39   You feel you might not be going.

S40   And the worst thing is that it really doesn't seem to matter any more. I don't want to fight for things any more.

C41   You feel you would rather just kind of withdraw than fight any more for things that mean anything to you.

S42   No, because another thing I want very much is to go away by myself and, you know, travel, like I told you. And something like that I don't feel there will be much fight on. I'll just go. I'll be eighteen. There won't be too much of a fight. I'm just tired now. Maybe that's why, I'm kind of tired. I haven't been getting too much sleep lately.

C43   You feel kind of beat out.

S44   Mm-hmm. There are these little things. As I told you, my other counselor, the one that did meet her, my mother, said that. What did she say? There's another thing that she said, that I often decided things in my own mind and then I would say that she said them, or that she implied them, and so I've gotta be careful about what I say she said. Well, she did say I want to make a comparison between my mother and myself, but she said that my mother was a driving ambitious woman, and this is something I think was in my own mind, that I am like my mother, and so I do everything I can to be unlike her, except for a few qualities that she has that I want, and she does everything she can for poor people. In fact that's one thing that got to be really bad in our house, because she was doing everything for everybody else and not staying home and things like that, but I do like that trait as long as it doesn't interfere with my family life. I just don't want to be like my mother too very much at all, because she's, uh, I don't mean to say unbalanced, but not consistent at all. One minute she'll be pouting around the house, and she does pout just like a little child, and the next minute she'll be asking my dad to go out for a ride, or let's do this or that, and it's one thing or the other. That's, uh, I forget the point I was making.

C45   Well, you feel you're like your mother but there are some qualities in your mother you don't like, and so you try very hard not to be like her.

S46   Very much. I lost a lot of confidence in myself, in the last year in school especially. I used to feel that there was nothing I couldn't do, and this last maybe year and a half I started feeling like there was almost nothing I could do, even though I tried very hard. I think I can see where there is just one thing that I am working for, to be a little bit unlike my mother. I am succeeding a little bit but then there's the other thing, where I am deathly afraid, and I'm afraid that it's still in me that I am, I do have certain characteristics of her that I can't get rid of. One is the nervous state I always seem to be in, worrying all the time.

C47   In other words, this one characteristic of being quite nervous you kind of fear. You worry about it because you feel that you show this.

S48   Mm-hmm. I do, and I never ask anybody whether they think I'm a nervous person because it seems to me an egotistical question, and so I don't ask and I'm afraid that it is there. Even my best friend I won't ask. It's something I'll have to live with if I've got it, and if I don't have it, well, it's just as well.

C49   In other words, you're not quite sure really if you have it. You don't want to ask someone, but you feel if it's there you're going to have to live with it, if it is there.

S50   Mm-hmm, yes. I guess I've got it, kind of have to. What I really want is a happy family life for me, and not like mine. And I want it to be a calm, serene atmosphere, not like ours. And yet, I want it to be in this way like ours, but everyone is very independent in our house. Whether they were brought up to be that way, or forced to be that way because of the situation at our house, the stamping, the yelling and the swearing, I don't know, but it is there, and therefore everybody has gone their own way, with Judy and I anyway. We're the only ones that are developed. We're the oldest ones. Let's put it that way. Judy is going into art and I'm going into creative writing, if I can, and I don't know what Charles and Madeline will do, but Madeline has a lot of art talent, too. What she'll do I don't know, but even if she doesn't go into art she's got it behind her now, rather got it in her, and maybe she'll keep it up no matter what she does. But what I want at my house is the same kind of thing, and I want intelligent children. I do want them to be intelligent, and if not intelligent, I want them to be pleasant individuals and not always worrying about whether someone's going to like them, like I did. I want them to feel more security at home so they won't have to worry so much about what other people think, as I did. That's why this characteristic bothers me, because I feel if I have it, if I can't control it, then my children won't feel that, because I won't be able to give it to them, give them the feeling of security.

C51   You feel that this characteristic and things that you think about and worry about quite a bit, you feel that if you have this then you won't be able to give the children the calm, peaceful atmosphere that you would like to have in a home.

S52   Mm-hmm.

C53   As compared to your own family.

S54   Mm-hmm. And then . . . I don't always read this column in the paper, but there's this "Dear Jane" column. I glance through it and every once in a while if there's something I want to read, I do. And there was one about a young mother who had three little babies, three young children, and she was so worried because her parents-in-law have shown so much favor towards the youngest baby who was a boy.

C55   Mm-hmm.

S56   Did you read it?

C57   No.

S53 Well, she felt they were doing this to the little boy and her other two little girls, the older ones, were going to feel slighted, very much, because when she was a young girl she was an orphan and she was adopted by an elderly couple, and she felt that they didn't love her very much. And she, I guess what it is is that she wants her daughters to feel security, and she doesn't want them to experience this favor thing, and Jane Lee, or whatever her name is, told her that she has got to stop seeing the situation through her childhood eyes and stop worrying about her daughters, because the situation has changed and things like that. That's another thing that bothers me, that if I don't stop worrying so darn much about certain things that I want to be, then it's just all going to be neurotic.

C59 Well, you feel that you almost over-worry about things.

S60 Mm-hmm, and I don't want to do that. I don't know. Sometimes if I don't talk it out, like I do with you, then it just gets worse and worse.

This counseling situation is looked upon very positively by the client.

C61 You feel that talking it out kind of relieves the pressure and tension.

S62 Mm-hmm. By the way, I left a folder in that outer room there.

C63 Yes. I have it for you.

S64 I was going to call and ask you to save it for me. I wrote down some things about the book I was reading in the library, a whole bunch of quotations and stuff that I wanted to read this summer. I went out and then I realized it was gone. I'm glad that I left it here so that I didn't lose it. There was a paper in there that I had written one time when my mother was stamping around and yelling at me. I don't know why I've had it in there. It was about

Client possibly left folder with wish for me to read it.

going to church. Actually, after I read it over it was a better paper than I thought it was. There were a whole bunch of weak spots in it but it does express how I feel quite a bit. I wrote I can't believe in God and, yet, no matter how much I try I still feel that, uh . . . this is one thing that I wanted this folder for, that I wrote down this summer. Exactly what he said I can't remember, but he said something about he supposes that a basic, or an inborn, or innate, something or other that is drawing him toward the immortality, and something or other of a god, and, yet, his practical mind, or something, just won't have any truck with it, and that's kind of how I feel, that I want to believe in God but I can't. If I can't believe fully then I, if there's any weakness in the whole thing I can't believe at all, and then finish the saying. And, yet, even when I talk with my best girl friend, Betty, about the most serious kind of weakness we have, I hope I've got it meaning that even though I say I can't believe in God the most important thing is that I want to, and I feel very alone without it because there is not much else for me to believe in at my own house, I think. As far as security goes, it just has always seemed to be an insecurity, more than a security. If it wasn't . . . I was always afraid that my mother and father didn't love each other because they were always yelling at each other, and the biggest arguments we ever used to have was on Sunday mornings when we had to go to church, and I always hated to go. I can't even remember what all these darn arguments were about. Sometimes it was what we were wearing. I didn't want to wear . . . my mother, inci-

Client equates yelling with being rejected and not loved.

dentally, does have a certain taste in clothes. She seems to be able to pick out things that are going to be high fashion, but I didn't want to wear them. Funny bows she attached to furry stuff. That's the hat I remember the most, that I didn't want to wear. It was a red fur hat, a bow-shaped kind of thing, and even now we still wear them, but I didn't want to wear it, though, and I cried like mad. And then we felt real stupid wearing them, and we didn't want to, seven and nine years old, and that was the kind of thing it was. There was no security there. I didn't even understand what was being said at church because we went to a church where they spoke Latin, and I didn't understand. It's all very beautiful now. I like to go, but there was nothing there, and, also, there was the thing that my mother and father were always, it seems constantly, arguing and yelling back and forth and they never showed any signs of affection toward each other. They still don't. Maybe in their own way they do. Now I can see that, but never outward signs of affection, which I think young kids should see sometimes. Maybe I was a dumb kid, but I just felt that they didn't love each other.

C65   You felt very often when you were younger that because there wasn't any display of affection at all that they didn't love each other, and you thought about this a good deal.

S66   I worried about it and I cried about it. I always used to cry. I always tried to make things more, I don't know, cover up. I always was worrying about where Judy was. She was always off gallivanting around. Someone always went to get her and bring her home. Then my

dad would yell through the house and
swear around, and my mother would
always say, "Get out in the middle of
the street and yell, then everyone on
the street will hear us." She would
either do that in her rebellious mood,
or she would say, "Jane and Judy,
close the windows, close the doors so
that no one will hear your dad." He
was so loud everyone would hear anyway, and it was just one big mess. So
now there's more of a security, because
I want very much to go away, and
there's so much whether I go to Arbor
or what. I don't care where I go. I
want to go away. They won't say I'm
going and they won't say I won't. I
feel my dad wants me to make the
decision. He hasn't said it but he does,
and he wants me to say that, "I'll stay
home, Dad, and give up Arbor." Yet,
I don't feel like I really have to.

C67 You feel your father is kind of antici-
pating a decision on your part to remain home, go to school in this area.

S68 He'd like it very much.

C69 But you don't feel this is justified. You
don't want to do it.

S70 No I don't. I want Judy to go away, too.
If it comes to one or the other, it's going
to be her that goes away to school but,
as I said, I think it might just come
down to where I won't stay home any
more because I won't be able to study,
I think. You just can't study at our
house. With all this yelling going on
how can I? I stay up till 3:00 now,
every night, and I get up no later than
9:00. That's six hours of sleep. I never
could start my school work until 9:00,
when everyone was settling down and
maybe watching television, and maybe
my mother was at work, and Madeline
was getting tired already, and Charles

stopped yelling and stamping around. I couldn't study before then because there was too much noise in the house. But Judy would go downstairs and work on her things, and she had a big room kind of, like with a big desk and all that stuff, turn on the radio with television blaring, and all that. I couldn't study, so then I was never studying until 9:00 and staying up until midnight, maybe. So now it gets to where I work at home all day, you know, cleaning up the house and things that don't take too much thought, and I read my books at night and then it gets to around midnight. There's one television program . . . I never watch television except for this Jack Paar. I think he's real good and so I watch him, and he doesn't go off until I don't know what time, maybe 1:00. Then I can't go to sleep until I look around for something to read, and I just don't fall asleep until 3:00, maybe. I think it's my own fault, and I suppose I could get into another habit. I should. I'll have to if I go away to school, but that's how it is. I just don't feel like I could study too well at home.

C71   You're pretty certain that the conditions at home would be a little bit too much to allow you to study, because you found this to be so in the past.

S72   Well, I could do it. I know I could, but I don't want to. I'm tired of doing it.

C73   You feel you could but you've had enough of it. You feel it's justified, you've earned something more than that.

S74   I hate talking about what I deserve and what I've earned and things like that, because no matter how hard I've worked there are other things that I've done

that take away everything that I've
earned. In other words, I feel guilty
about some of the bad things that I do
do. Bad things. Funny word, but I
mean like the times that I do lose my
temper and say some awful things to
my mother, and that usually is enough
to erase any other thing that I've done,
because I haven't been brought up with
respect for my parents, and so I don't
feel it. My dad I do, because he seems,
he practices what he preaches and my
mother doesn't. I feel that I have maybe
picked up a lot of my own characteristics from my mother, just from what
she has told me as well as from experience, but she hasn't There are so
many things which she has always
told us to do that she doesn't do. She's
sloppy for one thing, and I keep my
own place neat because she has always
taught us to be neat and things like
that. When I had this special counselor
in high school she asked my mother if
I could have my own room because I
wanted my own room, and so I have
got my own room. And Judy has to
share hers with Madeline, and Charles
doesn't even have a bedroom because
he has a day bed that he sleeps on,
but there I am No matter how hard I
work I also have the privilege and
extra privilege, because I do work hard.
Not because I do work hard. I work
hard because I've got the privilege, but
I do have the privilege that the other
kids don't and so it's all pretty balanced, how hard I've worked, for I've
received also.

C75 You feel that the privileges and the
extra things you've gotten has kind of
balanced out some of the good things
you've done and sometimes you've lost
your temper. It's kind of balanced out.

S76   Mm-hmm. And so this college business
      to me isn't a question of what I deserve
      and what is coming to me but more a
      question, to me right now, of my deci-
      sion, not theirs.

C77   You feel your college career ultimately
      will be decided by you. It's your deci-
      sion.

S78   Mm-hmm. I also think that maybe be-
      cause of all the decisions my mother
      and father have made for me, that it
      gets to where if they say one thing, well,
      I want the other right away, and I try
      to work on that, too, but I can see it.
      Even when I think of it right now I
      can see that I would go to Warren. I
      would probably be more willing to go
      to Warren if I didn't feel that my
      parents wanted me to go there. I can
      see it. I'm pretty sure.

C79   You feel pretty strongly that often your
      decisions, and you feel even your deci-
      sion in the future is made because your
      parents make one decision and you feel
      you have to take the other side.

S80   Mm-hmm, and if I go to Warren then
      they'll always be there making these
      decisions, and whether I follow them
      or not I'll always have to be fighting
      them. My mother doesn't like the way
      I dress and sometimes when she sees
      the things I have on, it just is enough
      to ruin her whole day and therefore it
      ruins mine. Even around the house
      she doesn't like what I put on. One
      thing my mother doesn't like is for me
      to wear a clean blouse around the
      house, to take a fresh blouse out of the
      closet and put it on. And I don't get
      it at all, and so I'm going to do my
      own wash and ironing, and I do.

C81   You can't quite understand why she
      objects to you wearing a clean blouse

around the house when you do your own laundry.

S82 Mm-hmm, and I'll admit some of the things I do are funny, because I'll take a good blouse, a really good blouse that I have, and wear it if I feel like it, but I think clothes are to wear, period. And, so I wouldn't wear this blouse painting, of course, but there are some things that I do that she doesn't approve of. Oh well! Both of them had a difficult childhood. I should understand that, too.

C83 You feel knowing your parents' background should help you understand them because they did have it difficult.

S84 Mm-hmm. They very much did. My dad, I don't know, he wasn't even going to go to his dad's funeral. He hated him so much. It seems my dad now . . . I never bring it up now but a couple of years ago, or when I first became aware of it, or decided that I would say something about it, I asked my dad something about. . . . Well, it always has seemed to me that my dad was always saying that he hated his father very much, and that he was the son of a bootlegger. I found quickly enough that it was something that I shouldn't bring up and I kind of think that my dad wanted his dad to be a little better than he was, because he was a bootlegger. To be truthful, he was, and he wasn't very scrupulous. He had ten children and was rather strict with his wife, and he was very strict with his children and he was the man of the household, as far as I can see. My dad didn't like him at all and, well, one of the middle sons, my Uncle Harold, ran away from home and never came back and didn't go to the funeral and

In speaking of her dad's feelings towards his father, client also is speaking about her own feelings.

never associated with the rest of the family most of these ten years, except for my dad. Now why this is I don't know. My dad's the oldest one but my Uncle Harold, when he came back from the war, he came to live with us and now that he's married, and he married a divorced woman, or whether she's divorced or a widow I don't know, but she's a very nice woman. She's an artist and talented and she turns out all kinds of things. She's got a son that he adopted. He didn't adopt him as a matter of fact. My Uncle Harold associates only with my dad and the rest of our family and why this is I don't know. Both of them hated their father very much and Uncle Harold enough to go away from home, and my dad just plain hated him as far as I could see. I kind of think that my dad actually didn't hate him and wanted his love more than he got, and so I don't know why.

C85   You kind of feel that although your dad gave the impression that he hated his father it really was something more, that he wanted more love and attention from him.

S86   Yeah. I think so. He didn't get it and he was forced to go to hate. Another thing is the religious background. You know my dad was forced to go to a parochial school, and to hear my dad describe the parochial school is comical, actually. It didn't add to my reverence, to tell you the truth. It really didn't, because my dad won't go to church and he quit school when he was quite young and he was forced to go to work. And on top of that, he used to do the rounds with his father, who was a bootlegger who delivered the liquor, and come in contact with the underworld, actually. I think there was a meeting in Chicago, as far as this Capone thing and my dad, maybe he was bragging or exaggerating to make it sound more important, but he said he did meet these people infrequently. But at least he did, and things like that, and while he was still very young, and he was a dandy and made money and never finished school, I think. That's another reason he wants us all to go to school. It's been put in my brain, and I always wanted to go whether my dad and mother did or not, I always have, but then my dad's childhood really is quite a mess, but he made the best of it and he's quite a successful man now. He had a bad childhood and so did my mother. My mother's mother was divorced twice and one of her two husbands just died a couple years ago. He was in Massachusetts in an old persons' home and we would always go and visit him. He seemed like quite a nice man. He was very old and he had hardening of the arteries. Well, enough of him, but that was my mother's childhood and they both had, well, it was depressing. On my mother's side, my grandmother had eight children and only three lived. And it was tough at that, no father, and my mother was working when she was fourteen in a factory, and she never finished school. I really should be a better girl to them and show them more respect and, yet, I can't. I just don't have it, and as far as I am concerned if you don't feel respect it isn't there and is just a surface thing.

C87 Well, you're kind of bothered because you know of your parents' background and you appreciate it for it, the trouble and difficulty it brought them, but yet you still can't quite feel the respect for them that you think you should, or that they want you to have.

S88   Mm-hmm. Especially for my mom. I can feel it for my dad. I actually do, because I think he's done a great job with his life but she seems to have missed the boat. They say when you're seventeen, something about when you're young you think about how dumb your parents are and then the next year, or when you're twenty-one or something, you're marvelling to see how much they're worth, but it does seem to me right now that my mother missed the boat somewhere, not getting enough education, not gaining enough control of herself. I do wish she'd get it, go back to school. She has a lot of potential. She's creative and she's working right now to put Judy and I through college. She's working at Andersons and she can improve her position and she can get more money but she's afraid to. She wants to quit working. She doesn't want to go on working, but she's doing it so we'll have enough money to go to school.

C89   In other words, you kind of hope that perhaps your mom would go back to school or take the time to kind of better herself, improve herself. You feel she could do this, but you feel somewhat badly because she's continuing to work solely to put you kids through school.

S90   Mm-hmm. She is. That's one sure thing. If there are many things I'm unsure of, that's one thing I do know. She is going to work to put us through school. And another thing is that it's not only going to be us. After we get off, let's see, there's four years' difference be-

tween my brother and Judy and I—he'll
only be getting in. And there's seven
years' difference between Madeline
and Charles and no sooner than he'll
get off, she'll be going in pretty soon
again. I just take it for granted that
they're all going to school. Well maybe
by the time Madeline goes, Judy and I
will be helping her through, and maybe
even Charles, because I think Judy'll
be a success. She gets along very well
with people and, besides, who knows,
maybe she'll marry a rich oaf, guy.

C91   You feel that maybe you can kind of
help out at home.

S92   Mm-hmm. Once I can start making my
own money, well, then I will be able to.

C93   You feel that you want to, once that
you're able to make some money, you
want to help out at home.

S94   Mm-hmm. I do. And then there's also
the thing, well, I think these few years
right now, the couple of years that
have passed and the couple of years
that are coming, are going to be the
most difficult for our family because
we are . . . I suppose, aside from the
time when Judy and I were born, which
was a financial strain on my parents,
we are also creating a big expense now,
both of us going away to school. Besides, my dad has a pretty good chance
of improving his position and he might
be making more money, and so that's
why I feel that while he's not doing
it now, he'll be making more money,
too, and so will we when we get out,
and things like that. And it won't be
so hectic.

C95   In other words, you feel that you're
somewhat concerned because you feel
that the next couple of years are going
to be pretty critical in your family,

because it's going to be a big financial expense for your parents to put both of you through school.

S96 Yes. Oh, it definitely will be, especially since right now my dad's worried about his job. Did I tell you that? He's, uh, the plant that he's working at is, has been going out of business as far as he's concerned, period, for five or six years and it might fall through at any time. He's worried about that. He's got a high position, supervisor, plant supervisor, something. I don't know. They make missiles, components, gauges, and tools and things. He can't tell us too much about it. I should know his position, supervisor. Yeah, he's plant supervisor. There's the guy also who's plant manager and from what my dad says—he gets pretty carried away because he can just see the whole thing sliding under him and he can't do anything about it, but from what he says the plant manager is a dumbbell. He over-staffed the supervisory staff with his relatives and friends, and things like that, and he doesn't give the right dates, and stuff like that, and I think my dad has had his sights on plant manager himself, anyway. If only this plant could. . . . He's got fifteen years in there and he applied for a new job just last week. I had to type out the resume, and the plant where he applied for he said was favorably impressed with him, but he doesn't want to go to work there, so what is he going to do. He doesn't know what to do. He's very insecure in his present job, because if he keeps the job if the plant goes under, well, there he is: a guy who's forty-nine, as he is, and putting two girls through college and raising two young kids, and doesn't have an-

other job. He could get another job.
I'm sure he could, but that's not the
point. He's got fifteen years in here
and if he hangs on a little longer, then
he will get another promotion. And
then there's also the thing where he
says that, "I think pretty soon is coming
another pay cut because of the financial
situation," and instead of pay cuts he
should be getting bonuses and in-
creases, and he's not. One year he took
a 24 hundred dollar pay cut. That
nearly killed me. That's the year I
went to Europe, and yet he still put me
through. He still sent me. Judy doesn't
worry about the money he makes, or
doesn't make, because she just isn't too
interested, but I do, very much, and I
try to find out. They don't like me to
know. My parents don't like us to know
what money's coming in and what
money's going out.

C97   Jane, I think our time is up for today.
I forgot my watch again, too. Would
you like to come back Thursday and
talk some more?

S98   If you have enough time I will. I'd like
to.

C99   Good. Would you like to come back
Thursday? I'll tell you what. Let me
give you a call. We might not be here.
I'm uncertain of the time as to the
morning or the afternoon. Can you
make it either time?

S100   Oh sure.

C101   Let me give you a call at home and see
if I can arrange a schedule for morning
or afternoon, and it will either be here
or perhaps we'll go to the institute.
It's a real beautiful building, and
maybe we'll meet over there Thursday.
OK?

S102   Mm-hmm.

C103   Fine.

Case Summary and Counselor's Comments

Case Summary.

   Client began the first interview by saying she was sick of talking about herself and then started talking with relish about her problem. She immediately brought out her difficulties in adjusting to her family and her intense feelings of competition and jealousy with her twin sister. She wanted help from her parents in order to go out of town to college and yet is confused and reluctant to accept their financial assistance. She expressed further confusion as to what she wished to study in college and whether she would be successful in her studies.

   Much of the material which emerged in the first interview was concerned with her problem of dependence and independence in relation to her parents. She told of her desire to refuse to go to church and parental pressure on this issue. She was quite upset about her parents' concern with financial problems.

   She repeatedly referred to the fact that her mother is undergoing menopause. Her criticisms were directed more toward her mother than toward her father. She is afraid that she is too much like her mother. She resented the strictness in the home and the controls imposed upon her. She feels that her sister is not under the same restraint. She constantly compared herself unfavorably to her twin sister. She feels that Judy (the sister) is more mature socially and gets along better with people.

   The remainder of the initial interview was devoted to client's description of the conflict with her mother, particularly in regard to client's choice of friends.

   In the second interview, client repeated many of the same themes. She complained of being "bossed around" on a job, a situation analogous to that in the home. Her conflict with her sister was discussed in further detail. She made several positive statements about the counseling situation. In S39, she said, "Something I do want to do is tell you how glad I am that you turned out to be the way you are, because, I don't know, I, did I tell you how suspicious of people, wary of people, sometimes I am? I feel this is not a good trait, but I am." There is an implication that the first interview had some cathartic effect.

   Feelings emerged around her father. In speaking of her beauty shop employer, she said in S45, "Yes, they were discussing me when I was sitting there, like a little girl, and I didn't go there for him to be my father either." She resents her father treating her as a little child.

   In S63, client showed a partial awareness of her strong feelings of jealousy toward the twin sister. Time and time again during this interview, she reiterated these feelings. In S77, client stated that it is unusual for her to talk about Judy. "Never done it before in conference with my counselor at school."

Client has gained some insight about her mother. She sees her mother as trying to identify with her—living her own life over again through her daughter.

She referred to several personal problems including a great concern about overeating. She is aware that she overeats when she feels nervous.

She showed considerable resentment about the rejection of her friends by her mother and also resented her mother influencing her father with respect to her friends.

Client began the third interview by saying that little has happened since the last interview and she didn't feel like talking. She then talked freely and volubly. She was fearful that she will not be allowed to go to Arbor, but feels strongly that she will leave home regardless of whether she attends college. The chaos and disorder in her family around preparations for college is quite upsetting to client.

Client is struggling with problems around her identification with her mother. She is aware of being like her mother in many ways and is anxious about this.

In S60, client again referred to the counseling situation, saying, "Sometimes if I don't talk it out like I do with you, then it just gets worse and worse." She began reminiscing about her childhood and the big family arguments on Sunday morning about going to church.

Throughout her series of three interviews, she frequently returned to the problem of college, and was concerned about the financial strain on her family which would be entailed if she and her sister go to college. She expressed guilt feelings about taking money from her parents. Each of the interviews was ended by the counselor because of time limitations. Client seemed eager to continue the counseling interviews.

(The interviews were terminated at this time due to the closing of the laboratory and the counselor's inability to continue the case since she was leaving the city.)

Counselor's Comments

Client seems deeply involved in an adolescent crisis with her family. She is trying to assert her independence, and is fearful of the consequences. Her oedipal conflict is quite strong. She shows strong feelings of rivalry with her mother for the affection of the father. She resents her father's treatment of her as a child rather than as a mature woman. Her rivalry with her twin sister is equally keen. Many of the comments in all three interviews indicate that client feels inadequate and sees her sister as being the family favorite. It is interesting to note that client barely mentions her other two siblings. Her own sexual anxiety is revealed in her overconcern and frequent comments about her mother's menopause. This probably serves to intensify her oedipal conflict. Her wish to go out of town to college is complicated by her desire to leave home and the guilt that is consequently aroused.

She seems to have gained considerable superficial insight through previous counseling interviews with her high school counselor and visiting teacher. Client is reaching out for help and may be able to benefit considerably from psychotherapy. This particular sequence of three interviews seems to have afforded her an opportunity to relieve some anxiety and tension around her current difficulties. They seem to have had mainly a cathartic effect. The opportunity to criticize her parents and sister without disapproval from the counselor may contribute temporarily to an improved attitude at home.

Counselor's Self-Evaluation

In a short series of counseling interviews, I do not feel it would be very effective to make many interpretations. Since they would be quite tentative and could possibly open up areas which would have to be handled over a longer period of time, extensive interpretation seems inadvisable. I feel that by accurately reflecting many of the client's thoughts and feelings, a considerable amount of material emerged in the relatively short space of time.

There were, however, many shortcomings in my interviewing technique. I was somewhat weak in beginning and ending the interviews. Small talk was not necessary, and it was careless on my part not to have a watch available in order to terminate the interview at the proper time. Sometimes I did not reflect accurately and injected some of my own feelings. There were a few instances in which I tended to negate the intensity of the client's feelings, which must have annoyed the client.

On several occasions, the client made statements relative to me which I ignored. In retrospect, it might have been better to deal with these transference feelings. Client seemed to be exploring whether she could trust me, and perhaps I did not give her enough encouragement in this respect. There was one instance where I inappropriately reassured the client which may have stifled a flow of new material.

I do feel, however, that client did relate well to the counseling and related many of her thoughts and feelings. If I made interpretations or suggestions in these early interviews, it would not have been conducive to a long-term counseling relationship.

Case Reviews

EDWARD ROEBER

As a counselee, Jane appears to be an "old pro." Her story is replete with sibling rivalry, oedipal conflict, guilt, rejection, nervousness, withdrawal, anxiety, and frustration, to mention a few of the terms used by Jane and her counselors. It is not difficult to classify Jane's symptoms according to psychological labels—there are plenty that seem appropriate. She has been counseled by a school counselor, special counselor, and finally a practicum counselor—in addition she has talked to one or two "intimate" friends—and apparently she is ready at the drop of an "un-huh" to tell her tale again and again. Her resources for expressing feelings are boundless. As a matter of conjecture, I see Jane as ideal material for a coached client, one whom a supervisor could use regularly with counselor candidates. Jane's repertoire would challenge them all.

Seriously, though, Jane's predicament raises two basic questions. To what extent can Jane's symptoms be associated with normal adolescent processes? What is the prognosis in her case? The question of normality for an adolescent is at best only a series of hypotheses—and Jane's case is no exception. In some respects, Jane discusses a number of conditions which plague all adolescents. She feels that her sister is treated differently from her, that many of her problems would disappear if there was only something to believe in, that she should appreciate more what her parents have done for her, that all would be OK if she could get away from home, that she is fully capable of responsible independence from the family, and that no one else has ever experienced the same "problems" during adolescence. These feelings to some degree seem within the normal range of adolescent feelings, but Jane's reactions apparently have been intensified as a result of temporary "independence" while in Europe. She finds it difficult to return to a family role once she had escaped it, even though she knew it would be only a temporary arrangement. In this latter respect, she also indicates a reaction within the normal adolescent range.

Looking at another set of hypotheses, Jane expresses a number of attitudes which may or may not fall in a normal range, depending upon the degree to which she overdramatizes her feelings:

> ". . . I was always afraid that my mother and father didn't love each other because they were always yelling at each other . . . they never showed any signs of affection toward each other." (III S64)

157

"I kind of think that my dad actually didn't hate him (her grandfather) and wanted his love more than he got . . ." (III S84)

"I want them (her children) . . . not always worrying about whether someone's going to like them, like I did." (III S50)

"I don't like to have many friends either, and that sounds funny, but I just don't like to feel obligated to a bunch of people." (I S115)

". . . did I tell you how suspicious of people, wary of people, sometimes I am?" (II S40)

"I do have to make an effort to make friends." (II S43)

"I don't know, or like being obligated, sort of like. . . . If I could get chummy with the teacher, then especially, I wouldn't like it because then he would just give me the mark or something like that." (II S91)

"He's (her boyfriend) quite good with people, too, and so I feel . . . that he can carry us both if he has to." (II S177)

This set of quotations, and there are others, indicate a type of attitude which can be very frustrating to the adolescent. Somewhere in the matrix of family relationships Jane has failed to learn how to give and receive affection. Because of inconsistencies in the effective behavior of mother, and even father at times, Jane apparently finds it difficult to trust her affections to anyone unless that latter person is willing to reciprocate considerably more than the average individual. Unless she is able to overcome this fear that people will take advantage of her, if she gives or receives affection, Jane may find herself moving from one group to another, or one job to another, searching always for a place where people freely give their affections and where she can comfortably receive their affections. Such a goal can be so idealistic that prognosis in Jane's case might not be too encouraging.

In *The Case of Jane,* there is a dedicated commitment by the counselor to a client-centered methodology. Diagnostically speaking, the counselor may have considerable evidence to support an approach which encourages counselee self-discovery. Using a series of clarifications, the counselor attempted to help Jane gain further insights into her relationships with parents, siblings, and other people. Apparently the counselor, from her self-reports and self criticisms, felt that her responses were consistent with her aspirations.

In the first interview, when asked her purpose for counseling, Jane indicated "trouble" with her own self and maybe with her family. (S23) The counselor immediately indicated in a response, supposedly clarification but more likely interpretation, that Jane found herself "confused and mixed up." This was the first of several questionable leads, some bordering on interpretation and some clearly repetition of content. This series of interviews demonstrates the almost continuum-like relationship between an interpretation, and a clarification or reflection. Between clearcut clarification and obvious interpretation, is an ill-defined region in which a given lead may fall, having both these characteristics. Take, for example, the lead, "You feel somewhat guilty about not going when you did before." (I C36) This lead goes beyond Jane's feeling, is clearly the counselor's hypothesis, albeit perhaps a good one, and ends up an interpretation. On the other hand, "You get pretty discouraged talking about it and thinking about it," (I C58) is probably "on target" as a clarification of Jane's feeling. Also in the first interview, the counselor states, "You are looking forward to school with a little bit of anxiety about college." (II C54) This lead falls in the gray zone between clarification and interpretation. In a sense, it probably reflects Jane's feeling in S53, but it contains an element of interpretation. Jane was expressing a feeling that if she can get away from home she is sure that she can handle the demands of studying at college. The counselor went beyond the feeling expressed by Jane, and yet it was qualified by "a little bit" which makes it applicable to almost any situation. This conclusion is not meant to place a value judgment upon the goodness of interpretations or clarifications. Actually it assumes importance only when a counselor, such as Jane's, attempts to use, primarily, clarification leads.

Another concern is the terminology used by Jane's counselor. An expression, such as "in other words," can be very irritating to an adolescent. It can also imply that Jane is not communicating very well and might reinforce feelings of inadequacy. Reinforcements of another kind could also occur when a counselor persistently uses such words as mixed up, confused, anxiety, guilt, nervous, and upsetting.

Taking into account the three interviews with Jane, I would nominate her counselor for the "Purple Heart"—especially for the latter's self control under a diarrhetic verbal barrage. On the whole, the counselor indicated more than ordinary talent for counseling—and this conclusion might be even stronger if it had been possible to see the nonverbal cues.

BUFORD STEFFLRE

This case illustrates the value of being able, not only to study the typescript, but to listen to the tape recording of a counseling interview. The written case, for example, would give us no reason to believe that Jane is crying in the first interview from S109 to S115. The fact that she does cry at that time tells us a good deal about her relationship with the counselor and the counselor's skill. Neither does the cold typescript give us any idea of how reassuring the counselor is in the first interview at C106. There are other places, too, where the tape does much to pad out our knowledge of the case.

One of the difficult things to understand about this case is why Jane continues to do such a good job of exploring her situation even though it appears that the counselor does little more than respond with restatements of content. (See, especially, the first interview from C158 to the end.) It may be that the counselor's manner and appearance provided a bridge that isn't apparent in her actual statements. On the other hand, it is possible that Jane was either "counseling prone," or had learned through her previous "special counselor" how to play the counselee role properly. In any event this case seems to me to be a good example of personal social counseling with a high school student, but it is difficult to identify the elements that made it so.

It might be helpful to look first at some of the things which the counselor wisely and skillfully did not do. These might be called her skills of omission. First, the counselor does a very good job of not pressing for clarity in unessentials. In the first interview when Jane is talking about her friends Lois and Mary, in the second interview when she discusses the problem of her art class, and in this same interview during the confusion of the case of the two Pablos, she sometimes is faintly reminiscent of Eisenhower at a press conference. The counselor, however, very wisely does not press for what must be unimportant accuracy in detail. Second, the counselor does not insist on turning these interviews into educational-vocational counseling. In the first interview at C34 the counselor makes what is apparently a fallacious statement of the problems which, if it had been accepted by Jane, would have turned the counseling toward vocational planning; but when Jane moves on to more personal matters the counselor attempts to stay with her. In summary, the counselor's skills of omission are at a high level.

I wish it were possible to discuss this case with the counselor because I would like to raise some questions with her, and I would be sincerely interested in her reaction to them. I first would like to ask her why she did not respond to Jane's concern regarding her femininity and her attractiveness. From the counselor's comment, she apparently recognized that she was not responding to Jane in this regard in the first interview (S129-S133), and that her lack of response caused Jane to change the subject and talk momentarily about her grades. A similar situation arises in the second interview when at S157 Jane stumbles and has great difficulty with the words "attractive" and "unattractive." When the counselor does not help her look at the meaning of this difficulty, Jane goes on to talk about her boy friend. Is this a way of getting back at the counselor by saying in effect, "Other people think I am attractive even if you don't"?

The second question that I would like to raise with the counselor deals with her response in the first interview when Jane, in S107, indicates her concern that she had previously been assigned to a "special counselor." The counselor responds, in C108, with "You feel it's kind of upsetting to always have to *lean* on someone." I wonder if the counselor thinks that she responded in this way and in this manner (with a slight emphasis on lean) as a way of saying to Jane, "Don't expect to lean on me." In any event, it seems possible that Jane interpreted it as a rejection, since she begins to cry. Is the counselor's attitude toward this passage related to the fact that the typescript itself does not indicate that Jane is crying?

There are several other places where Jane indicates that she is quite concerned about her mental health. (See, especially, first interview S105, second interview S143, third interview S46 and S58.) Was the counselor's lack of direct response to this concern a deliberate attempt to keep from opening up problems in Jane, or was it a way of avoiding an area in which she did not feel comfortable?

Because the counselor has some apparent interest in psycho-analytic interpretation of behavior, it might be interesting to discuss her response in the second interview at C48. Jane has said that she resents being treated as a little kid and the counselor responds, "Well, you feel you, that you understand you don't want to be a little growing boy." Is the word "boy" used to refer to Jane for some obvious reason that escapes me, or is it a slip? If it is a slip what is it expressing?

My final question would have to do with the counselor's psycho-analytic theoretical framework. It appears to me that while she uses a very consistent theoretical framework in analyzing the case, she does not use this theory to guide her activities in the interview. In fact, her persistent restatement of content would seem to me to bear little relationship to any current counseling theory. I find her analysis interesting, however, and I think it helpful, but when she suggests that Jane is having problems in defining her sex role, has she really told us very much that helped us understand Jane? Would not the base rate for sex concerns among seventeen-year-old girls be very high? To guess that a seventeen-year-old girl is concerned about her sex role is like guessing that an unknown jockey is small. In this same context, what does the counselor's theoretical framework suggest that she might do with regard to the transference which apparently was taking place in these interviews? Can this counselor really continue to operate in terms of analyzing behavior from one theory when she does not use this theory to guide her behavior in the interview situation?

There is some indication here that the school previously considered Jane in need of therapy. While this is not altogether clear, it appears that she had daily interviews for a long time—possibly with a school social worker. The counselor in this case also indicates in her analysis that Jane could profit from therapy. While the distinction between therapy and counseling is not an easy one to make, it seems to me that Jane is presenting almost a classic case of an adolescent in need of counseling. Her concerns are with the standard developmental tasks of adolescents. She is concerned about achieving a feminine social role, about accepting her body, about achieving emotional independence from parents, about achieving economic independence, and about achieving socially responsi-

ble behavior. On the basis of the little we know about Jane, she seems
no more in need of therapy than would any typical seventeen-year-old
girl. As a matter of fact, if all our seventeen-year-old girls had the insight
and maturity that Jane has we could count ourselves very fortunate as a
society. Jane would typify the kind of case that a high school counselor
should be equipped to deal with. His goal might be re-education in some
areas and support in others, so that Jane might have some help in master-
ing the developmental tasks which our culture asks her to learn.

Finally, while we can only catch glimpses, through the eyes of Jane,
of the special counselor who dealt with her in school, I find these
glimpses provocative. This counselor did a number of things which Jane
found helpful. She apparently did some very direct teaching about the
problems of middle-aged mothers (second interview S115). She did some
environmental manipulation by arranging for Jane to have a private
room (third interview S74). Finally, there is an indication that she provided Jane with a warning that reality is a criterion against which we
should check the validity of our notions (third interview S44). In at least
these three matters the counselor seems to have actively intervened in the
life space of Jane. From what we hear in the present case Jane found
those interventions helpful. Furthermore, I would hypothesize that the
success of the present case is due in part to the fact that the special
counselor taught Jane how to be a "good" client.

My over-all reaction to this case is one of optimism regarding counseling
with adolescents, of respect for this counselor's analytic abilities, and of
enthusiasm for Jane as a client who knows how to use the counseling
opportunity.

Dugald Arbuckle

Session 1. It is unfortunate that the typescript cannot reveal the
rapidity and the intensity with which Jane speaks and that the words so
often sound very much different than they read. The counselor indicates
her awareness of her own nervousness, as indicated by the excessive
structuring which takes place. A very casual reference to a microphone or
a one-way mirror is all that is needed, and some would even question the
need for this, unless it is brought up by the client. Actually, in C14, the
counselor states what would seem to be an untruth, since this reviewer
could hardly be reading this material if it was to be limited to counselor
and client!

The counselor's criticisms indicate her awareness of a tendency to go
beyond the client, and to impose on the client her own frame of reference.
While she is generally acceptant, she tends to be somewhat intellectual
and pedantic, and talks more than is necessary, particularly at this stage,
with Jane as she appears to be. The client-counselor relationship, how-

ever, appears to be good and counselor misinterpretations, such as in C46 and C48, do not appear to have any negative effects.

As I listened to the tape, I got the feeling that the counselor was continuing to intellectually understand Jane, but that she was not going along with the level of her feelings—she was understanding, but she was not empathizing. The counselor indicated her own awareness of this in her comment after S105. In the next few comments this counselor remoteness is particularly noticeable. Might it be that the counselor is not with Jane here because of her own uneasiness about the possibility of deeper involvement? Might she be afraid to feel Jane's fear? This discrepancy between intellectual understanding and a feeling involvement is indicated again in S121, in the counselor's comment, and C122. C154 was one of the few counselor comments at this point in which the counselor *sounded* as if she felt what Jane was expressing as well as understanding what she was saying. Toward the end of the session the *you feel*'s have become almost mechanical.

Session 2. The second session follows very much the same pattern as the first, with the client intense, pouring out words and feelings, and the counselor reacting predominantly to the content of the client's statements. The counselor possibly gives some indication of a reason for this aloofness in her comment after S107. The client very likely is indicating a sexually related feeling, but the counselor might possibly be more effective if she could empathize with Jane as she is expressing this feeling, rather than being diagnostically concerned with the meaning of the client's expression. The words in C108 read well, but the counselor does not sound as if she feels the discomfort of Jane.

As Jane progresses I get the feeling that she moves closer to herself, then moves away, but the counselor always appears to be somewhere in the peripheral area rather than being in the boat with her. If in C166 the feeling, the expression, the communication that is coming to the counselor is one of client discomfort, why not communicate this feeling back to the client. The closeness of feeling between client and counselor would appear to be the essential ingredient, with the "why" being relatively unimportant. It might even be difficult for the counselor to answer my somewhat didactic question of, "Why be concerned with the why?" How much more difficult is it for us to reveal intellectually the confused and complex "why's" of the various aspects of our behavior. Can we consciously discuss what is possibly subconscious?

Session 3. Client and counselor continue in Session 3 much as they have in the previous sessions, with the counselor continuing to react in a "content" fashion rather than in a feeling fashion. C51 is a good example of a counselor comment which tends to encourage the client to think, rather than to freely and feelingly express oneself. Such comments contain enough in the way of intellectual content to encourage the

t to *think* about the counselor's statement, and it tends to produce
ntellectual discourse between client and counselor. Often, of course,
the client is so immersed in his self that he pays no heed to the counselor's
attempted direction, and this appears to be the case with Jane. It reads,
and sounds, in S52 and S54, as if Jane is continuing in her own direction,
and not allowing the counselor to distract her.

Case Summary

The anxious and fearful girl that I heard on the tape, the girl who
talked so fast, and was near to tears at times, the girl who skirted deep
and probably repressed feelings does not, somehow, seem to be the same
girl that I read about in the case summary. In these three sessions the
counselor was with Jane, but usually only in words, not in feeling; she
understood intellectually, but she did not empathize. This is a summary
of a "case," not of a girl named Jane, and too frequently in our counseling
sessions, we appear to be working with cases rather than with real life
human beings.

Counselor's Comments

No comment.

Counselor's Self Evaluation

The counselor here seems to be confusing reflection of feeling with
repetition of intellectual content. A "reflection" of a "feeling" must contain the feeling it is reflecting. When a client expresses a feeling of fear
and says, "I am afraid," a reflection of feeling reflects the fear, and the
words are simply a vehicle for the expression of this feeling. Far more
often than not, in these sessions, Jane's expressed feelings were not being
reflected. Most of the counselor's comments were intellectual, with bits
and pieces of the counselor attached to them, and rarely was there a deep
empathic expression of the totality of the client's expression of feeling.
One may get an impression of closeness in reading the sessions that is not
quite borne out when listening to the tapes.

I would question whether the feelings that Jane expressed toward the
counselor could be described as "transference feelings" in a psycho-
therapeutic sense. They would appear to be a more conscious expression
of feelings of one person toward another.

The counselor's opening statement that, "In a short series of counseling
interviews, I do not feel that it would be very effective to make many

interpretations," and her last statement that, "If I made interpretations or suggestions in these early interviews, it would not have been conducive to a long-term counseling relationship," are interesting—the implication is that the only time that interpretations should be used are when a counseling relationship has been well established. I cannot but wonder here, that if the counselor has got along without interpretations up to this point, why bother bringing them in at all?

SIGNIFICANT QUESTIONS FOR DISCUSSION

1. Is *The Case of Jane* the kind that a school counselor should be prepared to handle? (A counselor educator who reviewed this book in manuscript form differed quite strongly with Stefflre on this point.)
2. This was the first counseling ever conducted by the counselor. After the first interview she said to her supervisor, "I felt somewhat overwhelmed by her deep feelings and particularly was bothered when she began to cry." (This happened after S107.) How would you have responded to this beginning counselor? What are some appropriate ways for school counselors to deal with emotional release, e.g. crying?
3. How might a counselor's own attitude and value orientation have interfered when Jane expressed her feelings about church and religion? Are there other areas where the counselor's attitudes and values may hinder the counseling process?
4. If you had been the counselor, in what ways might you have handled this client differently?
5. If you had a chance to talk with the counselor, what would you have wanted to discuss with her after each interview?
6. Where do the reviewers agree and disagree in their review of *The Case of Jane?* What are your reactions to the reviews?

The Case of Jack

Purpose of the Interviews

Jack stated that his reason for coming to the counseling laboratory was for testing to help determine the type of work for which he was best suited. The school counselor's referral expressed concern about the boy's poor accomplishment and lack of enthusiasm in school. Though test ratings showed high intelligence, he did no better than C or D work. It was the referral counselor's hope that contact at the laboratory would help him to formulate better future plans, and that this direction toward a goal would prove a helpful influence toward raising the level of his scholastic performance.

(It is perhaps worth noting that Jack stated in one of the later interviews that the referral to the laboratory was arranged by the counselor with Jack's mother and was not discussed with him.)

Background Data on the Student

Jack was, at the time of the interviews, a rather husky and healthy-looking sixteen-year-old in the eleventh grade in high school. His father is a welder, his mother a housewife, and he has one younger brother, eleven years old. The family lives in the suburbs of a large city and is apparently comfortable financially.

The latest intelligence test scores on Jack give him an I.Q. of 120. However, his academic record shows straight D's in English and French, C's in geometry, and an occasional B in science or algebra.

On the referral form, Jack stated that in school he liked aglebra and geometry best, and English least. Much of the form was left blank (characteristically), but he did indicate that he was undecided as to whether or not he would attend some other school after high school, that he had some interest in flying, and that he wanted to discuss, "What am I best suited for?" His opinion of school: "It's OK."

The Interviews

	FIRST INTERVIEW	COUNSELOR'S COMMENTS

C1   Hello, Jack; sit down. Picked a warm day to come down, didn't you?

S2   Mm-hmm. (*Looking around*) Two-way mirror, huh?

C3   Yeah, that's right. Did she tell you about it? So that if there are people studying to come here to observe, they can do that. That make you a little uneasy about it?   *Reflect and accept suspicion.*

S4   Yeah.

C5   Well, if there are any, there's no one around today, and if there are people who come, they will be people who are studying advanced work in college, and they're not much interested in you or in me, as persons, it's just the way the counseling goes. So that's a little comfort, maybe. (*Pause*) It's kind of strange, isn't it, the first time?   *Reassuring.*

S6   Yeah. (*Pause*)

C7   Can you tell me a little about what you, ah, came down for?

S8   Well, uh, my counselor told me that you would give the tests to find out what I'm best suited for.

C9   Um, is that what you're interested in, about your future job?

S10   Mm-hmm.

C11   Well, can you tell me a little bit about that? What have you considered?   *Encouraging.*

S12   Well, so far about, ah, the only thing I've really thought of is welding. My father's one and I can weld a little bit. Be a good job. And, ah, I've thought of flying, something like helicopters, that would be a good job.

C13   So you've considered welding and being some kind of a flyer.   *Fairly adequate reflections.*

S14 Mm-hmm. Forest ranger wouldn't be bad either, something like that.

C15 Think you'd like that kind of outdoor work?

S16 I like the woods and all that.

C17 Uh, huh.

S18 But I don't know, any one of the three'd be OK.

C19 Mm-hmm, and where do you go to school, Darwin?

S20 No. Lewis.

C21 And Mrs. Coleman said, uh, what did she tell you about coming down?

Attempt to clarify situation, find how he wants to be helped.

S22 Well, she told my mother. We took that Kuder Preference Test, and, ah, I didn't do so hot on it, you know. I guess there was three subjects that I was, you know, about medium, and then three others that were lower, and then music, way down. That's the only one I know what it was.

C23 So, it didn't give you any clear ideas about what you should do?

S24 No.

C25 So you don't have, yourself, then, very many clear ideas about what you like, eh?

S26 Well, I like quite a few things, you know. Most anything is OK, ah, I can do most anything. But . . .

C27 But what?

S28 I mean, you know, whatever one works out is OK with me. Just as long as it's a good job, you know.

C29 Mm-hmm. It doesn't really matter too much to you.

Good.

S30 No, just as long as it's a good job, you know. I can do it, most anything.

C31 Mm-hmm, and a good job?

S32 Yes, I'd prefer a good job.

C33 I mean, what does that mean?

S34 Oh, good pay, something I like, you know.

C35 Mm-hmm. So it seems like you don't
ask for too much, then.

S36 No. (*Pause*) Pretty sly the questions you
ask.

Uneasiness in client.

C37 (*Laugh*) Well, I'm not trying to be sly;
I'm just trying to understand why you
came down here, and what I can do
for you.

I reassure.

S38 Well, like Mrs. Coleman said, that you
would give the tests, you know, see
what I was best suited for. That's mainly
why I came down.

C39 That's about the main thing you had
in mind? Would you like to see what
kind of tests we have, that you could
take?

S40 Yes, I would.

C41 I have a sheet up here handy. So you've
already had the Kuder, heh? (*Nods*)
Now, here are some of the kind of tests
that we have. Now this here is one
test, the California Test of Mental
Maturity. And that's what you call an
aptitude test, and it's supposed to show,
that is, this shows something like your
ability for school work. You've probably
had tests of that sort at Lewis, along this
line, like an intelligence test or an
aptitude test, to test your ability, for
school work.

I might have omitted the
name of the test.

S42 We had the Kuder Preference Test, and
that's about it.

C43 Mm-hmm. Well, let me explain what's
on here, and then we'll see if we can
get a better idea of what you want. Now
this is all one big test, here. It's called
the Differential, this means a lot of different aptitudes. It tests your ability in
a lot of different things, in verbal, see,
in words, in numerical abstract reasoning, space, mechanical, clerical, and
then language, do you see?

S44 Mm-hmm.

C45 And that's all one big test. Each part of

this takes about a half hour. So you can take that whole thing if you want to, that will take several hours, or you can take any part of it to see if you're very strong in verbal, here, then that goes along with perhaps certain kinds of work, and numerical with other kinds, do you see? There's a kind of relationship, maybe, with abstract, with something like space relations, drawing, engineering, something like that kind of work, do you see?

S46   Mm-hmm.

C47   Now these interest things, you remember what the Kuder was like, where you make choices, you know, and then it shows . . .

S48   I'll tell you something, on that Kuder, though. Uh, I don't know as I really took that serious. I know quite a few of the kids didn't. I mean, I took the test and that, but I don't know if I, you know.

C49   Yeah, I know what you mean, a lot of things in there that didn't seem to make sense to you and so you just plunged in and . . .

Too quick to assume I understand.

S50   No, people, you know, kids come in and . . . Kuder Preference Test, I can't see any reasoning in that test, so they, eh, the heck with it.

C51   So you think if you took it again more seriously, maybe it would show something more, hey?

S52   Oh . . . it's possible.

C53   That's a possibility then? Well, now, this thing here, this Strong is similar to this. This one, again, asks you a lot of questions which, I don't know, maybe you won't see any sense to, see, if that's the way you feel, but I know, I took this one recently, and it says, uh, how do you feel about, see, you check like and dislike, how do you feel about making a speech, about writing a letter, about digging in the garden, and so on, you know a lot of questions like that to try and figure out what would be your vocational interest. (*Pause*) Now, this down here, Mooney Problems Check List, this is a long list of a lot of different kinds of problems that people of your age have, like making friends, getting along in school, getting along with your parents, girl friends, God, smoking, all sorts of things, see, and this gives you an opportunity to go through and mark the things that bother you, and then perhaps talk about them later. You see, people come down here for all kinds of reasons. This one, Survey of Study Habits and Attitudes, this one, again, is a list where they ask you a lot of questions about how you study, about how you do your school work, and then they add this up and see how you compare to people who are very good in school work. You see? And then this last one down here is about reading, that tests your reading ability if you have trouble in reading. Sometimes that points out what the trouble is. (*Pause*) But, as I say, people come down for a lot of different things, sometimes to take tests, sometimes to talk about things that are on their mind, sometimes to find out more about their future job. Or, "To find out what's wrong with my study habits, how come I don't get better marks?" I think Mrs. Wagner told you, I'm not trying to be sly or pry into you or anything like that. This time is yours, and you can get up and walk out, or stay, or take these, or whatever is on your mind. I'm trying to be helpful. (*Pause*) Any of these sound like anything you wanted to take, or are there any things you wanted to talk about?

Far, far too many words. It could be done much more simply.

Structuring.

S54 Well, I think I might take that Kuder Preference Test. And the Vocation Interest. And possibly this one. [*DAT*]

C55 Do you think you'd like to try all parts of this?

S56 I think so.

C57 Mm-hmm. Well, this will mean you'll have to come back a few times to get all these in, you understand?

S58 Mm-hmm. What would this Clerical Speed and Accuracy be?

C59 Well, this is a little test that really is quite simple, but it is supposed to test whether or not you are good at the sort of things like clerical work, like checking off a list of numbers, let's say, or filing something in the right place. They might have a list of four numbers here and four numbers there, sometimes on this kind of test, and they say, "Are they the same or different?" Well, it's very easy to see if they're alike or different, except that you're supposed to go real fast and see how many you can get done.   Too many words.

S60 What's abstract reasoning?

C61 Ah, now, that's supposed to test—that's supposed to test your ability to, uh, something like think, or to solve problems, something like that. That one will have a lot of different, I'm sure you've had tests like this, where they have some kind of a funny looking figure, and over here are four like it, which one is the same turned over, or something—that sort of thing. It's supposed to—instead of saying, "Do you know the meaning of a word?" it tests your ability to think outside of words.   Would have been better to say: "It tests your ability to think in symbols rather than words."

S62 Language Usage, what would that come under?

C63 That's like your English classes. Is it right to say, I did, or I done?

S64   (*Laugh*) I'm pretty good at guessing.

C65   Yeah.

S66   I get the same mark in English as I do   Some warning here.
in French, both D's. French helped me
quite a bit, with English. There's a lot
of things I didn't know, like conjuga-
tion of verbs. Never heard of it before.

C67   Language teachers say that sometimes,   Poor response.
that they teach grammar more than the
English teachers do. Has English been
hard for you?

S68   Pretty much. Spelling, quite a bit. Now
French, I got a D in there, and, uh, just
the marks in there, in class, were C's
and B's, but I flunked every test.

C69   You did the daily work all right, but   Good response.
not the tests.

S70   I could read, and my daily work was
all right, and everything else. I just
couldn't take the tests. Spelling, I believe, was coming in there.

C71   Oh, when the book is closed . . .

S72   I know the word in my mind, but I
don't know how to spell it.

C73   So that handicaps you as far as the
mark is concerned.

S74   Mm-hmm. Otherwise, I could get pretty
good marks in that class. And, uh,
numerical reasoning is pretty good. Geometry, I, what'd I get, C. I understand
that pretty well.

C75   That's a pretty hard course, too, isn't   Poor response.
it?

S76   Oh, it's hard if you don't study.

C77   What I mean is, many people find that
hard.

S78   I didn't find it too hard. Some of the
quizzes we had were rather hard to
figure out.

C79   Mm-hmm. But it wasn't something that
was way beyond you, or anything like
that?

S80   Yes, I caught on pretty good. (*Pause*)

So, if you'll line those tests up. Let's see, July 11, we're going on vacation. We'll be gone two weeks. Then after that we can come back again.

C81 We ought to be able to work out some-thing like that. If that's what you're interested in. 'What do you think, shall we start on . . . where do you want to start on these? Now, here's another thing, we have this time now when we can stay till a quarter to five or six, or some-thing like that. You could take one of these back and take one of these some other time. You can sit and talk. . . .   Suggesting.

S82 Which one could I take now?   He rejects the suggestion to talk.

C83 Well, like this Kuder, would you like to take that or any one of these here? We could get one of these in. They all take about a half hour.

S84 I believe I'll take the Kuder then.

C85 All right. Want to do that right now?

S86 Mm-hmm.

C87 All right. Now, ah, just sit tight a mo-ment until I find out if she wants you to take it in here, or if there's another spot where it's cooler. (*Leaving*)

[Administered Kuder Preference Record]

SECOND INTERVIEW (*Two days later*)

Summary: Interpreted Kuder Preference Record. High areas are Computa-tional, Scientific, Artistic, Clerical. Also took *DAT* Verbal Reasoning, scored 85 percentile.

THIRD INTERVIEW (*One week later*)

Summary: Asked to see test results. Seemed thoughtful and interested by results but did not comment. I asked, "Is this helpful?", replied, "Yes."

He seemed very pleased by the high score on Verbal Reasoning. Finally warmed somewhat and discussed school. He feels that he has ability and can get C or D without studying. Tends to put it off and forget. "I just don't study, that's all." I said, "So this would be the problem if you wished to improve your marks."

He also expresses criticism of several teachers.

Soon he seemed to tire of talking and asked to take another test. Administered *DAT* Numerical Ability. Score, 65 percentile.

Relation much improved.

FOURTH INTERVIEW (*Three weeks later*)

Summary: Jack has been on vacation. Says he gave some thought to future, plans to "try" in school. He feels confident that he can do the work but does not try because he has no interest in it.

He talks of having an easy-going personality, doesn't worry ahead or make detailed plans. Takes things as they come. He has considered welding and forestry, but not deeply.

Asked for further testing. Administered *DAT* Space Relations, Score, 97 percentile.

Considerable counselor direction in urging consideration of further schooling, improvement of marks, etc.

FIFTH INTERVIEW	COUNSELOR'S COMMENTS
C1 Hi. I saw you waiting out there. You're always very punctual.	Build rapport.
S2 What? (*Pause*)	
C3 Have some things you wanted to talk about today?	Good start.
S4 Well, I thought about doing the school work, but I couldn't think about anything much.	
C5 You have been giving a little thought to it, eh? I suppose coming down here keeps it in your mind and makes you think about it. (*Pause*) But you don't see any way out or anything.	
S6 No. Just do it when I get home. Say I'll do it, and then do it. (*Pause*)	
C7 About the only thing that seems clearer is that if you want to do it, you're going to have to do it.	
S8 Mm-hmm.	
C9 About all there is to it.	
S10 That's right. (*Pause*) That's all. (*Laugh*)	Resistance.
C11 About all you have to say, huh?	

S12   Mm-hmm. (*Pause*) Caught a cold some place.   He changes subject.

C13   Oh, did you? That's bad in the summer, isn't it?

S14   Sure is. Had a head cold, and now it's going down into my chest.

C15   That's uncomfortable in this kind of weather. (*Pause*)

S16   Well, we could take a few tests. (*Smiling*) Good old stand-by.   He sees tests as an escape.

C17   It seems as though when you don't know what to say, why then you can always take a test.   Interpretative.

S18   Yep.

C19   Tell me, did I hear that your mother was interested in talking to me, or finding out about what's been happening?   I initiate subject, request information.

S20   I don't know. She didn't say anything to me.

C21   I don't know where I got that idea. I thought it was from you. But she hasn't said anything to you? Does she ask you about what's happening?

S22   Well, I tell her I take tests and all, give her the results.

C23   You said as we were going out last time she's always interested and nagging at you to do better.   Again, deliberate attempt to start the client.

S24   Yeah. Just plain nagging. That's more like it.

C25   Chiefly about the school work?

S26   Oh, little bit of everything. (*Pause*)

C27   So she's on your back, kind of then, huh?

S28   Mm-hmm. That's one reason I don't like to drive when she's in the car. All the time, "Oh, you're going too fast, or, you're doing something wrong." Never do anything right.   It succeeds.

C29   You feel as though she's rather critical.

S30   Yeah, and then you go out, and, you know, you watch her drive, you know, and she makes more mistakes than you did. Like coming up here, I'd rather drive myself, alone. I think it's safer. Jeez! We didn't even get off onto Van Born, you know. She pulls up there and stops. It's clear coming east, and there was a milk truck, just pulled out, nothing else behind it. No, she couldn't go. He might step on it. She had plenty of time to go. So, after that goes by, she creeps out, she's sitting there in the middle of the road, you know, and by that time they were coming from the east, and kind of fast like, you know. I looks over, the cars is coming, you know. Whew!

C31   You figure she shouldn't be criticizing your driving.

S32   Yeah, I mean I don't say anything, I do and I get knocked down, but . . . (*Pause*)

C33   The feeling is kind of that you, you know, you have a mind, and you're growing up, and like to have some judgment, too, eh?   Interpretative.

S34   Mm-hmm. I mean, I don't do it perfect, no, but still, I mean . . . she's always saying there's something'll happen. Like a little kid runs out in the road, a half mile up the road, you know, I've already seen it. About five minutes later, "Oh, watch out for that little kid!" you know. I've already slowed down and all like that, and, "Oh, you're going too fast." I don't like it.

C35   Spoils your easy going personality.

S36   Yeah!

C37   Always criticizing.

S38   Yeah. (*Pause*)

C39   Yeah, I know what you mean. (*Pause*)

S40   You get in the car and about the first thing, "Oh, you're doing this wrong, you're doing that wrong." I went out one time on Telegraph, 45 mile zone right there, I was doing 35, "Oh, you're   This is the most he has ever said. In this sense, my direction and suggestion has helped the process.

going too fast." Cars are zipping on by me, you know, weaving out around. Coming up here, you know, going home, she'll, she won't cut across traffic on the expressway. When you come off or on, you know, heading north, you're trying to get on the westbound Edsel Ford. You cut down on the John C., you cut over on the other lane, just keep on like that. There's just a short distance in between, but there is enough to get over, if she'd get over, but she just, the car's got the power and all to do it, but she won't, there's a car coming, you know. He's a thousand foot back; she won't go. There's plenty of room, you know, a couple of car lengths where she could duck in, but she won't duck in. She's got to have the road all to herself.

C41   So you find as much fault with her driving as she does with yours.

S42   Yeah. I notice she runs quite a few stop signs, too. I mean, she slows down and all. Like she'll stop, if there's a line of cars there, she'll stop once, and that's it. When everybody goes, she takes off, too. You're supposed to stop at the stop sign, no matter how many times you stop back there. She takes off; she doesn't know whether cars are coming.

C43   I guess this is a kind of a feeling that comes when you're growing up and when you start feeling like you know something, and you have judgment of your own, and you resent being still treated as though you were a child and didn't know anything.   *Didactic approach.*

S44   Well, I mean, yeah, I will make some mistakes; I won't see some of the things, but . . .   *Ignored.*

C45   You're not saying that you're perfect.

S46 But as for everything, it's kind of ridiculous.

C47 And does this come over into school work?

I thought he might be ready to explore this.

S48 Well, not too much. But she, uh, nags quite a bit in that, you know, nags.

C49 She kind of wants you to do better.

S50 Yeah.

C51 I imagine she says you could do much better than that.

Suggesting probing.

S52 Well, in the morning, you know, when I get up for school, sure, I take it easy, there's no rush-rush. I always make the bus. I don't see that, you know, go out there and stand for fifteen minutes in the cold or something. Stand around and do nothing. You know, I'll take my time. "Oh, you're going to be late! Oh, you're going to be late!" Bus comes about quarter after, she wants me to leave about eight o'clock. Sometimes, I'll leave at eight o'clock. I'll go to the kid's across the street, sit over there, watch TV a while. Then we go up and catch the bus. (*Laughter*) You know, it's a lot easier.

He changes to a safer subject.

C53 So you feel, don't you, that she rides you and bosses you around a little?

I wish I had said, "So, outwardly, you do what she says."

S54 Sure. And then, coming down here, she's getting ready and, "Are *you* ready?" You know, I've been ready for half an hour. "Are you ready?" So!

C55 Her personality is quite different from yours. In that sense of she's flighty and wants to get all ready to go, and you're more easy.

S56 Mm-hmm.

C57 So you probably rub against each other in that way.

Probing.

S58 I mean, I can see leaving, you know, early for coming down here, because there's the traffic, and you can't tell just what is happening. But, uh, I don't want to leave two hours early, just to come down here. There's no real sense to it.

C59 That's right. Just wait anyhow.   Judgmental, encouraging.

S60 I mean, there ain't going to be that big of an accident or anything else that would hold you up that much. (*Pause*)

C61 Tell me, Jack, is she kind of dragging you down here? To this?   Request for information to clarify his feeling.

S62 What do you mean, dragging me down?

C63 To the lab here.

S64 You mean, did I want to come? Well, I didn't even know about it until she told me I had to go.

C65 Oh.

S66 I mean, I'm coming. I mean, if I didn't want to come, I wouldn't come. That's it.

C67 Oh! Well, I kind of wondered sometimes, you know, if it was that you were being forced to come and didn't especially want to.

S68 Well, see, my counselor, she didn't say anything to me. Just called my mother up. It was arranged through her.

C69 And said what? Do you know?

S70 Well, like she recommended that I come down here. So my mother said, "You got to go. Get the slip and apply." So, I did.

C71 But it wasn't your idea.

S72 I didn't even know about it, till I was told I had to go. I mean, it's an OK thing, though. I can see some good in it, I mean, you know.

C73 You feel like it has some value, eh?

S74 Yeah.

C75 Well, as I say, I've wondered sometimes, you know, if it seems like you're being sent in, and, uh, you're a little unwilling about the whole thing. But   Clarification.

you feel like it isn't going to hurt you.

S76 No, it won't hurt me, much.

C77 Well, we have good luck sometimes, if people are concerned about something, and talking it over, and sometimes the tests do help, you know, make it a little clearer. But it takes the person to be concerned, the person has to feel like he wants to come. That's why I wondered about you. So, it has been a little bit of use, eh? *Structuring.*

S78 Mm-hmm.

(*Opening window*) [Comments about weather.]

C79 So, you know what I'm curious about is whether the relation with your mother has any influence on the way you do your school work. If there's anything there. *Clinical pursuit of information.*

S80 Yeah, it's quite possible. I can't think of how, but it's possible.

C81 You haven't given any thought to this.

S82 No.

C83 Well, the only thing is that from what we know so far, it seems that you have very good ability, and your school work is very mediocre. So, this immediately makes us wonder, is there something that's keeping you . . . *Interpretative.*

S84 Yeah, it might be instead of hanging around, I get out, or something like that. You know, instead of doing school work, I take off.

C85 Yeah, sometimes people find that it's something like that, or, there's a lot of different kinds of reasons, and that's another way we can sometimes be helpful. If this becomes clearer in your mind, why you see where it's taking you, and whether you want to do that or not. It's your own, always your own decision. (*Pause*) But, you say . . . is this a thing that sometimes happens? You enjoy getting out of the house? *Structuring, clarifying role.*

S86 Mm-hmm. Sometimes I get mad and

take off, and I don't go over to anybody's house. I just take off and walk.
I get back I'm still mad, you know,
but . . . (*Laughter*)

C87   You feel like it's a situation you just   Went too far.
want to get out of sometimes. Before
you say the wrong thing, I suppose?

S88   Yeah. (*Laugh*) (*Pause*) What'd I get on   He changes to safe subject.
them questions I took last time?

C89   I made a little chart out here. This is
for this whole set of these tests here,
and the one you took last time is Space,
and you scored just right at the top
on that. Very outstanding ability in
that field.

S90   It's easy. All you got to do is think,
reason.

C91   Well, don't undersell this. This is a
thing that some people see and some
don't. That particular one drives a
lot of people crazy. You know, this
folded thing here, and what's it going
to look like when you put it together.
But you felt as though you had feeling
for that, though?

S92   Yeah. Actually, I didn't even, I didn't
construct the figure in my mind, you
know. Some people say construct it in
your mind, you know, it helps out. I
just look at the sides, look at the other
figures, you know.

C93   Just comes to you, uh? (*Pause*) You see   My usual overdone test inter-
what we have here? The way this is   pretations.
interpreted is, this along here, this percentile business, fifty, here, that means
average. See, this is your average line
right along here. That means what an
ordinary person of your age and your
grade would get is along in here. That's
what the majority of the people get.
That fifty there means fifty per cent get
less, and fifty per cent get more, and
they're mostly around in here. Now,
you've had three parts of this: verbal

ability, you score very high, ninety, better than ninety per cent of the people; numerical, a little less, about sixty-five, but still, that's well above average; and then space is very high, that's about as high as you can go on that. (*Pause*) Now, if you wish to come back enough times, it would be interesting if you want to, to fill in all of these and get the whole complete profile.

S94   OK, we'll do that.

C95   This one says, in the manual, that this is related to things like reading blueprints, like drafting, maybe to some kind of like architecture where you have the idea of visualizing what this is going to look like, these forms, in space. (*Pause*) That sound like anything?

His frequent pauses and lack of response cause me to try to direct the interview.

S96   (*Laugh*) No. Architectural things like that, I can do them and all, but I do them generally just for fun. Doodle quite a little bit. I can draw a square, any other kind of figure, make it, I don't know what they call it, you know . . .

C97   Uh, perspective.

S98   Yeah.

C99   That reminds me, that's probably related to your art interest. Remember, on the Kuder. So there is a definite kind of an indication there toward that sort of thing, art, or architecture, or mechanical drawing. Have you ever had drafting, mechanical drawing?

S100 I had mechanical drawing, some stuff like that.

C101 Mm-hmm. And you didn't like it too well?

S102 No, I didn't learn anything I didn't know before.

C103 Maybe more advanced work like architectural drawing might be more along your line.

My personal opinion intrudes.

S104   Possibly, but like I said, that's more
       like a hobby would be.
C105   It doesn't seem to you like a work that
       you'd go into, is that what you mean?
S106   Yeah, that's about it.
C107   Have you given more thought to that,   I again initiate subject.
       what kind of work?
S108   Well, I, no, not too much. (*Pause*)
C109   Well, would you be able to stay and
       take some more of these today, or
       come back? We're only going to be
       here three more weeks, for the summer
       session.
S110   I'll take them next week. I'll take two
       days I'll come in.
C111   Yeah, that'd help, so we could get it
       all in.
S112   How about Friday?
C113   Yes, we can come Friday.
S114   OK, I'll take one now.
C115   OK. Do you have any preference about
       what you want to take now?
S116   Um, let's see . . .
C117   This is a half hour, this is a half hour,
       this is about ten minutes, this is a half
       hour, and this is about ten minutes.
       Something like that, you know.
S118   I'll take the abstract.
C119   All right, abstract.
S120   Save those ten minute jobs for when
       we just got a little time.
[Administered *DAT* Abstract Reasoning]

SIXTH INTERVIEW (*One week later*)

Summary: Administered *DAT* Mechanical Reasoning. Score, 75 percentile. Language Usage. Score: Spelling, 30 percentile; Sentences, 40 percentile.

   Talked to Mother a few minutes while Jack was testing (she drives
him to the lab). She says he has high ability and will not perform in
school. He is stubborn and resents being told anything. Will balk at advice
and suggestions. Mother feels he needs direction. I suggested this was the
area of conflict, her wish to guide him and his resentment of it. She

agrees, but she sees no way out of the problem. (Many signs of maternal dominance.)

SEVENTH INTERVIEW (*Two days later*)

Summary: Jack asked for results of last session's testing. Says they are about as he expected. He knows he is weak in English.

Still much hesitancy. I asked, "Talking in a situation like this doesn't come easy to you?" He replied, "No." Later he said, "You better think of something to say, I'm about talked out."

Gradually he warmed and began a long description of a science fiction story he had been reading. Then he switched to hunting incidents. He also mentioned tentative plans to go to Lawrence Tech to study welding. Good rapport. The relationship continues to improve. This is the first time he has ever talked through an entire session.

EIGHTH INTERVIEW		COUNSELOR'S COMMENTS
C1	Sit down. How are you?	
S2	OK.	
C3	Your ma come down with you?	Conversational opening.
S4	Mm-hmm.	
C5	She object to coming late?	
S6	No. She just told me to drive.	
C7	Oh, yeah? Did you enjoy that?	
S8	Don't bother me.	
C9	You like to drive.	
S10	Yeah. I prefer it in the country, though.	
C11	You don't have too much experience yet, eh?	
S12	Had quite a little bit. On occasion I drive quite a bit.	
C13	Yeah. Well, going home in the expressway is no fun, that's for sure.	
S14	Kind of jammed up coming in.	
C15	Mm-hmm. You get into a lot out that way, a lot of Ford traffic. (*Pause*)	Waiting for him to begin.
S16	Well, you know you were talking about thinking about the job? Well, uh, got a good idea for after school.	
C17	Yeah?	
S18	Join the Coast Guard.	

C19 Oh, yeah?

S20 Take up flying.

C21 When you get out of high school?

S22 Mm-hmm. I mean, you know.

C23 So that seems like a possibility, eh, looking into that? Where did you hear about that?

S24 No place, you know. I know they got flying. If I was going to join, I think I'd like flying.

C25 Mm-hmm. And then think about that as a career?

S26 Yeah. Say helicopters.

C27 It's interesting. The last guy I had down here wanted to be a flyer.   Unnecessary.

S28 I don't know. Air Force is out. I don't know why.

C29 Don't like that?

S30 No. I mean, it'd be the best one of Army, Navy, or Air Force, you know, but, I don't know, I guess the Coast Guard would be better.

C31 Yeah. Something about it seems a little more attractive to you.

S32 Mm-hmm. (*Pause*) So, (*Laugh*) that's   Still hesitant to talk.
about it.

C33 About all, eh?

S34 Mm-hmm.

C35 But you still are kind of considering the future?

S36 Mm-hmm. (*Pause*)

C37 Do that instead of welding, is that what you meant?

S38 Yeah, I guess so.

C39 But it's still kind of up in the air right now, huh?

S40 Mm-hmm. (*Pause*)

C41 I suppose in a way, by taking tests   Trying to keep it going.
and things like that, shows you there are many things you could do.

S42 Yeah. Like I said before, I can do most anything.

C43 Mm-hmm. So a little bit depends on what, uh, what looks good to you, what interests you, something like that.

S44 Mm-hmm.

C45 And these things might change as you go along, too, I suppose.

S46 Yeah. (*Pause*) Have you seen the satellite yet?   He changes to safe subject.

C47 No.

S48 I've seen it three times.

C49 Have you really?

S50 Mm-hmm.

C51 I didn't know it had gone over.   Conversation continues.

S52 Yeah, it's been going over quite a bit.

C53 Is that right? The big balloon?

S54 Mm-hmm, *Echo I.* Let's see, I've seen it, uh . . .

C55 I did see in the paper it went over the other night about midnight.

S56 Saturday, Saturday night, I think it was. Yeah, Saturday. Saw it twice. Last night I saw it once.

C57 How do you know when it's going to come?

S58 Well, it's got a time schedule. It's in the paper. In the *Times,* they've got it.

C59 In the *Times?* I haven't seen it.

S60 Uh, what time was it? 10:46, I think, I'm not sure. Last night it was beautiful for something like that. I mean, there wasn't, you could really see. It was clear. Saturday, it was clear and all, but it wasn't quite as distinct.

C61 Mm-hmm. What time did you see it?

S62 Last night? 10:04. No, yeah, four.

C63 I wish I'd known about that. No kidding, I'd like to see that. And it re flects the light of the sun, just like the moon, I suppose.

S64 I guess they put that into an orbit where it would. They'd planned it that way. Stay in the sun about two weeks. So that the gases would stay in a gaseous state instead of turning to a solid.

C65 That sort of thing interest you?

S66 Yeah. (*Pause*) Yeah, you can see it for about fifteen minutes. It'll come up from about west, just a little, about south southwest. Wait now, *west* southwest.

C67 Yeah, anyhow right in there between south and west.

S68 Yeah, I'd figured out the time. I figured out my own schedule; I didn't know if they'd have anything. And, uh, I just left out the six tenths. It's orbitual time was two hours, one minute, and six-tenths, I guess it was, and I left out the six-tenths. Little bit of a difference. I figured it out for Sunday. Figured it out Saturday night for Monday, too. And when I added it all up it came out quite a bit of difference.

C69 When will it be back again now?

S70 Well, it's going around all the time.

C71 Yeah, but when can we see it?

S72 I'm not sure, ten something, I believe, 10:46.

C73 Tonight?

S74 Tonight, mm-hmm. If it's clear.

C75 Well, I'm going to be out. Maybe I'll have a chance to see it.

S76 I don't know, I'm not sure of the time. But, uh, do you get the *Times?*

C77 No, we get the *News.*

S78 I don't know about the *News.* It was on the front page. Someplace in the *Times* is a, uh . . .

C79 Schedule . . .

S80 A schedule of it. I think it was on the front page.

C81 The kind of interests you have are very typical of a kind of person who has a little feeling, a little ability, you know, like this. (*Pause*) And, as you think of occupations, for instance, or jobs in terms of being on a ladder or a pyramid, or something like that, starting down with someone, starting at the

Trying to come back to a consideration of his future.

bottom with a person who, uh, washes dishes, sweeps floors, things like that, going all the way up, you know, to someone like who designed this kind of satellite, things like that, the differences usually run in their ability levels. Usually a person who has mind enough to construct this satellite is not happy as a dishwasher, and so on, do you see? That's what I was kind of concerned about for you. You have good ability. Maybe you should raise your sights up to some of these things up here. I suppose other people have told you that?

S82 Yeah. (*Laughter*) (*Pause*) Yeah, when we first, Saturday night when we was looking for it, in the paper it said to look toward the northwest.

C83 Mm-hmm.

S84 It come from the southwest. We only caught it by accident, you know, and it was right up top of its orbit.

C85 Is it about the size of a star?

Conversation, yet this is an improvement over earlier interviews.

S86 Mm-hmm.

C87 Can you see it moving clearly?

S88 Yeah, you can see it moving. It's not fast. It takes about fifteen minutes . . . to go. And, uh, when it gets up, right above, it's just a little bit brighter than most any other star.

C89 Mm-hmm. I'll be very interested to see that.

S90 Kind of weird, you know. Think about that thing up there.

C91 Funny thought, isn't it.

S92 We'd sight it up with a tree, standing on a . . . I was over this kid's house, and uh, went through this orbit, took it right straight through, same exact place, as the day before. Funny thing, it looks like it was weaving, you know, wobbling back and forth. I don't know what would cause it, maybe it'd be the twinkling of it, or . . .

C93   Yeah, maybe something in the atmosphere would give that impression. You mean you saw it two different times, and the second time seemed to be in the same orbit? You lined it up on the same tree?

S94   Yeah, mm-hmm. We lined it up. There was a hole, you know, in the leaves, and we lined it up, and it was the same place. Fact, first night we seen it was about twenty minutes to twelve—twenty minutes to ten, I'm sorry—and the papers had predicted it would come by twenty minutes after twelve. Quite a difference in time. Maybe made the wrong orbit. We didn't know whether that was it or not, you know. Figured it might have been some other satellite, we didn't know.

C95   I guess there's all kind of junk up there now, eh?

S96   Yeah. (*Laughter*) (*Pause*) It don't move real fast, but it, you can detect movement. It was really nice out last night. You could see most everything, you know.

C97   Cool and clear.

S98   You see a lot more stars out.

C99   Yeah. (*Pause*)

S100 I started something, it's your turn now.   Asking for encouragement.

C101 (*Laughs*) What do you want me to say?

S102 Words. Let's not waste the tape.

C103 Well, we got plenty of tape. Hot as usual, isn't it? (*Opening window*)

S104 Yeah.

C105 Well, I'll tell you one thing, this is the   Structuring final session.
last time I'll be able to see you. So I would be interested in your summarizing, telling what you have learned, or anything like that. What it has meant to you. Do you have any questions? Did you get what you came down here for?

S106 Yeah, I guess so.

C107 You guess so. (*Pause*) Talk to me about that a little bit then, did you get what you came for, is there anything, do you have any questions, anything you want to know?

S108 No.

Frustrating client to deal with.

C109 Then did you learn anything, coming down here?

S110 Yeah, I'm pretty good at most everything; I should get better marks at school. Except English.

C111 Mm-hmm. And not as good in English as in technical things, apparently. What else?

S112 That's about it, I guess. (*Pause*) Sounds like a lot, doesn't it? (*Grinning*)

He still hesitates.

C113 Doesn't sound like much, does it? (*Pause*) You kind of knew this before, that you had pretty good ability?

S114 Yep.

C115 This kind of affirms it, then, doesn't it?

S116 Mm-hmm. (*Pause*)

C117 I guess you could say in that sense then, that you have considerable choice in vocations.

Leading.

S118 Mm-hmm.

C119 A considerable number of things that you could do. (*Pause*) And we could also say that it would be possible for you to get better marks, if it meant enough to you that you wanted to, and would try.

S120 Yeah.

C121 Care to go into that at all, talk about that?

S122 Not much.

Resistant.

C123 (*Laugh*) You want me to do it.

S124 That's the best way I can keep my mouth shut.

C125 Trouble is, I can't do it, though.

S126 No, guess you can't.

C127 Nothing I can do about your marks.

S128   Yeah. (*Pause*) I've also got a very great   Subject change again.
       ability for cracking the knuckles. (*Dem-*
       onstrating) Bones. Knuckles and wrists,
       elbows.

C129   That's a great skill. That's probably a
       bad sign of something.

S130   Nervous. (*Pause*)

C131   Are you a nervous person?

S132   Mm-hmm. I don't know, like you get   Still ill at ease in lab.
       up in front of a class, I don't like it,
       you know. I don't like to be watched.
       I feel cornered. (*Pause*) Just like that
       thing. (*Indicating the mirror*)

C133   Yeah.

S134   I don't like it.

C135   I can see it bothers you a lot, doesn't
       it?

S136   Mm-hmm. I just don't like the idea,
       you see. I don't know who's in back
       there.

C137   Yeah, I understand.

S138   I just don't like it.

C139   That's probably handicapped us a little
       bit, hasn't it?

S140   Yeah, quite a bit in English.

C141   Huh?

S142   Quite a bit in English.

C143   No, I mean us here.

S144   Oh, well, here, too, yeah.

C145   That is if we were somewhere else,
       maybe it would be easier to talk.

S146   Um . . . (*Pause*) on the knuckles, you
       know, you said that could mean some-
       thing. Got so now, I got to.

C147   Or else they hurt?

S148   They'll get stiff. I imagine it'd go away,
       you know, but in between there, you
       know, I can't move the fingers.

C149   You got them loused up good, eh?

S150   Yeah.

C151   I heard once that, I don't know if   Interpretative.
       there's anything to it, but this was sup-
       posed to be a sign of hostility, you

know. Someone that was always making a fist, popping his kunckles, you know, all this sort of thing. Supposed to mean that he wanted to hit somebody.

S152   That's an idea, I would like to have a fight about now.

C153   (*Laugh*) I hope it's after you leave here.

S154   I've been looking for one every night I go out.

C155   Yeah? You like to fight?

S156   No, I mean, I ain't going to go out and start one, but, uh, anybody tries anything, you know, I'm rcady.

C157   Gives you a chance to relieve some of your feeling, eh?

S158   Good chance to have some run. In gym we were always wrestling or something. Go out nights, you know, somebody wises off, and, you know, pop 'em. I don't start it, you know, but I'll help it along.

C159   Now see, this is the first time in eight weeks that I've learned anything about you, as a person.   Encouraging.

S160   Yeah, I was covering up kind of good, wasn't I?

C161   Yeah. I guess before we could, you know, if we were ever going to find out how to help you to get better marks or deciding what was preventing you from doing it, why we would have to know more about you.

S162   Yeah.

C163   But maybe it's clear to you. You're a smart kid.

S164   Oh, yeah, a brain.

C165   Seriously. Maybe it is. Might be that, you know, coming down and thinking about it like this makes you think about it in between times, and you've decided on some things. Either you're going to let it go this way, for some reason, or you want to change it. (*Pause*)

S166 Aw, I don't know. (*Pause*)   Still hesitant.

C167 Is Mrs. Coleman going to notice a change in you in the fall?

S168 I don't know. I try to stay away from her.

C169 Yeah? Are you in trouble at school? Fights at school?

S170 No. None at Lewis. I had a couple at Salinas.

C171 I thought maybe that had made bad feelings between you and the counselor.

S172 Mm-hmm. (*Pause*) Naw, it's just that I don't like her and she don't like me. Mainly why I don't like her is that, uh, unexcused stuff, you know.

C173 Yeah, you mentioned that the other   Initiating subject.
      day. (*Pause*) Are there many teachers over there that you dislike?

S174 No. There's some, but not many. (*Pause*) The librarian, but, of course, who doesn't? That's common. Then, an English teacher.

C175 Man or woman?

S176 Woman.

C177 You don't like her. Who else?

S178 Um, that's about it.

C179 All women. (*Pause*)   Interpretative.
                                             No response.

S180 Then my homeroom teacher, he's a crab. But I figure it this way, on him I got it made. I'm playing brownie, see, I sit up in front of the room, you know, and I, he wants anything done, you know, I do it.

C181 Oh, yeah.

S182 And, uh, if I end up with him for any class, I got it made. He's supposed to be the roughest one in the school.

C183 Yeah, what's his subject?

S184 Uh, Civics.

C185 That the term after this?

S186 Mm-hmm.

C187 Playing the angles, eh?

S188   Yeah. It's kind of dangerous, though, he gets mad, you know. He gets mad, he carries these keys around. Gee, he throws them into my corner. Just misses me, you know. (*Pause*) That Soffer, you know, she—I don't know, maybe she's just on to me all the time.

C189   This the English?

S190   Mm-hmm, English. I don't know, there's other teachers that didn't do me any good.

C191   But you dislike her especially because she was nagging at you, eh?

S192   Naw, I ignored her.

C193   But was this kind of a trait of hers, kind of needling you, pick on you, something like that?

S194   No. I don't know. It's just her, the way she did things, you know. She'd give an assignment, you know, and if you didn't get the date or anything, you know, she'd never ask for it. She'd never ask for anything, and, uh, that was just too bad. You had to get it in. Quite a few of the kids, I guess, didn't get it in on time.

C195   She makes it easy for you to get in trouble, get behind.

S196   Yeah, and uh, quite a few of the times I'd have the stuff done, you know, it was in my notebook, but she never called for it and I didn't hand it in. (*Pause*) And, uh, you didn't learn some things, you know, the book, you know, you give magazine reviews. You get a magazine, and, uh, she'd give you a mimeographed sheet and you had to answer questions. You ask her and she'd answer them for you. No sense to it. I didn't get anything out of it, and I don't think anyone else did. Cause, uh, there was nothing to it, you know, you go through, you run through real quick, you only got an hour, so

An exceptionally long speech for him.

you run through quick. You know, it'd been different if you'd had time to look at each different one, you know. But just run through quickly was nothing. Kills the week, you know.

C197   Kind of a waste of time, eh? And, uh,   Interpretative.
Jack, you aren't exactly the kind of kid who would just smile and do what the teacher wants, and say, "Yes, ma'm," you know, and never have a thought about whether this was something worth while or not.

S198   What do you mean?

C199   I mean, you kind of have a mind of your own. You know, you don't do something just because the teacher says, "Do it." Is that right?

S200   No, I generally do it.   He resists.

C201   (*Laughs*)

S202   I generally do, you know; lot of things, I don't.

C203   Well, let's say you do it, but you just kind of do it. You don't put your heart into it.

S204   Yeah. I mean if it's not an interesting subject you don't, you do it, but that's it.

C205   Mm-hmm. The kind of subjects you would enjoy most you probably never have had. Like if you were at Lawrence Tech or something like that, some of the things they have there if you were doing, you'd probably find very fascinating.

S206   Mm-hmm. I've got chemistry coming up, there's one I think I'll enjoy.

C207   And then will your mark in there be better, would you say?

S208   Yeah, I imagine so. That's pretty simple, you know, I mean, chemistry.

C209   Yeah, that's one of those snap courses.

S210   Yeah.

C211   Well, that'll be one interesting thing to look, you know, if we can get together

again next year, to see, does that fact
that you like chemistry and enjoy it,
does that mean you got a better mark
in there, or not. Or doesn't it have any
influence on it, you still get C or D.

S212 I like the class, so I'll get a better mark,
you know.

C213 You're pretty sure of that.

S214 Mm-hmm. Unless we get a bunch of
goof-offs in the class, I mean, you
know . . .

C215 [Inaudible]

S216 My history class last semester, the fat
slob sits up there and reads a book.
Playboy or something He's trying to
look real intelligent, you know what I
mean. We're in the back of the room
playing basketball, throwing paper
towels out the window, something else,
you know. I mean, there wasn't anything else to do. Had to do something,
break up the boredom.

C217 That's a waste.

S218 Yeah, he'd sit up there and read a
book. Every day he'd read a book.
So . . .

C219 So naturally people horse around, eh?

S220 Yeah.

C221 Well, what I was trying to say before is,   Interpretative.
there were probably many people in
the class that, uh, read the assignment,
wrote in the notebook, or whatever
they were supposed to be doing.

S222 Yeah, but, you know, I usually don't
remember the assignment, and I'll do
the assignment, you know, and I'll have
it. I won't bother to write down when
it's due.

C223 I don't seem to be able to make this
point that I'm trying to make, and
maybe it isn't a good one. (*Laughs*)
What I'm trying to say, and I still
think there's a point, is that, let's take

a girl, for instance, there are many quiet little girls in the class?

S224 Yeah, and they're always taking notes.

C225 Yeah, and who would never, if he was sitting there and reading a book, they would go ahead and study or something like that, you know, that they were supposed to do, and you're not like that. I'm not saying you should be, you understand.

S226 No.

C227 I'm saying you're a kind of person who has a mind of your own, and you resent getting gypped like this.

S228 No, I mean, I know most of what's in the book.

C229 Yeah, and that's another factor in it, see. If you were not, if you were . . .

S230 I mean if it was something new, I didn't know something about, I could probably go ahead and read a book. I mean, biology, you know, I was glad to go through the book. I was always going through, you know.

C231 You found that very interesting, too.   Summarize.
You have a definite lean toward math and science and technical things, and away from English and languages and history, right?

S232 Mm-hmm.

C233 See, that's a very clear idea about your   Interpreting.
future work. That's a big help.

S234 Yeah. That biology teacher I had, I didn't like her too much, but she was OK, you know, she was a good teacher. A good teacher and all, but, I mean I liked her better than some teachers, but, you know, there was just something about her. I would have preferred some of the other teachers. Course that might be because of some of her tests. The weirdest questions, you know. Some of that stuff you never even heard of. (Pause)

C235 Are there some teachers you get along very well with?

Probing.

S236 Yeah, I guess so.

C237 Fair.

S238 Mm-hmm. My biology teacher, I was going along OK until she jumped all over me for doing something I wasn't doing. Yeah, she jumped all over me for talking. I mean, you know, I usually kept my mouth shut. I don't talk that much. Jumped all over me for talking. I was about ready to tell her off.

C239 You don't like being criticized like that.

S240 Well, I mean, I could see it if I'd . . .

C241 Especially when it's unfair.

S242 If I'd been talking, I'd have sat there and took it, you know. I didn't do anything, no, but I didn't want to get kicked out of the class. But I'd about had it there, because, I hadn't been doing anything, and what the heck, I couldn't see that. (*Pause*) Think of something else I could say.

C243 I was thinking, you don't like to be pushed, or pushed around, treated unfairly, criticized for something you didn't do. And I guess you're subjected to a certain amount of that in school.

Interpreting.

S244 Yeah.

C245 I guess that's happened to all of us.

S246 Yeah. (*Pause*) I have this one teacher, she's always, you know, kind of an emotional nut, always yelling in class, or something like that, you know. Some girl was doing her homework from some other class, she starts yelling, rips it all up.

C247 Big scene.

S248 Yeah. You're sitting there, you know, and you're studying, and she gives out a yell and everything goes flying. Right about there, you feel like quitting, you

He is warming. Much more talking than usual.

know, and you usually do. I mean everything's all nice and quiet and she lets out a yell or something. Well, it's not the best conditions to work in.

C249   Yeah. I think that might be important, that that has an influence then on the way you do your work. Doesn't it?

S250   Mm-hmm. I guess so. I mean, I can work in most any kind of, uh, if it's noisy I can work, if it's quiet I can work, but someone starts yelling, I can't. I mean, you know, if it's quiet and all of a sudden someone starts a fight or something, I can't work. Or if it's sort of people talking, you know, and all of a sudden everybody quits talking, you know, I quit working.

C251   So these kind of flighty and emotional teachers, or cross ones, probably have an influence on what kind of work you do.   *Interpreting.*

S252   Yeah.

C253   And maybe a little more on you than on some other people. Maybe some other people just pass it off and go ahead with their work. I think it affects you a little more strongly, probably. Agree with that?

S254   Yeah.

C255   To a certain extent, eh?

S256   Mm-hmm. To a certain extent about   *Always resistant.*
everything.

C257   Well, it's just, it's interesting to think about these different things that influence, you know, your work. I think that's probably one thing, that's probably part of it; the way you react to these different kinds of people. (*Pause*) Is your dad like you?

S258   Hum?

C259   Is your dad like you? Are you like your dad?

S260   Yeah, I guess so. On some things.

C261   How about your little brother, is he   Again probing, looking for
     like you?   subject which will start him.

S262   Nope. No, uh, I sort of keep calm.
     When I get mad, I get mad, you know,
     but he's always getting mad. Chases me
     around the yard with a baseball bat
     or something. Want to sword fight
     with the bats or something, you know,
     and he gets hurt, he gets mad.

C263   (*Laughs*) And I suppose you get the
     devil?

S264   Yeah. "Little brother, you know, you
     mustn't hurt him." Half the time I'm
     just trying to keep him from beating
     my brains out.

C265   (*Laughs*) Yeah.

S266   Sunday, when we went out to the lake,
     we was going to, uh, you know, and we
     was throwing mud. And we was play-
     ing keep-away with the ball awhile, and
     he gets mad, and he came with the
     mud, you know. Pretty soon, he went
     in on the dock and was throwing, you
     know. We were, we'll fight you, you
     know. Fun is fun. Picking on little
     brother? He starts it. Lot of times, he'll
     just want to play, you know. He gets
     hurt, then he gets mad. "Well, you
     shouldn't be playing like that!"

C267   More or less whatever you do, it doesn't
     come out right. I mean, you're being   Understanding.
     told about it.

S268   Like, I'll do something, "No, you're
     doing it all wrong, you're doing it the
     other way." I'll do it the other way,
     "No, you're doing it all wrong, should
     be doing it the other way." Like doing
     dishes, you know. She's always com-
     plaining I never do the dishes. I'll go
     in, I'll do the dishes. "What are you
     doing here? Go on, beat it," or some-
     thing, you know. "You don't have to
     do them now." Something like that,
     you know.

C269   What you mean is, you try to do it right, try to please, and it doesn't work out.   A client-centered response! This is possible once he has started to unfold feelings.

S270   Yeah, and I get mad, so I quit. I don't do anything, I don't do it, period.

C271   Yeah.

S272   Why should I if I know Mom, if I know I'm going to get cussed either way.

C273   That is, if what you're trying to do doesn't work out right, you just won't do it at all, you figure, eh?

S274   I mean, there's two different ways to do it, and both ways are wrong, you know, you gonna be, catch it either way, why, uh . . .

C275   Why try?

S276   Yeah, you gonna catch it, why try? Why waste your time?

C277   Better to just coast along, take it easy, and let it roll off.   Understanding.

S278   Yeah. I can see that, you know. I mean, I'll do the dishes, and she'll, "Oh, you're splashing too much water." I'm the one that cleans up the floor. "Oh, but you're splashing too much water." She's always worrying about I'm splashing too much water. I always clean it up.

C279   And so, as a result of this kind of thing, you don't want to do the dishes because you're just going to be criticized.

S280   Yes?
       (Knock at door. Told we have five minutes left.)   The pressure of time limit encourages him to go on.

S281   What time is it, ten after?

C282   Mm-hmm. That's about right.

S283   Like last night. I stayed up and watched a movie. Finally asked me, "how long you going to be up?" I said, "I don't know, about twelve-thirty, one o'clock." One o'clock, I was up there.

C284   How do you mean, up there?

S285   Upstairs.

C286   To bed?

S287   Yeah, and took and got cleaned up, and went in and got, winding my watch. Father comes in, "Get to bed," you know, little more strongly, and, uh, says something about me getting up, and I says, "Yeah." "Don't you sass me." "I ain't sassing you. I was up there when I said I would." And he says, "Ah, you should have been up earlier. You shouldn't stay up so late." I could see it if I was staying up every night like that, you know, but I don't stay up that late very much. In fact, I hardly ever watch T.V.

Real unfolding taking place.

C288   But here you were doing something you thought you had permission to do, and it was all right, and he still criticizes you.

S289   Yeah.

Poor word choice.

C290   And especially in a way, like hollering at you, that you object to.

S291   Oh, I don't object to it. I'd prefer not to be hollered at, but I don't object to it.

C292   Well, it bothers you, let's say.

S293   He's gonna holler, he's gonna holler. I ignore him, you know, like tune him out.

C294   And so you kind of develop that kind of a personality of letting things roll off, and, you know . . .

Interpretative.

S295   Yeah, I guess so.

C296   Like you say, your little brother is always mad, right, and you're not. You more or less kind of . . .

S297   Yeah, I get mad when I get mad, but . . .

C298   You ordinarily tend to try to not waste it.

S299   Wouldn't do any good to get mad, you know.

C300   But still, this anger probably comes out somewhere?

Interpretative, leading.

S301   Yeah, at times I'll get mad and go down in the basement and bend a few iron bars or something.

C302   Where else does it come out, do you think?

S303   That's about it, I guess. Sleep it off.

C304   Well, you think about that, about where else does that anger go when you are bossed around and criticized and treated unfairly.

Since this is last meeting, I want to clarify.

S305   Well, you were saying on the hostility, now, how about pounding? I like nothing better than to get out, swing an ax, sledge, something like that. That I like, you know. I go out to a lake, and I split wood. No good at it, you know.

He reacts to earlier comment about the knuckles.

C306   It helps to release some of this.

S307   I like the feel of it, an ax or sledge or something. It's doing something, you know.

C308   Yeah.

S309   It's just like making a radio or something, something like that. Not all the time.

C310   Very different kind of hobbies, eh?

S311   Mm-hmm.

C312   I was thinking, I saw an article the other day, a woman said that people like me, she was writing this about women, that people who sit all day, and are under tensions, should play softball. She said that's a good way to work off all your energies, you know, to hit that ball, and throw it, real hard, and slide, and all that stuff.

S313   I was reading in *Reader's Digest* where the, I think it was in the Sahara, the oh, it was that book I've got, *Island Rescue*, I think it was, guys were supposed to keep a little pile of stones right outside their bunk, and uh, they throw them to get rid of tension.

C314   Oh, yeah? (*Laughs*)

S315   Me, I'd go out and bust them with a
        sledge, you know.
        (*Knock on door to indicate time up.*)

C316   Well, I'm still, I'm interested in where   Pressure of the final interview
        else this hostility might go. That's easy   makes me press the point.
        to see that you want to throw some-
        thing or hit something.

S317   Walk them off. I get mad, I'll walk a
        couple of miles.

C318   Still another way, I think. How about
        in defiance and not doing what you're
        supposed to do, and not what I want
        you to do? That ever work?

S319   I don't know. I never think about that.
        I usually just, before that, I get mad,
        you know, and take off.

C320   Another way is to pretend to do what   Interpreting.
        you're supposed to do, but not really
        do it.

S321   Well, usually, you know . . .

C322   Not really do it right or do it well.

S323   If they get me mad or something, I'll
        go in the basement or get away, before
        I really let somebody have it. If I hit
        somebody, you know, I'll bust their
        jaw. Cue you in on that.

C324   Well, when you're angry it must be
        very satisfying to hit somebody.

S325   Yeah, I imagine it is. I don't try it
        very often, don't get practice. Like I
        say, I go down in the basement and
        bend a few iron bars. I cleaned up in
        the basement today. Found some iron
        bars where I'd wrapped them around
        my hand.

C326   Well, that sounds like a considerable
        amount of tension.

S327   Well, that's a good way of getting rid
        of it, though. Kind of run out of iron,
        though.

C328   Yeah, and that isn't always with you,
        like in school.

S329   Oh, around school I don't get mad   We have finally arrived at the
        that much.   heart of the problem.

C330 It's just at home.

S331 Yeah, them I can ignore easy. There's nothing to ignoring them in school. You know, you got a book, you can always make like you're reading in the book, or something.

C332 Well, this is your marks, isn't it?

S333 Yeah, I guess so. (*Pause*)

C334 But the ones at home are more deep and harder to laugh off.

S335 Well, yeah, you know, usually you're not doing anything else that you can, I mean, you know, it's a lot easier to ignore somebody if you can, you know, even count, like on that there, you know. Count the rose petals. You know, you can block them out like that.

C336 Just turn it off.   Understanding.

S337 Mm-hmm. That's a real easy way, you know. Only in school, you know, you count the letters, something like that. At home, you can't. About the best way is just to get out.

C338 I think an important thing here is that this turning it off in school, this is what happens to the school work, in some cases.

S339 Yeah.

C340 This is the first real talk we've ever had.   Very warm feeling evident here in expression.

S341 Yeah.

C342 I wish we could go on.

S343 I'm about talked out, though.

C344 I think you're just starting now.

S345 Maybe we've just started on the subject, but I'm about talked out for today.

C346 (*Laughs*) Yeah, I mean for today, but for the future maybe we could find out some other ways to get rid of this tension, this anger, so that it wouldn't interfere with your school work.

S347 What would be a suggestion of getting rid of it?

C348   I haven't got any quick answer for you. Maybe part of it is to try to keep it from arising in the first place.

S349   Like how?

C350   Yeah. It's hard to be an adolescent and not have these.

S351   I'm all for stopping it, and everything. It starts, yeah, but I don't start it.

C352   Think your parents have a role here, eh?

S353   Yeah, quite a bit. Like my mother, you know. She, I, uh, didn't get up too good this morning.

C354   Cause of the late movie, eh?

S355   Naw, I never get up easy though. I get up a lot better if I sleep in. I can do that, you know, I'll sleep later in the day. Well, she got mad, I guess, I don't know how come. She dropped something, anyway, she heaved a bowl at me. I was over making a sandwich. Broke the bowl. Caught me on the back. Didn't hurt or anything, you know, but I didn't like it.

C356   Things are that wild, eh?

S357   Mm-hmm. And, you know, she's always getting mad. Lot of times I don't do anything like that would cause it, you know what I mean. Like I'll come in, I mean, you know, I'll be out, and I'll come in, she's mad already. Then, cause I don't come in with a big old smile on my face, and get slapped down a couple of times or something, you know, I'll come in, I'll, I just sort of keep out of the way, you know. And the next thing I know, "How come you're so darn mad?" You can't win. I guess that was what it was about this morning, that I never smile. I don't smile in the morning. She don't either! She don't smile until about the third cup of coffee. Me, I don't smile until I'm awake. Takes about an hour.

> More feeling than he has expressed in all the previous meetings.

C358   Not so long, eh.

S359   Yeah, they're always saying, "You don't smile, you're grouchy," or something. I ain't grouchy. I just don't smile. I don't come in laughing or anything, you know.

C360   You're just not like that.

S361   No, I mean, I laugh when there's something to laugh about. I don't just laugh for the fun of laughing. Laughing ain't that funny, I mean, you know. I'll laugh when I hear a good joke or something, you know, I'll laugh, but uh, she'll say I'm talking with a wrong tone in my voice. I'm yelling, something like that. Half the time she'll, "What'd you say?" You talk louder, "Don't yell at me," something like that.

C362   Bad feeling most of the time.

S363   Yeah. I turn and ignore them, though.

C364   Well, I wish we had some more weeks to work on this. I wish you had better feelings for your counselor at school and could talk to her about it.

S365   Well, she ain't got quite the facilities for something like that, though.

C366   Crowded office?

S367   Yeah, small office, and, uh, right across from the gym and all. I don't talk very good when there's a crowd. I've set some rather surprising records. Gave a speech in history, one hundred and five "uh's." Nobody topped it. Closest was forty-five. I was supposed to give a speech in English. I didn't give that one. I put that one in history off for quite some time, about a week. "Are you going to give a report today, Jack?" "No, not just now." Put it off. I finally did it, yeah, but, I had one for history. I handed one in written, but I wasn't going to give it.

C368   Not in front of the class. Well, we're going to have to quit, Jack. Do you

think you'd be interested in coming
back here next term? Be a different
person, still the mirror and everything.

S369 Yeah. (*Laugh*)

C370 Well, bear it in mind if you get in
trouble, or things seem to be getting
worse, why, bear it in mind. All you
have to do is go to Mrs. Coleman and
say, "I'd like to come down." She'll
arrange it for you.

S371 OK.

C372 And, uh, I hope it's been of some help,
and keep in mind this, about what the
anger is doing to you, and what you
could do about it, if there are any
ways of dealing with it, and, what
could, you know. That's the thing
you'll have to work on. Well, we're very
late.

(*Leaving*)

Case Summary and Counselor's Comments

Case Summary

The client said that he came to the laboratory for testing to determine
the field of work for which he was best suited. His school counselor was
evidently interested in helping him to improve his marks and recommended the visit to this mother. In the course of the visits, the client
took the following tests:

Kuder Preference Record: Outdoor, 74 percentile; Mechanical, 65 percentile; Computational, 93 percentile; Scientific, 94 percentile; Persuasive,
34 percentile; Artistic, 83 percentile; Literary, 18 percentile; Musical, 1
percentile; Social Service, 10 percentile; Clerical, 80 percentile.
Differential Aptitudes Test: Verbal Reasoning, 85 percentile; Numerical
Ability, 65 percentile; Abstract Reasoning, 85 percentile; Space Relations,
97 percentile; Mechanical Reasoning, 75 percentile; Language Usage:
Spelling, 30 percentile; Sentences, 40 percentile. Combined VR and NA:
85 percentile, equivalent to an I.Q. of something better than 115.

Jack stated that he has thought of becoming a welder, a flyer, or a
forest ranger, but he has not looked deeply into any of these. He always
seemed pleased, though not surprised, by his high test scores. It is apparent that he is well aware of his good ability for school work. He is

critical of school and of teachers and states that he often simply does not try to do the work.

In the beginning, Jack displayed considerable suspiciousness and hostility toward the physical aspects of the laboratory, such as the microphone and the one-way mirror, and he was reluctant to enter into a counseling relationship. His manner was guarded and resistant throughout most of the interviews.

However, as the series of interviews continued, he began to unfold more significant material, and it became apparent that he has considerable friction with parents and teachers. The subject on which he is most verbal is his antagonism toward his mother. He resents her authority and tends to reject her advice and suggestions. The client also feels that he can do nothing to please her (she criticizes him if he does a household chore), and he therefore chooses to do nothing instead. For example, Jack could have driven to the laboratory, but he so resents his mother's criticism of his driving that he refuses to do so.

The mother describes Jack as stubborn and indicated he was inclined to balk at her suggestions regardless of their merit. Since she feels it her duty to guide and direct him, she sees no way out of the dilemma.

It appears that much of the client's negative behavior is attributable to adolescent striving for independence from his mother's dominance. This carries over to rejection of adult authority, and is characteristic of his relations in school.

The anger which the client feels at what he considers unfair treatment by his parents is extreme. Consider such bits of behavior as bending iron bars around his hand, and wishing someone would provoke him into a fight. However, this unacceptable aggression is largely denied expression, is repressed, and finds substitute outlets in such things as surliness, knuckle-popping, and refusal to follow directions in school. Parental reaction to this behavior intensifies the feelings.

It seems evident, then, that it is this adolescent conflict with parental authority which is responsible for the client's poor performance in school, and that it is this conflict which must be dealt with if we wish to effect improvement. Perhaps awareness of the situation will provide the school counselor with cues for handling him in the future to avoid entering the conflict as a mother surrogate. The school counselor is also in a position to confer with the parents toward steps for ameliorating the home situation and giving the client more independence. A case conference of the client's teachers might develop ideas of how to handle him to generate less rebelliousness, and the boy himself needs further counseling to clarify his feelings and to see how they influence his behavior.

Counselor's Comments

This was not an easy client with which to deal. In fact, the hostility which he displayed on his initial visit made me doubt that he would return to the laboratory. That he was guarded and resistant is evident, and he was well aware of this. He often remarked, "I said something, now it's your turn," and he asks for further testing as a way out of pursuing a line of self-investigation. Yet, he did continue the contact and seemed almost to challenge the counselor to discover his needs. It was partially this attitude that encouraged me in my probing.

Gradually the relationship deepened, yet it was not until the eighth and final interview, as the time was running out, that he made evident the scope of his hostility. In those few moments, he opened the lid on his feelings in a way that he had not done in all the previous meetings, and it appears that, for him, this was a major step.

How much was accomplished is uncertain. The experience at the lab may have given the client some insight, and helped him to see his situation more clearly, but the main achievement, probably, was the building of the relationship. Jack needed help and encouragement to overcome his resistance and to accept the counseling help. It seems to me that this was accomplished. He finally faced the strength of his feelings of rebellion and the ways in which these feelings are now disadvantageous to him. The stage is now set for further help in working through these aggressions and finding better ways of dealing with them. It is unfortunate that the end of the semester caused the laboratory contact to terminate at this time.

It appears that Jack has the ability for superior scholarship, in some fields, particularly, and that he is capable of a higher level of aspiration than he is presently considering. Unfortunately, the energy for such work is being dissipated in conflict with the parents. It is to be hoped that the school counselor, having this insight into his behavior, and the opportunity for continuing contact, will be able to be helpful to him.

Counselor's Self-Evaluation

An evaluation of my handling of this case poses several questions and will doubtless elicit contrary responses from advocates of different schools of counseling theory. Though usually given to the client-centered approach, I have in this instance experimented with taking a more active and directive role, and I have mixed feelings about the results. In these interviews, I find myself asking questions, initiating subjects, probing and interpreting, and generally committing heresy to Rogers. Is it in spite of this, or because of this, that the relationships continued and deepened?

In a case like this, where the client is frankly resistant and lacks readiness for counseling, the client-centered approach seems a further burden to the relationship, almost, in fact, a form of rejection. Perhaps such a person needs the help of counselor direction and encouragement. How otherwise do we account for the fact that the questions and the interpretations lead the process forward and bring about the unfolding of significant feelings?

I have been encouraged in this experimentation by the belief that it is not wise for the beginning counselor to be too parochial in his philosophy. It has been my feeling that with students who are not ready to relate to a counseling situation, a rigid adherence to Rogerian technique creates in me a sense of helplessness, in what is supposed to be a helping relationship. I was also recently influenced by observation of the didactic approach of an Adlerian counselor, by reading in various schools of counseling thought, and by statements such as this one, attributed to Harry Stack Sullivan: "The therapist should remember that he is an expert in interpersonal relations, and the patient should feel from the very first interview that he is learning something which will benefit him." Sullivan is referring to analysis, but perhaps there are implications here also for the counseling situation.

This is not to minimize my own technical shortcomings—the many missed feelings and faulty interpretations, the conversational replies, the tendency to talk too much. Apparently giving up the internal frame of reference makes one especially prone to these failings. Yet, because the boy felt that the process was meant to be helpful to him he continued the contact. Thus it may be that he was helped, not in a problem-solving way, but by being supported and encouraged to enter the relationships and focus on the problem areas.

I do not delude myself that I can solve another's problems, and I dislike advice and pat solutions. I feel strongly the rightness of Rogers' philosophy and deplore my lack of facility in his technique. However, I am not convinced that his is the only valid system. Since the present client did not seem to respond to non-directive methods, I decided to forget the rules, to respond not in preconceived ways, but to be sensitive to the present gestalt. It is a question of fitting the approach to the needs of the individual. I feel that this client was helped to form a relationship and to disclose his feelings, and that it would not be possible for him to take more initiative in dealing with the problem and improving his adjustment.

Case Reviews

WILLIS DUGAN AND DONALD BLOCHER

The Case of Jack is a rather difficult one to analyze for two reasons. First, cases of underachievement in adolescent boys are usually quite complex, and when the low motivation which the client has for school carries over into the counseling process we have a problem which is challenging to the most expert counselor. In this instance, unfortunately, the problem of analyzing the case is complicated by the fact that the counseling is not expert. It becomes difficult to decide whether what is happening is the result of the client's resistance, or poor motivation, or whether it is simply the result of inept counseling.

All through the three interviews which are presented, we find gross mechanical errors which would be difficult to excuse in even a beginning interview. Multiple questions, yes or no questions, counselor overridings, judgmental statements, and personal references are found throughout the series of interviews. These gross errors, of course, make it difficult for even a well motivated client to express himself, and in the case of a boy like Jack, they are nearly fatal to any worthwhile outcome in counseling.

Perhaps even worse than the mechanical errors which are evident is the obvious confusion with which the counselor goes about trying to establish a relationship. This case is fairly typical of the beginning counselor who buys wholeheartedly a dogmatic, theoretical approach to counseling only to find that he has neither the intellectual understanding nor the personal attributes to make the approach work for him in an actual counseling relationship.

The counselor begins the case, obviously committed to a rather strongly Rogerian approach. He opens by reflecting feeling, but fails to develop any structure, or to establish any real relationship. Indeed, it is not until the fifth interview that it becomes clear that Jack has been involuntarily referred for counseling! When the client reacts to the nondirective approach in the beginning of the initial interview by saying that the counselor's questions are "pretty sly," the counselor is unable to accept or reflect these feelings of distrust and suspicion, but instead finds it necessary to defend his intentions. He then retreats into a confused description of a lengthy series of tests in which he apparently has little faith and which he obviously does not understand.

By now, far from having a client-centered relationship, the situation is really "test-centered" and supposedly vocationally oriented, with almost complete responsibility in the hands of a counselor who knows very little about either tests or vocations.

At this point, the counselor is understandably panicky. He discards his pseudo-client-centered veneer and begins to use a variety of counseling techniques, including probing, depth interpretations, reassurance, and urging. These are employed in what must be pretty close to a random order, with little apparent direction or rationale behind their use. Worse yet, having failed to establish any kind of professional relationship, the counselor tries to keep the entire situation from collapsing by forming a sort of "buddy-buddy" relationship with the boy. The counselor adopts slang, shallow flattery, and tries to be "one of the boys." In this relationship the counselor subtly reinforces the youngster's feelings of hostility by implying that the parents, the school, in short the world, is wrong and Jack is right. This approach does result in two outbursts of hostility which may possibly have some therapeutic value. They are not, however, accompanied by any real insights or any willingness to accept responsibility for his own behavior. In between, is sandwiched some hours of dreary, contrived, and boring conversation which is designed, as Jack puts it, "to fill up the tape."

The result of this confused approach to the client is, of course, predictably disastrous. In the eighth interview, Jack is still nervous, tense, and suspicious, as evidenced by his knuckle-cracking and concern about the mirror.

Obviously, the counselor has not been able to present himself as a trustworthy, dependable, consistent person. He has not been able to communicate himself unambiguously, because he has been too busy fishing for techniques, defending himself, and generally manipulating the situation. The subtle evaluation by which the counselor encourages Jack to vent his hostilities backfires as soon as the topic shifts to Jack himself or his possible shortcomings. Here Jack resists or changes the subject because he is afraid the counselor will be as evaluative about clients as he has been about parents or teachers. The result, here, is that the counselor is reduced to counting a moral victory when, after eight interviews, the client is able to put together more than a few monosyllables and to vent some superficial hostility which is undoubtedly present in all adolescents.

The above criticisms seem harsh. Unfortunately, they are not atypical of the work of beginning counselors, particularly those who have not taken the time to develop a personal point of view toward counseling. It is much easier to read the theories of authorities, to jump on this bandwagon or that, than it is to internalize concepts, to examine one's own attitudes, and to begin the laborious and sometimes painful process of building a personal theory and philosophy of counseling.

The counselor in this case apparently had no clear goals of his own in regard to what he wanted to accomplish. He clearly had no idea of how tests, for example, might or might not be useful in terms of such goals. He knew about many techniques, but did not know when or how these might be useful to *him* in counseling. He showed a good degree of general psychological sophistication and seemed to understand the client in an intellectual sense. He was not able, however, to translate this understanding in the actual relationship into some behaviors which would be helpful to his client. Above all, he did not understand how his own feelings and attitudes would influence his counseling behavior.

This case seems to point up the necessity for a thorough counseling practicum which forces the counselor-trainee to synthesize all which he has learned, and to fashion these lessons, individually, into a set of tools which can be genuinely helpful in actual counseling relationships.

BUFORD STEFFLRE

The National Defense Education Act provides substantial amounts of Federal money, ". . . to enable the public secondary schools to set up programs of guidance to encourage students with outstanding aptitude and ability to complete their secondary school education, take the necessary courses for admission to institutions of higher education, and enter such institutions." How realistic is such a goal?

In *The Case of Jack* we have a counselor trying with conspicuous lack of success to "encourage," and feeling, at once, guilty because such heavy handed encouragement is contrary to his belief in individual autonomy, and at the same time, frustrated because the illicit encouragement doesn't encourage. His stated goal follows the party line of counseling (I C37, C53—last four sentences)—to be helpful with a minimum of preconceptions as to what form his helpfulness should take; but, he acts out a goal which stems from society's concern that bright boys do the things we want bright boys to do—behave at home and get good marks in school. As he shifts from an internal to an external frame of reference, his encouraging remarks probably begin to sound increasingly familiar to an already well-nagged Jack.

If Congress wants bright children in college it had better not leave the job to guidance workers, in the expectation that the counselor will be able to pull off some flashy trick which will obviate the need for the total push of school and society which is needed to change the values of youth. Jack got his ideas about himself, and about learning, from sixteen years of interaction with his family, community, and nation; eight, or eighty, interviews with a counselor are unlikely to change them so long as his environment remains the same.

The counselor, however, does a good job of disclosing, to his and the reader's satisfaction, that Jack's behavior is an example of the middle class delinquency which vents its frustration in the genteel aggression of underachievement. Jack, too, seems to see the relation between his anger and his poor marks and finds the insight mildly interesting though not personally meaningful. Jack's relationship with his school counselor is not a good one, and this case suggests that centralized counseling services may have merits which have not been properly assessed or used. Getting away from the school, where he so assiduously acts out his role of the "don't give a damn" adolescent, permits him, gingerly, to experiment with other ways of behaving. Perhaps the day will come when more school counselors and administrators will be sufficiently secure to see that their activities may be properly supplemented by centralized and more specialized counseling services.

Another factor highlighted by this case is the problem of parent counseling. We do not need to take Jack's complaints at face value to agree that his mother might well profit from a chance to talk about her sullen sixteen-year-old spawn. But who is to suggest this confrontation? Only a very daring or skillful school counselor would imply that the mother might benefit from counseling. Certainly, the school needs to consider the family relationship, especially in a case where it seems so central to educational purposes, but how this should be done and who should do it is not clear. Of course, it might be better if Jack and his mother went to different counselors to lessen their "he said and then I said" tendencies, but we have here a more difficult problem—most parents would like us to comb the child's hair without taking off his hat.

Now, let us look directly and critically at the counselor. At the outset, and in balance, he seems to me to be flexible, conscientious, intelligent, and on his way to being a professional counselor of a high order of competence.

However, like most of us, he is shrewder at analyzing others than at seeing through himself. He is dealing with a difficult, hostile adolescent whose behavior may set up some historical harmonics in the counselor. It might have been more profitable to respond to Jack's, "Pretty sly, the questions you ask," (I S36) with a recognition of the hostile resentment and anxiety implied, rather than with the subtly rejecting, "Well, I'm not trying to be sly; I'm just trying to understand why you came down here, and what I can do for you." (I C37) That the barb struck home is suggested by the unseemly haste with which the counselor accepts at face value Jack's purpose as being, to take some tests to "see what I was best suited for."

This meaningless cliche on the record, the counselor spends the next several interviews on tests which contribute nothing except to ease a strained counselor-client relationship. Jack (I S48, 52) senses that testing is a red herring with little relationship to his real problem. (Wouldn't it be refreshing if we could persuade school counselors to make referrals by saying, "The counseling center is a place where they do *not* give tests and do *not* tell you what you are best suited for—you'll like it there!") Surely, the counselor knows that tests will not do what Jack alleges he wants them to do. Why then, does he reach with such relief for the test list? This action only makes sense if we assume that ten minutes of Jack's spiteful anger was all that the counselor could take. (That word "sly" stung enough so that the counselor finds it necessary to throw it back, I C53. The counselor calls this counterattack "structuring" and, I suppose, in a sense it is.)

As an exercise in "clinicsmanship" we might review the statements in interviews V and VIII, which precede the counselor's getting up and opening the window. As I read interview V the counselor has said in effect (V C67 to 77), "You're a bad and ungrateful client," and when Jack ignores a direct plea for reassurance (V S78) the counselor throws open the window.

In interview VIII the client says (VIII S100) "You're not much of a counselor or it wouldn't be so hard for me to talk to you," and again the window is opened. Certainly there is no objection to opening windows as a way of relieving psychological pressure, but I wonder about the counselor's plans for winter. Pneumonia can be even worse than injured feelings.

In the last interview the counselor asks several times for reassurance (VIII C105, 107, 145, 342, 372), scolds a little, preaches some, but stays with Jack and seems determined not to be put off by his anger and diffidence. In spite of his tendency to fear "committing heresy to Rogers," this counselor is on his way to being his own man, free to examine himself and others in their terrible and beautiful complexity. His sense of disappointment stems, I believe, from his unrealistically high expectations.

A reasonable goal for a counselor in *The Case of Jack* would to be simply supportive to the boy, and, if possible, to his mother until time dries up the running adolescent sores. Jack is a junior as he starts counseling. In a year he will be at the age when our culture will permit him to part from his parents with face saving on all sides. In the meantime, let us try to help them live with the love-hate relationship so twisted by hidden reasons, both genetic and historical. I would think that Congress might be getting as close to its money's worth as it could expect if Jack had help in growing out of his anger, even if he never became an engineer, or a physicist, or an elementary teacher, or whatever it is we must have this season. This counselor is not doctrinaire. He appreciates subtleties and limitations. His next step should be to face his own fears more clearly.

DUGALD ARBUCKLE

It is a beautiful day outside my office, and a cool breeze off the Charles chases a few fleecy clouds. I have read the typescripts on Jack and listened to the tapes, and I think, and I feel, "Man is a remarkable fellow —here we have Jack, who is troubled and bothered, and here we have counselor, who is also troubled and bothered, not so much by Jack, as by his own unresolved conflict over his self. And yet, the humanness of the counselor shows through, and it is to this that Jack reacts, and likely grows, and becomes a stronger person. He has experienced something new in the way of a human relationship."

Several points appear to stand out in the case of Jack:

1. The so frequent unintentional hypocrisy of the use of tests: they *may* have helped to get Jack to the counselor's office, and they *may* have helped Jack to get started, although to this reviewer they appeared to hinder both Jack and the counselor, and give them both good reasons for avoiding more meaningful issues. They appear to have been pointless in terms of content (why give the Kuder twice?). It is interesting to note that Jack, early in S22, says about the Kuder, "I didn't do so hot on it," (apparently there must be "bad" and "good" scores on even the Kuder) and the counselor elaborates the distortion in C23 by saying, ". . . it didn't give you any clear ideas about what you should do."

2. Reading the typescript, particularly at certain points, gives only a shallow picture of what Jack is saying and feeling when one listens to the tape. The counselor had the visual advantage of seeing Jack, and yet, over and over again, he reacts to the bare-bone words that Jack has used and ignores the basic communication in Jack's voice.

3. The counselor sounds and talks like a teacher (is he one?). Again and again, it seems that he just can't help directing and shoving and probing. There is counselor domination and direction throughout the interview, and yet the counselor seems surprised when Jack, used to parent and teacher domination and direction, and sensing a similar dominance in the counselor, does not appear too interested in talking deeply about his feelings. Is Jack hostile, or is he reacting in a most natural fashion?

4. What sort of counseling services are available in a school system which must refer individuals such as Jack? We might wonder about the professional self-concept of the school counselor who feels that he must refer a rather ordinary fellow such as Jack. Isn't the school counselor supposed to do any counseling, or does counseling in a school consist of direction, advice, a presentation of information, and referral?

5. Every now and then the counselor, briefly and fleetingly, becomes "a counselor." We can be optimistic and believe that this is the real counselor, but that he, too, as a product of the same system as Jack, cannot yet accept the idea that he and Jack have within them their own answers—different answers, to be sure, but for each the right answers. When the counselor finds his, as he no doubt will, then he

will be able to establish a more effective helping relationship with any of the thousands of Jacks who sit in American classrooms.

Session 1.   The counselor's first few comments indicate his own uneasiness. He is, most likely, reassuring himself more than Jack, and this is not unreasonable; counseling behind a one-way mirror can hardly be expected to add to the comfort of any counselor! In S28 the counselor gets a feeling which he does not follow, but instead continues the direction, and so gets the S36 response.

In C39 the counselor rushes the testing business, and, yet, this is the natural dilemma that faces the counselor who feels that he has a testing job to do with a client, and who has a client who has been told that this is what he will get when he goes to see the counselor. Whatever the reason may be, the counselor apparently goes along with the testing routine, and it is he who pushes the testing, not Jack. The detailed test descriptions which follow would appear to be more for the counselor than for the client.

C49 hardly seems to be what Jack has been saying in S48. Is he saying, "Ah, they tell you to take them, so we take them, but . . ."?

Jack quite frequently shows that he wants to talk, but often the counselor gets in his way. The last sentence in C67 is a good example of this. C71 is an extraneous comment, but instead of accepting the client's reaction the counselor has to defend his remark in C77.

Session 2.   Apparently, there was no consideration given to Kuder number one. How many times does one take the Kuder?

Session 3.   The two comments indicated here on the typescript are interesting. The relationship would have to be very honest and secure to have the young client respond with anything other than "yes" to the counselor question, "Is this helpful?" This is somewhat like the teacher saying, "Do you like me?" To the client's possible expression of feeling in, "I just don't study, that's all," the counselor brings a directing, "Let's talk about school . . ." remark rather than going along with the client.

Session 4.   It would appear from the counselor's remarks that he functioned as a school teacher rather than a counselor.

Session 5.   Jack starts off, and the counselor goes along, but by C19 it seems as if he can't stand it any more and goes back to his directing role. He gets himself in a hole, but the client helps him out, and keeps on anyway. The counselor's comment about his direction and suggestion having helped the process is at least debatable; it may have hindered it instead. In any case, Jack is rolling for a while. He keeps on, despite the somewhat didactic comment in C43, the "Let's get back to school" comment in C47, and the "Tell me for me" comment in C61. The counselor starts to push and dominate, ignoring the client, until finally in S88 the client says very reasonably, "Let's stop this and talk about the nice safe tests." The counselor, even here, could have reacted to feeling, but instead he obliges, at length, about tests. By C95 the pattern of counselor direction is established. From the tape, it sounds as if Jack knows and feels that the counselor is the boss, and so he reasonably enough waits for the questions and the direction. The session never does get off the ground again, and it ends on a final note of counselor domination—the administration of a test.

Session 6. Does counselor's involvement here with mother have any effect on his relationship with Jack? I would think it would.

Session 7. This sounds, from the brief typescript description, as the session which may have come closest to being a real counseling session.

Session 8. Again, Jack gets going, but the counselor periodically intrudes. He pushes a bit in C41, and then in C43 and C45 he says, "Talk for *me*—*I* want you to talk;" so Jack says, "OK—let's talk about the satellite."

In S66 Jack's "yeah" is very expressive. It gives me the feeling, as do most of his other yeah's, that he does not really feel personally involved but is saying, "It doesn't matter to me. . . ." In the comments that follow, Jack seems to be saying, "I don't want to talk about me," and the counselor, in C81, says, "But I want you to talk about you." When he becomes personally involved with his "That's what I was kind of concerned about for you," Jack comes back with another of his expressive yeah's, laughs, and continues about the satellite. Having talked, as directed, but not about himself, he then, in S100, says to the counselor, ". . . it's your turn."

We can certainly understand the counselor's frustration by S108, yet we see here the frustrated counselor, rather than a frustrating client. Jack is reacting in a completely normal, ordinary, human way, but the counselor is frustrated because he won't do what the counselor wants him to do. By S132 this reviewer was getting frustrated too, and feeling, "Can't the counselor reflect, or ever react to any feeling at all?" In this comment, and others, there is much feeling, but the counselor either passes them by, or, as in C139, misses the feeling entirely.

S164 expressively disagrees with the counselor's previous comment, obviously saying just the opposite of what his words read, but the counselor rejects Jack's disagreement. For a number of comments that follow the counselor probes and digs and interprets, and Jack says, "No thanks," and keeps going his own way. In C197 the counselor goes along, but then he has to go beyond this and take over and get into difficulty. The counselor seems almost determined at times not to go along with the client, and each time Jack gets going the counselor pulls him back. C221 and C223 are "teacherish." The counselor is so busy *talking to* the client that he misses the tone and meaning in S224 completely and continues in C225 in the same vein.

Jack's "Mm-hmm" in S232 sounds very much like, "If you say so, boss." The last sentence of S242 indicates the client's concept of the counselor. Despite all this, Jack begins to talk as he wishes. The counselor is right in saying that C269 is a *client*-centered response, but it is now a technique. A client-centered counselor would not feel that he had to wait until the client "started to unfold his feelings," although there would appear to have been a rather continual unfolding of feelings which the counselor has missed. Jack continued, and the counselor wavers back and forth. It almost seems as if the counselor were saying to himself, "By golly, maybe this fellow can do this himself," and then his more dominant self says, "Of course he can't—get in there and do it for him." The counselor, as he says, wants to "clarify," but can one didactically clarify complicated attitudes, feelings, and emotions?

If C330 is "the heart of the problem," why does the counselor turn Jack away from it in C332 and then pull him back to it in C334? In C338 we can see an excellent example of the counselor missing the deep expression of feeling in S337 and thus restricting the client to a "yeah." Having missed the feeling, the counselor then pushes and tries to get back to it. Again, in S353, where there is a long pause between "Like . . ." and ". . . my mother," there is a deep expression of feeling, which the counselor missed in C354. Despite all this, Jack comes forth in the latter part of this session, and it would seem reasonable to assume that the basic strength of the counselor has somehow got through, and it is to this that Jack is reacting. It certainly can't be to the sort of comments that are typified by the last one, where the counselor once again stands on the teacher's desk and comes forth with a few final words of wisdom.

Case Summary and Counselor's Comments

The counselor appears to feel that Jack's anger was extreme, and that he was very hesitant. This, in turn, seems to be considered as a valid reason why it is difficult to be acceptant of him. Surely, a professional counselor does not equate his acceptance of the client in terms of the client's acceptance of him. Jack's hostility seemed neither extreme or unusual to this reviewer, and we may hope that the day will come when the school counselor will find no difficulty in being truly acceptant of Jack, rather than trying to manipulate him to become what he wants him to become.

The counselor's self-evaluation is interesting. He would appear to be involved in the process of self-development, but not yet too certain of just who he is or where he is going. When one says he is "usually given to the client-centered approach," it sounds somewhat like one who says, "I am sometimes democratic," or even, "I am partially pregnant." Even though the comment about "committing heresy" is doubtlessly said in jest, it still indicates the feeling that in order to be a true blue client-centered counselor, there are some things you *have* to do and other things you must *never, never* do. Any counselor who is doing something, or saying something, only because the book, or the man, or somebody, or something, has said this is the way it must be, must surely be ineffective as a counselor, since he is not being himself, and is, quite likely, unaware of his self. The beginning counselor must be eclectic in his learning, since at this stage he doesn't know who he is or where he is going. Even when he has achieved some degree of self-consistency, he will still be involved in a process of change and modification, but this will be a modification of the self, not a change of technique or procedure because of the demands of others. The client-centered counselor, at least, is a free man, free enough and secure enough to be acceptant of his fellows without prior segregation into acceptable and nonacceptable categories.

The unknown counselor here, too, should not deplore his "lack of facility in . . . technique," since one's technique is merely a secondary expression of self, and while change of self will result in change of technique, change of technique will never result in a change of self. I would hope, too, that the counselor would never become convinced that Rogers has "the only valid system." Carl Rogers, as far as I know him, anyway, doesn't feel that he has the only valid system. Nor do I. Once the counselor feels that he has the ultimate, final, and conclusive answer, he must surely be lost in a parochial world of absolutism that will render him quite ineffective in a helping relationship with another person. Finally, let us hope that the counselor will continue to "forget the rules," and not bother "to respond in preconceived ways," but will also continue with his own self-analysis, so that he may come to better understand why he says what he says, and why he does what he does. Then, he may possibly move to some modification of self so that he can become the counselor who can develop a deep and meaningful relationship. He has started along this road with Jack.

Edward Roeber

The Case of Jack might be suitable for publication in *True Detective Magazine* or as script for the *Perry Mason* television series. At least the counselor's behavior gives me an image of the intense detective or lawyer who, in spite of hell and high water, intends to get to the "bottom" of the case. Here he certainly reached the "bottom" of something. Before hanging the counselor in effigy, though, it must be recorded that he alone was not the only accomplice to intrigue.

In terms of his verbal expressions, Jack has been referred to the practicum counselor by his mother and school counselor. Communication of purpose compounded the network of probable confusion: "My counselor told me that you would give the tests to find out what I'm suited for" (I S8), "Well, I didn't even know about it (lab) until she (mother) told me I had to go" (V S64), and, "Well, see, my counselor, she didn't say anything to me. Just called my mother up. It was arranged through her" (V S68). Did the school counselor naively feel that tests would help Jack find a suitable vocational goal which would in turn "motivate" him? Or was this a ruse for getting him to go to a practicum counselor in hopes that he could be straightened out? Of course, no one knows the answer, but I would lean heavily toward the latter assumption, based upon hostilities expressed by Jack toward both his mother and the school counselor. Experience with cases of this type in a practicum indicates both a mother and a school counselor all too frequently plan strategies intended to trick or trap unwary students into a counseling situation. The unsuspecting practicum counselor and the student are the innocent victims of the plot.

Jack is an adolescent boy who has learned to handle hostility and aggressive tendencies in ways which are partially acceptable, i.e., going for a walk (VIII S317), bending iron bars (VIII S301, S325), splitting wood (VIII S305), and watching a late TV show (VIII S283); and partially unacceptable, i.e., itching for a fight (VIII S152, S154), cracking his knuckles (VIII S128), and underachieving in school. If we can accept at face value Jack's statements, his home is characterized by tensions and frustrations. From a low to middle-class home, his models (mother and dad) apparently have not controlled their aggressions nor provided understanding and support. He has become very perceptive of inconsistencies in the behavior of others and extremely sensitive to any imposition of limits by adults. Inconsistencies in adult behavior have led him to a "what's the use" attitude, to a "what you don't say can't hurt you" policy, and to a "I'll stay out of your way, you stay out of mine" type of behavior. Thus far, he seems to have controlled his impulses to strike out and fight back, but one wonders how long it will be before he rebels and overtly acts out his aggressions.

Looking at the practicum counselor's behavior, I am struck by his dogged, if not perceptive, determination to ferret out *the* problem. He apparently sensed that the referral was not handled well and that Jack was reluctant to express his true feelings about the visit to the lab. He did not stay with Jack's apprehension about the mirror, Jack's tendency to feel that the counselor's questions were sly ones, and Jack's use of tests as a way out, even though he seemed to sense them as indicators of resistance. Unfortunately, he did not follow his intuition and help clarify Jack's (and his own) ambivalence toward mutually derived outcomes for testing and interviews. He made some unwarranted assumptions, such as, "I will go along with the testing and get at the real problem later," "Jack will become accustomed to the mirror as we develop a sound working relationship," and, "Any kind of a relationship is better than no contacts with a student who needs help." In the verbal exchanges between Jack and the counselor, there was evidence of mutual frustration with each other. The counselor had a tendency to confuse and even irritate Jack with his ineptness to choose words free from stereotyped and double meanings. This problem in semantics is crucial. Here are a few illustrations:

> "A lot of things in there that didn't seem to make sense to you and so you just plunged in and . . ." (I C49) Jack simply did not see any value in the test. The counselor implies that Jack is either not bright or the test is confusing. Jack probably interpreted it to mean he was dull.
>
> ". . . you're a smart kid." (VIII C163) Jack, probably, could interpret this as being impolite, bright, a goat, or a child.
>
> "Is your dad like you? . . ." (VIII C259) Jack, because of poor enunciation by the counselor, took this to mean "does" instead of "is."

These illustrations are only a small sample of the counselor's provincial, and other types of expressions, in addition to changes in voice, which could seriously affect the development of a relationship with Jack. That the latter did as well as he did was a tribute to Jack's tolerance and not to the counselor's skill.

Another matter of critical importance is the counselor's persistence in the last contact to open old wounds, knowing well that it was the last interview. Were the attacks made upon Jack's present set of defenses sound? Would the development of new ways to handle his anxieties and aggressions be any more acceptable than his present ones? Or is there something more basically necessary to Jack's understanding his problem than merely understanding how he reacts to, or other ways in which he could react to his environment? In any case, the counselor proceeded to move very rapidly and could have stifled any desire to go to another counselor. Feeling the pressure of time, a counselor can change his pace and jeopardize his relationship with a counselee. I cannot agree with the counselor's optimism in his summary statement regarding the beneficial effect of the relationship. His pursuit became too intense.

A final observation related to general methodology. Frustrated by Jack's passive resistance and, finally, limits imposed by time, the counselor did not stay with attitudes or content, but interspersed responses which tended to close off or divert ongoing discussions: "But what?" (I C27); "About all you have to say, huh?" (V C11); "It's interesting, the last guy I had down here wanted to be a flyer." (VIII C27); "Well, I'll tell you one thing, this is the last time I'll be able to see you. . . ." (VIII C105); "Nothing I can do about your marks." (VIII C127); "That's a great skill (knuckle cracking). That's probably a sign of something." (VIII C129); "I hope it's (looking for a fight) after you leave here." (VIII C153); and

"I don't seem able to make this point that I'm trying to make, maybe it isn't a good one. (*Laugh*) What I'm trying to say . . . is that . . ." (VIII C223).

In his case summary the counselor indicates a deliberate attempt to experiment with methodology. Based on his responses, the variety bears out his intent. In his self-evaluation, the counselor says, "In a case like this, where the client is frankly resistant and lacks readiness for counseling, the client-centered approach seems a further burden to the relationship, almost, in fact, a rejection." This statement and a few others leave the impression that he did not wish to follow a rigid Rogerian methodology and the only alternative was a "smorgasbord" rationale, especially with respect to acceptance and rejection. Irregardless of the counselee's readiness for counseling and the counseling methodology chosen, responses that communicate acceptance and understanding are likely to be most productive—and they are not the monopoly of any single methodology.

The Case of Jack represents but one skirmish in the lives of both counselee and counselor. But it would be interesting to know how well their wounds have healed.

SIGNIFICANT QUESTIONS FOR DISCUSSION

1. What did the tests contribute in *The Case of Jack?* What were some shortcomings in the counselor's explanations of tests?
2. In the eighth interview the counselor (C81) uses a hortatory appeal to get the client to raise his level of aspiration. How did Jack react to this approach? Does this procedure work with many underachievers?
3. What might be some more appropriate ways in which the counselor might have tried to deal with the resistance presented by Jack?
4. If you had been the counselor, in what ways might you have handled this client differently?
5. If you had a chance to talk with the counselor, what would you have wanted to discuss with him after each interview?
6. Where do the reviewers agree and disagree in their review of *The Case of Jack?* What are your reactions to the reviews?

The Case of Edna

Purpose of the Interviews

Edna was referred to the laboratory by the junior high school counselor as the result of a request by the girl's mother for outside help. From Edna's point of view it is doubtful if she had a well defined purpose for coming, except that her mother wished her to come and had made the arrangements.

Mrs. Martin, however, had a distinct reason for sending her daughter. She said she had had trouble with Edna because of her poor grades in school, her defiant and rude attitude toward the teacher, and her unacceptable behavior at home with her mother, sister, and grandmother. She hoped that in some way the child could be helped to become more amenable at home, and that perhaps we could discover what her potential might be.

Background Data

Edna is a twelve-year-old, seventh grade student at Taylor Junior High School, Murray, Michigan. She lives with her mother, her fourteen year old, eighth grade sister, Angie, and their maternal grandmother, seventy. They are Negroes, and the girl wrote on her application that her mother had had two years of college and her grandmother had had a high school education.

The father and mother are divorced, and the father has remarried and has two small children by his second wife.

Edna was given group mental tests in 1955 and received a C rating; in 1957 her rating dropped to E. The *Iowa Tests of Educational Development* showed her to be a half year behind her present grade level.

She had attended Chase Elementary School in 1953, and later, Johnson.

Client listed the following as her favorite hobbies: riding, swimming, skating, bicycling, movies, radio, TV, art museums, dancing, societies, church. She reads *Post, Life,* and *Ebony* magazines.

When she first came to the laboratory she stated that her ambition was to be a doctor, her family wants her to be a doctor, and that she expects to be a doctor eight or ten years from now.

226

The Interviews

<table>
<tr><td align="center">**FIRST**
INTERVIEW</td><td align="center">**COUNSELOR'S**
COMMENTS</td></tr>
</table>

C1 Hello Edna. How are you today?

S2 All right.

C3 Do you mind the heat very much?

S4 No.

C5 Did you come all by yourself?

S6 Yes, Ma'am.

C7 Would you like to put your umbrella in the corner so you can be comfortable? And your purse you can put on the table, or somewhere. Would you like to talk to me today about something? Would you like to discuss things with me?

(*Short pause*)

S8 I don't know, I don't know what to discuss.

C9 Well, maybe you could tell me something about yourself so I'd know you better. How would that be?

S10 Well, I'll, do you want me to tell you how old I am, or where I live or something like that?

C11 Whatever you'd like to tell me.

S12 Well, I go to Taylor High School, and, I don't know if I like it or not. Because, see, first, we, nobody wanted to go there because we thought we were going to Darren or McLain. But, when we got there, I guess we learned to like it better because it was more differenter from the other schools.

C13 Mm-hmm.

S14 But, they don't, they don't have no school dance like the other school has, or nothing like that, or a, they just have clubs for the smart children. And they just, you know, like they have art clubs for the children that can draw

real well or either the, uh, chess club
for the children that are smart.

C15   Mm-hmm.

S16   Something like that. And, uh, I don't
get to do anything much.
(Pause)

C17   What would you like to do?

S18   I'd like to be a doctor.
(Pause)

C19   So, you, you have gone to this school,   Restatement.
uh, and you've been somewhat disap-
pointed with it. It isn't exactly what
you thought it would be?

S20   Yes, Ma'am.

C21   And you feel that the activities there
are just for, uh, what you call, smarter
kids.

S22   Yes.

C23   And that they don't include everyone.

S24   Yes, Ma'am.

C25   So, this makes you feel kind of bad.   She seemed scared and I
                                               wanted to show support so
                                               she would continue.

S26   Mm-hmm.

C27   Well, I can see how that would be. You   Poor response here.
can just tell me whatever you want to.
It helps me to understand you better.

S28   Well, we don't live with my father, and
sometime we don't get as much privileges as other ones, children, you
know. And . . .

C29   You say you don't live with your father?

S30   Uh-huh.

C31   Yes.

S32   And so, well, when we go over his
house, we used to go over there often,
sometime he would come over our
house, come and pick us up. But, then
he started talking about everybody on
my mother's side, and saying something was wrong with all of them, and
all like that. And so, we just didn't
start going over there any more. Then
we had a big argument, and so, then

(*Pause*) he doesn't hardly come over any more and we don't go over there. 'Cause he always talks about somebody on the other side of our family, and nobody ever talks about him.

C33 So you feel that, that, uh, when you do visit your dad, you don't really get out of it what you wanted to. You just get criticism.

S34 Yes, Ma'am. My grandmother, she always be beating on me and everything. She don't never beat on my, but sometimes she do. But, she always give my sister special privileges because she's older than I am. And she always accusing me of something that sometime I don't even do.

> This abrupt change from criticism of her father to her grandmother startled me—she was getting now to the thing uppermost in her mind.

C35 So you feel your age has a lot to do with the way your grandmother treats you.

S36 Yes, Ma'am.

C37 You feel that, that your mother, uh, goes along with this and that they sort of, uh, uh, maybe gang up on you because you're younger.

S38 No, my mother doesn't, but my grandmother does. My mother, she do sometime, but not all the time.

> She didn't accept this inference that her mother was at all to blame.

C39 Would you like to tell me something about your home and your family and your sister and . . .

> Probing—I was trying to bridge the gap between her criticism of her father and her immediate home life.

S40 Well, I don't have nothing much on my mother. But my sister, she teases me a lot and she's fourteen. And my grandmother, I already told you about that. And that's all.

C41 So you feel your grandmother and your sister are really, uh, more a part of your problem than your mother?

> I meant this as a reflection but when I heard tape I realized I had asked it as a question—thus, it was probing.

S42 Yes, Ma'am.

C43 And that your mother, you get along pretty well with your mother, but your

> Here I reflected as I had really meant to do in C41.

grandmother is sort of a source of ir-
ritation. She kind of bothers you.

S44 Yes, Ma'am.

C45 And your sister, uh, teases you and
makes you feel that you are younger
and that you don't have any privileges.

S46 Yes, Ma'am.

C47 Well, I can imagine that would be
pretty hard to take. I can see how you
feel. Does it make you nervous to
come here and talk to me?

S48 Yes, Ma'am. A little bit.

C49 Well, you don't have to be nervous,
'course, I don't know. I was going to
help you think about your problems
and see if you can figure out some way
so that it won't bother you so much. I
can understand how you feel. And
sometimes if, uh, if you think about it
and, uh, talk about it to somebody
then they can understand how you
feel and, maybe, two people thinking
about it can make it seem that it isn't
quite as bad. Maybe you can, maybe
that way you will, uh, really, uh, know
more how you do feel, then it won't
bother you so much. Do you think
that's possible?

> I was very nervous here and feel it was a very poor response, scarcely grammatical.

S50 Yes, Ma'am. My grandmother has thir-
teen children and hardly none of them's
ever taken her out or anything, like
they should do. And that's what makes
it sort of crowded sometimes.

C51 So, you do understand some of what
makes her the way she is.

S52 Yes, Ma'am.

C53 And, that's bound to help you.
(*Long pause*)

> She became very fidgety here, until I felt I must break the silence.

C54 Would you like to tell me something
about your school and about your work,
anything you can think of. Would you
like to talk to somebody about it?

S55 Well, some of the teachers are high

school teachers, and they be giving, they be tr—, uh, they expect you to learn as fast as a high school student. And, some of the work you don't catch on to. And, she makes us put our heads down and nap. And, then he say he don't want to keep none of us after school until we can be quiet. He has two groups. He has an A group and a B group. And the A group has only eight children in it, and the rest of the class is in the B group.

C56 So that you feel that the A group is a little bit more privileged? They get to do more things?

Again, I meant to reflect but didn't succeed very well. My question tended to prevent the client from a more fruitful response.

S57 Yes, Ma'am.

C58 And that they are . . .

S59 They have more differenter work than we have. They have some higher work.

C60 Mm-hmm. You feel your teachers expect too much from you and think that you know, you are able to do more than you really have?

S61 Yes, Ma'am.
    (*Long pause*)

C62 You feel, sort of as if you were only older than your sister, then you would be able to do some things now that you can't do?

S63 Yes, Ma'am.

C64 And, also, that if your, that if only your dad could, uh, if you could visit your dad, or he could visit you without criticizing, that life would be a lot happier for all of you?

S65 Yes, Ma'am. He does that to everybody, I guess.

C66 You mean, criticizes everybody?

I continually ask questions instead of reflecting the material.

S67 Yes, Ma'am.

C68 So that makes the visits quite hard for all of you to bear?

S69   Yes, Ma'am. He hasn't been over there since Easter.

C70   Well, I can understand how hard that must be for you. (*Long pause*) It must be very hard for your mother, too.

S71   Yes, Ma'am. Sometime when she be going to Cleveland, maybe for a church trip, or something, or Toledo, well he, then he starts, then sometime we go over there and sometime we don't. Maybe she be, maybe she don't be back until Sunday and he brings us home on Saturday night. Then he starts to fussing and everything. And, then my sister say we ain't going down there no more.

C72   So that these trips to your dad's are really a disappointment to you, and even worse when your mother isn't there.   Reflection.

S73   Mm-hmm. Then what he said; and we got a little brother and a little sister. Larry is seven and Lynn is about (*Pause*) six or seven months, I guess.

C74   Mm-hmm.

S75   But they're all right.

C76   Mm-hmm.

S77   And, uh, the only time we do have fun is, like, when we go up in Idlewild to my auntie's skating rink, or, uh, when he's not there, maybe he'll go out somewhere or something like that, that's when we have our fun.

C78   So, that your stepmother really is, uh, quite nice to you and you have a little brother and sister. . . .

S79   Yes.

C80   A brother and sister that you enjoy?

S81   Yes, Ma'am.

C82   But, uh, when your dad is there it's pretty hard for you?

S83   Mm-hmm. As long as he don't have nothing to talk about then it's all right.

But, then he finds something to talk about.

C84 Do you really feel that he picks at you and he thinks up things to criticize you?

S85 Mm-hmm.

C86 Then he picks at you.

S87 Mm-hmm. Those things he be making up. You can tell he making them up. (*Long pause*) I guess it's because he's laid off, 'cause Mommy said when he wasn't laid off he used to act a little bit better. But since he's laid off from work, well, he acts sort of crabby.

C88 So your mother does try. She tries to understand him and, uh, make excuses for him?   *Probing—I was trying to establish the mother's attitude toward her former husband.*

S89 Yes, Ma'am.

C90 And, you feel that because he lost his job this would be quite natural for him to feel that way?

S91 Yes, Ma'am.

(*Long pause*)

C92 As a young girl you can understand, how, even as old as you are, you can understand how your dad feels out of work?   *Trying to enter her frame of reference.*

S93 Yes, Ma'am.

C94 And your mother, even though she has, uh, she is separated from him tries to understand, too, what makes him this way.   *I was thinking that the mother was trying to be fair to the girl's father.*

S95 Yes, Ma'am.

(*Long pause*)

C96 Is your grandmother your mother's mother or your father's mother?   *I had a reason for probing —I felt the mother might resent the grandmother more if she were the husband's mother.*

S97 My mother's mother. My father's mother, she lives down south, her and my grandfather.

C98 So you feel, uh, in some ways that your mother and you (*Pause*) and your sis-   *Restatement of entire expressed problem.*

ter understand that your dad criticizes and your grandmother is, uh, a little crabby, perhaps because, uh, because, as you say, that he's out of work is one reason he's crabby and the grandmother is a little bit irritated because, although she has a lot of children, none of them come to see her.

S99   Mm-hmm.

C100   Also, or take her?

S101   Except my Uncle Randy and my Uncle Thomas, sometimes my Aunt Elizabeth.

C102   Mm-hmm. (*Long pause*) And you feel that your, your grandmother might, uh, be better, uh, or easier to get along with if she had more outside interests, maybe more of her children near her. . . .

S103   Yes, Ma'am.

C104   Could do things with her?

S105   Mm-hmm. Sometime they promise her things, they don't even come to see her, or come. They say they're going to take us downtown to see the, the new bus station or something like that, but they don't come to see her any more, except, maybe sometimes on Memorial day. None of them come and see her but, on Tuesday, I think. And, none of them called her 'cept on Tuesday. I guess that's the way it just is, like that.

C106   Then, you feel she does have somebody that cares for her, and that perhaps she, (*Pause*) she's disappointed by the promises and, and expects a lot of things that never really happen?

Here, I meant to say she has nobody who cares for her.

S107   Yes, Ma'am.

C108   Have you thought in your mind, thought to yourself, if only, uh, you could, uh, do something about this family situation that, perhaps, you'd be happier and, uh, better able to get along?

Probing to see if Edna had ever thought of a way out.

S109   Yes, Ma'am.
      (*Long pause*)

C110 Have you ever thought of anything that you might do to change some of this?

S111 One time me and my sister started to run away from home when we was living on Clearmore, but we didn't. And we haven't thought of any more ideas.

C112 You both thought of running away from home?

This should not have been a question, it should have been a simple reflection.

S113 Yes, Ma'am.

C114 So you felt that if you could just get away from it, that, perhaps, you could, uh, have a better life than you have, and, uh, that it would be, uh, do you think you would like to come back again and talk some more about this with me?

(Interrupted by knock on door. Five minutes remaining.)

S115 Yes, Ma'am.

C116 Would you?

S117 Yes, Ma'am, maybe I'll have more to talk about.

C118 OK, you can think about things, and you can think about what we talked about, and uh, perhaps, uh, you know, people are able sometimes when they think about things and talk about them, it makes their own mind clearer about them. You can understand things and people much better.

I expressed this very awkwardly.

S119 Mm-hmm.

C120 And, perhaps, as you think about your relationship to your mother and your grandmother, your sister and your dad, you can go on and talk some more about it another day.

S121 Mm-hmm.

C122 Well, uh, how would you like to go and make another appointment. We'll go and see Mrs. Walton. Would you like to do that?

S123 Mm-hmm.

C124 Come on, let's do that.

Unnecessary and too directive.

SUMMARY OF SECOND INTERVIEW WITH EDNA

Edna had asked for a second interview to discuss home problems and when she began to talk it seemed that she had so much to say that she could hardly get it out fast enough.

She was late and said it was because her mother insisted she eat lunch before coming and she had been late getting home from church school. She launched into an account of her grandmother's abusive treatment of her, showing her scratches, and mentioning that her sister had tried to defend her whereupon the grandmother beat Angie also.

Edna said she felt she was overworked because her sister attends summer school and she has to do Angie's work as well as her own. She discussed her dislike of having girl friends visit her home because her grandmother always embarrasses her in front of them, or else she treats them in a rude manner. The matter of carfare came up, and she said although her mother and she both wanted to come to the clinic again, they had no money.

Without considering possible results I said I might be able to arrange for the fare through the university, as I felt it might not be wise for her to think I would give it to her. After the interview I realized it was not a wise thing to involve the university, but I would probably do the same thing again as I could see no other way to insure her coming again, and I felt she wanted so much to return.

She gave vent to much unrelated hostility in this interview which was in striking contrast to the first, which I had considered almost a sterile experience. I thought she seemed to have thought about her situation and was eager to discuss it, but still perceived me as just another adult of whom to be wary.

SUMMARY OF THIRD INTERVIEW WITH EDNA

Edna told of one or two times when her grandmother had been rude to her girlfriends and had embarrassed her when she told the guest to go home.

She mentioned that the family had moved and her chief concern was the fuss her grandmother was making over the bedroom Edna's mother had assigned to her. She said the grandmother preferred the room Edna's mother had selected, which made further tension in the home.

In this interview Edna fidgeted and was unable, or unwilling, to concentrate on her problem. In fact, she asked me about the microphone and giggled frequently. She did ask if we could assign a "Big Sister" to her as she said Angie had one at the church school.

I was puzzled after this session and wondered if she was merely dramatizing her home situation and perhaps exaggerating it. I also felt that she might have wanted the Big Sister just so she could go home and show Angie she, too, had a Big Sister.

I felt that this interview didn't move at all.

SUMMARY OF FOURTH INTERVIEW WITH EDNA

Mrs. Martin had asked to have Edna have some type of intelligence test. We looked over the list of available tests and after I explained the purpose of the different ones she wanted to have the *California Mental Maturity, Short Form, Junior High Level, 1957.*

When Edna arrived she wanted to begin on the test at once. I had planned to go over the list with her explaining, as I had to her mother. However, she had brought her very young brother along, and as she seemed anxious to begin at once, I decided to give her the test without more ado.

She was very relaxed throughout and seemed to be trying to do her best. At the end she mentioned that her mother had a bus ticket yet for herself, and one for Edna, and that they would both see me once more before next week when the summer clinic ends.

It seemed to me that she was more at ease than she had been in any interview yet.

I had the feeling that Edna was serious for the first time and, yet, she was more at ease than ever. I thought it significant that her father had allowed her to come, because both she and the mother had thought he would raise a fuss. Apparently, though, he knew, as she said he was going to pick them up. Her little brother (a child by the father's second wife) was a very nice child and was so good even though he had a long wait in the other room. I could see he was very close to Edna and she seemed to know just what to do with him.

SUMMARY OF FIFTH INTERVIEW WITH EDNA

Since Edna had taken the *California Mental Maturity, S-1957 Form, Junior High Level,* she had asked for a fifth and final interview to have me interpret the test results to her.

I explained that she was a little low in comparison to others of her age and grade level, and she said she thought she did poorly. She wondered if her school counselor would put her in another school or in a Special Education Class.

She continued talking, saying that she knew she was going to study much harder the next year and, entirely unsolicited, said she knew the clinic experience had helped her. She even asked if it would be possible to continue in the fall.

I assured her that the laboratory would be functioning again later in the fall and that very possibly it might be arranged so that she could come again.

She seemed elated because her mother had made arrangements for her grandmother to go to another daughter's home for awhile. In fact, she had no complaints about her grandmother in this interview.

In the previous testing session Edna had asked me what one of the pictures on the test was. I told her that if she couldn't decide what it was, that I would tell her when she came to hear the test results. She asked me again, and when I remarked that it was a picture of a man's lapel she smiled and knew at once what it was.

	FIRST INTERVIEW WITH EDNA'S MOTHER	COUNSELOR'S COMMENTS
	[Missed opening minute.]	
C1	Would you like to talk to me about Edna?	If I could do this again I wouldn't lead her this way.
M2	Oh, I figured that's what you were going to do.	
C3	Or anything at all that you would like.	
M4	Oh no, Edna is a pretty good subject to start out about because I've been having a lot of little difficulties with her, and most of it stems right in the home and I feel that that's the reason why her schooling has been falling down for the last year or so. The way I found out about this place was that I called the school last year and I was talking to Mr. Pap. He said that in June they were going to start this clinic. So, in the meantime, conditions at home with her grandmother seemed to have gotten worse. So I told her, "Whenever you go down and talk to them and, tell them what's going on at home because they are trying to help you." So then Miss Walton said she would like me to come down. So, it is a problem there at the house with the children, and being the father and mother, and there	

is another generation there, represented by my mother. It is a problem.

C5   You feel then that because you have two generations in the same house, that it is a little hard for you.

I could do a much more thorough job of reflecting here if I could do it over.

M6   Yes.

C7   It has created problems for you.

M8   Yes, it really has. Well, right now, I don't know how to handle it because, like, if I make a suggestion of my own with the children in mind, and she's bumping it because . . . Whenever I'm working, she's in mostly complete authority, and if I'm not working, I think a little jealousy sets in because she likes to be boss all the time. A friend of mine told me, "I don't think your mother will ever really be happy unless she could be boss all the time and therefore it would be nice if she could have a kitchenette to herself." You see, because it is a problem with the children, you know. Then the altercation that happened, let's see, it must have happened about a week ago Saturday night, with Edna and my mother. Edna said she grabbed the strap when her grandmother was whipping her, and so, she threw the strap. Well, I didn't think too much of that. Any child will, you know. So I think she got a little hot—she told people about it. Well, I didn't say anything to her, my mother, about it because I was just tired about it all. I said, "While you girls are going down there to the Center, I want you to let them know. I'm not going to be arguing with her about it." So now what I do when I'm going to be out of the house for more than an hour, I take Edna with me.

C9   You find that your mother has a desire to dominate people, so you remove Edna to avoid . . .

Here, again, I didn't reflect fully.

M10   Yes, that's right. Edna, of the two girls,   Mrs. M. defends Edna here.
      Edna is the one that has been the most   Later she changes and ac-
      mousey one. She's not always sassy,   cepts what the school coun-
      but she's just plain-spoken. There have   selor tells her.
      been times when the older one will say,
      "Mama, Edna was just trying to ex-
      plain." Well, her grandmother resents
      that and she considered the child as
      being sassy.

C11   She really just doesn't understand that
      the child is trying to tell her something.

M12   That's right. It's really a problem. I   Here she begins on her own
      don't know how to handle it right now.   problem.
      So the last couple of weeks when I'm
      going to be out for a couple of hours
      or when I'm going to a party at night,
      I let her go stay with my cousin. She
      has two or three girls and I let her
      spend the night over there. When I get
      back home, she and Angie have gotten
      along all right. But Edna has always
      been the one that has felt, I don't
      know, it looks like to me—I told a girl-
      friend of mine she takes out on Edna
      what she resents in me. I said, "I could
      be wrong. I hope I am. I don't have to
      be right."

C13   You feel that she looks at Edna as a
      way for her to get back at you?

M14   That's right—for something she can't   She shows signs of being able
      get me to do, or see her way or point of   to direct her own life here,
      view. Like I always tell her, "Now   but hasn't realized it yet.
      Mother," I say, "A lot of things you
      say, I said, but I still have to go ahead
      with my ideas. I never let those chil-
      dren disobey her. I don't do it. When
      they come to me to let them do a cer-
      tain thing in a certain way, I see if it's
      all right and I go along with them.
      And some of the ways that you handle
      me when I was coming along, I feel I
      should use different tactics with them."

C15   You're a different person and you feel a
      different way. I mean you have your

own way with your own children.

M16 Yes, that's right. Angie goes over to the Church Youth Service and Edna is coming down here and so I tell them, "Whenever you go, you just tell them whatever happens." I talked with Miss Wilson last week and she told me she'd be out on the 14th to see my mother. I feel that it would be nice if she could live with someone else for a while. She said, "I feel that it would be nice if she could live with someone else for a while. I feel that it would be better even for you." She came out and had a long talk with me about two or three weeks ago, a little before I moved.

> This is the woman who was "going to tell her what to do." She finally never came to their home at all and hadn't yet at the last interview.

C17 She's from the Church Youth Service?

M18 Yes, that's right. And so she told me, also, that Angie acquired a "Big Sister," so Edna wants a "Big Sister," but I don't think this organization . . .

C19 No, it isn't set up that way. This is the kind of place where we think along with you and try to explore your problem and see if we—we feel we can help you best by having you ultimately decide what you want to do. So that's the type of relationship.

> I cut her off terribly here. In our text it says once in a while a counselor can interrupt, but I am sure this is not the type of place for it.

M20 I see. Well, Miss Wilson told me to talk to you about it and let her know. Maybe she could also get Edna a "Big Sister."

C21 Well, I don't know. We could see about that. I don't know what the possibilities might be, but I'll certainly try to find out for you.

> I knew we didn't operate that way, but I was uncertain what to say and thought it would give me time to think.

M22 All right. Now, just like when we moved Sunday, well a couple of days before we moved, she told one of my brothers, when she got out of the car, I told my brother she doesn't like this place.

C23 You mean the new place?

> They had moved the day before.

M24   The new place. She said, "No, it's too
        small, and this and that." And I said
        that I'm doing the best I can. I said,
        "I'm moving out of this larger place
        only because I couldn't keep up the
        rent." We are still in the nice neigh-
        borhood, we are just a block and a half
        away, and in fact, it's a nicer street.
        Because there are more home owners,
        and where we were living there was
        about five four-family flats right across
        the street, and the people there didn't
        keep their lawns up, and one flat has
        about twenty-four children in it. I
        don't exaggerate when I said twenty-
        four. And their mothers are not trying
        to keep them bathed or cleaned up.
        That was creating a problem too. So I
        said, "That this was even a nicer street
        and if I could have gotten a better pay-
        ing job, I would have kept the old
        place." All she said to me was that the
        place was too small. So I told her,
        "You know why I gave up the other
        house." So I just wouldn't argue with
        her. I can't argue any more. . . .

Here she shows a certain pride, and I felt it all the way through all the interviews—not unpleasant, but just showing she was quite particular about where and how they lived.

C25   In some ways, you feel you really bet-
        tered yourself, as far as the street goes
        and as far as the house, and it certainly
        is better for you because you are able
        to afford it.

I was trying to be supportive here as I felt she needed it.

M26   That's right. That's absolutely right
        because I was worried stiff after my
        checks got cut in February—all the pay
        checks were cut in February. I was do-
        ing some baby-sitting at the time. I
        couldn't even see anything from my
        baby-sitting money because by the
        checks being cut, it just replaced that.
        So I know after the winter was over
        I would have to get out and find some-
        thing a little cheaper, or even where
        the rent is included. So now I'm in a
        place where the rent is included and

This is the only reference to her job.

that takes the strain off of me a little
bit, you see.

C27   You're a bit better off financially?   Again, supportive.

M28   Yes, that's right.

C29   Have you discussed with your mother   This question was a great
      the reasons that, does she really under-   mistake. I felt it at once. It
      stand that you really were forced to do   stopped her.
      that?

M30   Yes.

C31   Well, how did she react to this? I
      mean, did you have an understanding,
      or how did she?

M32   Well, I feel like that she thought per-   She goes on (with probing)
      haps that I would be able to get a   but I think I spoiled a much
      house similar to the one we had, only   better response.
      with cheaper rent. The only one I
      found like that was only five dollars
      cheaper, and you don't move to save
      five dollars with that expense.

C33   No.

M34   You know what I mean.

C35   No, because by the time you have   Trying to reflect support.
      moved, and you've gone through all
      the expense of moving . . .

M36   Yes, that's right. And you have to pay
      to have the lights turned on again and
      the gas, you really haven't saved
      enough, not for five dollars. Now I
      would move to save ten dollars because
      I would feel that over a period of
      eleven months that the twelfth month
      would represent my moving expenses
      and I had come out ahead. But you
      don't move to save five dollars. Most of
      the places that I did find were five
      dollars cheaper and I needed to save
      more than five dollars.

C37   So you feel in your own way, that you   Summing up.
      really have done the best thing for you
      and your children?

M38   I do. I really do.

C39   You feel that if your mother could just   Continuing the reflection.
      be, live somewhere else, it would be
      much easier for you?

M40   I do because, see, she's constantly com-   Here she really began to go
      plaining and my children say, "Mother,   deeply into her problem.
      we both tell people," (Angie at the
      Center and Edna talks here) "that
      every kid [Inaudible]." I have other
      brothers and sisters and they don't seem
      to [Inaudible] look after my mother,
      but some of the other kids never take
      her around, they never take her out in
      the car for a ride when she's sick, and
      so she only has them to just [Inaudible]
      all the time, see. So it's really a prob-
      lem.

C41   She doesn't realize that maybe her   She mentions this in another
      other grandchildren would have faults.   way later when she says her
                                                relatives might hear her
                                                mother talk about Edna and
                                                they might think she is worse
                                                than she really is.

M42   That's what it is by her not going
      around them, see. She doesn't get
      around too good. Most of the boys
      have cars and a couple of my sister'
      husbands have cars, but they don't . . .
      on holidays that come up she's home,
      right there. It isn't fair because that
      means she feels left out. I don't have
      money to have picnics, even backyard
      picnics. If I have a little job and when
      a holiday comes along, we'll have a lit-
      tle something down in the yard. You
      know, I'll try to splurge a little, but
      when I'm not working, the kids will go
      to the show and she's left there by her-
      self, and her other children don't even
      come around her.

C43   So she just feels like an outcast, you   I think outcast was an un-
      think?   fortunate word here.

M44   Yes, that's right. She and Angie seem
      to get along pretty good. Mrs. Wilson
      is going to come out to the house.

C45   To talk to your mother?   Unnecessary, and should have
                                               been quiet and listened here.

M46   Yes, uh-huh. I think that's going to be
      about Thursday or Friday. Yes, my sis-

ters and brothers feel like I did a wrong thing to move. But see, they're not counting my expense, you see, because she's been complaining to them.

C47 They don't seem to be willing to have her live with them either?

M48 The fact of it is, no one has asked her. They see me struggling with two children, and myself and her, see, and . . . I have one brother who lives about five blocks from me, now that I've moved. We were about seven blocks, but now we live about five blocks apart. It's still within walking distance. I remember his wife told my mother, often asked her to come and stay with them awhile. I thought it should be arranged like that. I feel that it should be arranged where she could go and stay with this one for awhile and the next one for awhile.

C49 Did you ever talk to her about it? You know, come right out and ask her?

Poor time for question. She would have gone on soon.

M50 Let's see. Oh, I think I did. Oh, it's been about four or five years. I can't think back on the conversation now. I have had a sister ask Mother to come and spend time with them, but she always has an alibi. Well, see, most of the furniture where we're at is her furniture that my brother got her a long time ago, even as late as '51, just before my younger brothers got married, and so, perhaps, she feels like she should be around her things. Well, I can see that too, but I feel like, well, I can get out and get me some more furniture, if I have to buy one piece a month, or to go to the Goodwill.

Here she shows willingness to take action. (Movement)

C51 You feel that you, that she would not want to leave her own things and perhaps it hasn't occurred to her to really consider the fact that you would be able to replace those?

M52 That's true too, that's right. I don't

know how this will all work out. Because I look at Edna, and like I told
Mr. Pap, "I don't feel like Edna should
be promoted to the next grade when,
she is constantly failing with D's."
That's when he told me that this clinic
will be opening up in two weeks and I
had filled out an application about,
oh, six weeks before school had opened,
and then I called down to the Board
of Education and they said they were
going to analyze her in September. Because I feel like she has so many problems now, she can't learn.

C53   Do you think she is aware of these
problems or do you think she doesn't
recognize them?

I feel this question was justified. I hadn't been able to
elicit from E. why she had
come to the clinic. Here the
mother began to get very intense. I could hardly think at
this point as I was so much
in her frame of reference.
Looking back on it I feel this
was the start of much deeper
material.

M54   I don't know how to answer that. I
know she, like she told me when I took
her to the Detention Home. I took the
kids to the Detention Home just before
school was out. They upset me so I felt
just like screaming.

C55   You mean to visit?

M56   No, Ma'am! Angie had gotten into some
trouble at school, putting on lipstick
and such, and Edna, well she wasn't
being too bad at school, but she just
wasn't getting even fair marks, and
fussing and fighting at home. This was
why I carried them over. So I made the
appointment and they went the following Monday. I talked to Miss Rogers,
she's in charge of "girl-intake," and
that's how I was introduced to the
Church Youth Service. So, something
good came out of it, and something
good came out of it for Edna with this

organization, because I constantly kept in contact with Mr. Pap. He said, "Edna's greatest trouble is her attitude, her attitude is so bad." And that's true.

C57   You've seen this at home?

I asked this purposely because I wanted her to concentrate on her story and thought it would help.

M58   Oh, yes. Yes, I have. Her attitude is very bad. Just like I was talking to someone and they asked me had she started to menstruate, and I said, "No, she's twelve and one-half," and they said, "She's a little late for that." And so that chemical change is still working on her, and so . . .

C59   And so you realize that makes some excuse for her.

I think this is an example of interrupting which is permissible for support and to keep her going.

M60   That's true. She's getting so she sleeps all the time, and she's tired, and as long as she's outside playing, you know, she's all right, but if you ask her to do something, "Oh, I don't want to do it," with her face all turned up, and I don't know. I know if she's doing that in school, I don't care what school they send her to, she'll never learn.

Here she stops making excuses for E.

C61   No, you realize then that she is getting into all this trouble, and not only causing trouble in the home with your mother, but it's getting in the way of her learning.

M62   Yes, that's true. That's the first thing he said, "It's Edna's attitude," that's what he said. So the fact that she's, she and her sister are being raised in a broken home, then that's another problem. So like I told Mr. Pap, I said, "If I can get Edna straightened out before she's eighteen, or twenty-one, or whenever they're considered grown, I would feel that I've done my part by her in

Here she reinforces her new insight about E. She accepts Mr. Pap's account of E's behavior.

that respect." I'm not going to sit by
and not take her some place because her
problems, well, I can't handle them
myself. I just can't.   Intense here!

C63   What you're saying is that you do
recognize that it will get worse as she
gets older.

M64   I do.

C65   You really will give her a gift that will   I tried to reflect in different
be of value to her by straightening her   language.
out.

M66   Yes, that's true, that's just how I feel.
I told Mrs. Wilson that I'm going to
try to do everything to get Edna
straightened out. I said if it means that
I won't be able to work until maybe
the next five or six years, if I do no more
than that to get her straightened out.
I know I'll still have to work, that
doesn't bother me, but if it means
sacrificing some little things I would
like to have to get her straightened out,
I'm willing to do that.

C67   You're willing to give up luxuries to   I should *not* have used "lux-
get her adjusted.   uries." She didn't accept it.

M68   Because I have not been able to get   (Insight here)
through to her. Angie went through   I feel the same way some-
her little phase and I was able to get   times with Edna.
right next to her. She sorta broke out,
you know, and she kinda came to herself, but I can't get through to Edna. I
told the teacher, told Mr. Pap, "It
seems like Edna has a barrier built
right in front of her and just whatever
you say falls off."

C69   A barrier with everyone, not only with
you.

M70   Mm-hmm.

C71   So, she just doesn't react to people,
perhaps.

M72   But it's the funniest thing now, she's
like that with adults, but she's altogether different with little children.
Edna will take anybody's baby and take

care of it and you wouldn't have to worry. You could go downtown and shop, and she'll dry that baby, clean it, if necessary, put powder on it, give it its bottle and have it just as nice and neat. And where the baby would be laying she would clean that off and, you would think that she was somebody forty years old that had twenty years of experience.

Intense here.

C73 So she does take responsibility.

Reflecting in different form.

M74 She certainly does.

C75 She loves children and seems to have a mother's instinct.

Same as above.

M76 She certainly does. All the little children in the neighborhood that we live in love Edna. She can't walk down the street without children on both sides, "Edna, Edna." They want to follow her to the store, you know. But she just, it looks like to me she is an authority with smaller children and babies, but she resents authority from those who are older than her. I've really studied her, that's why I know that I can't help her because she's often moody and . . .

She accepts it.

C77 You do realize that she does resent authority and she exerts this authority over younger children and that makes her happy.

This was a poor response. I used same words she did. She accepted it, though.

M78 That's right. That's absolutely right. That's true because she had a great love for dolls. It was just like an obsession. I had to steal her dolls away from her, one by one, and only keep her with two because, it seems to me, they were keeping her from learning, and I used to have to take her dolls away from her.

She was in a world of her own at this point.

C79 At what age was this?

I thought I should ask this.

M80 Oh, that went on up until she was about eleven. And right now, we moved here Sunday, and I said, "Edna, it seems like to me you would give some of the dolls to the Goodwill or someone in the neighborhood." She has dolls that she had, that were given to her when she was about four, when she knew how to sorta hang on to them you know. The Goodfellows would give her a doll every year and someone in the family would give her one so she had a good collection, that would go across that wall just about. That's no joke, see.

C81 And she wouldn't part with any of them.

M82 She gave some of them that had the arms broke off or something like that and when we got ready to move Sunday, I looked into a larger bag we were putting some things in, and she had a little basket with a top of it I had given her one year, a play layette, you've seen them, and she had two or three in there. Then I gave her a great big doll, her last doll, that was when she was about eleven, I got it down to Sam's for about three dollars, and a great big Mama doll, it was just like a little boy, she kept that one, too. That part was OK, I was just saying how she just loved dolls.

C83 And this had really told you something about her. She has so much that is worthwhile about her if only she can be trained and be helped to see her own problem, perhaps.

I should have kept still.

M84 And do you know what she would do? She would go to the second hand store or the Goodwill, and I'm not telling a fib, Edna—all her dolls had bibs, bonnets, diapers, socks, shoes, blankets, everything. Everything. I told her, "That worries me, that's not a good sign." You know what I mean.

Very upset here.

C85   So you feel play is very real to her, perhaps it's almost too real.

M86   That's what I'm saying. That's right.

C87   At such a young age, too.   Unnecessary response.

M88   And just think Mrs., what's your name?

C89   Simms.

M90   This happened about five years ago, so you can imagine how engrossed she was with it then. And when she got about ten, she knew how to go buy these little things, you know.

C91   She just lives with her dolls.   Reflecting with different language.

M92   That's right, that's exactly the truth. We had a cot in the girls' playroom, and every night before Edna would go to bed, she would cover her dolls. She'd get up and go to school, and be running late, and come all the way back on a cold morning, and you'd think maybe she forgot her mittens or something, and go back there and she would be putting an extra cover, or coat, or anything, on the dolls. So I told her, "This just isn't right." I said, "I know it isn't."

C93   So, for several years, you had seen signs   I responded here because I
      of behavior that you don't think is   thought she wouldn't go on.
      normal for her age.   If I could only keep quiet.

M94   That's right. It just didn't seem normal. You're absolutely right. And then another thing I found out when I couldn't correct Edna in her writing. Right now she still, she can't master her writing like she should. She writes like a girl that's about in the third   She is really deep in the
      grade. That's what let me know that   problem.
      she wasn't learning like she should. And cries all the time. This crying went on even when she was about eight or nine, and most girls pull out of that when they're twelve and one-half.

C95   Did it seem to get worse then?   Poor response. She didn't accept it.

M96 Today she was crying about something.
I said, "Edna, I'm sorry," so she sorta
stopped you know, but she cries. I'm
trying to do my best. I want to help.
So she came home from school in June
and I saw her report card laying there,   Here she tries momentarily
and I said, "Oh, what's this? I'm not   to defend her.
going to whip you, but I feel now you
should go to a special school." I said,
"I'm going to do everything I can to
help get you in there, but you're just
not learning." I said, "I know that
you've been trying because . . ." all
her efforts were high.

C97 Up until this time?   Not a good response. It
                                                stopped her.

M98 She . . . Yes. She passed with all D's
and one, I think, C or two C's. And the
C's were in a class like Swimming, and
I think something like Hygiene, you
know. In her other classes where she
had D's, she had high effort marks, so
that let me know that Edna was trying. But it just isn't fair.

C99 So you realize that perhaps she has low
ability and perhaps it is beginning to
show up now in her adolescence.

M100 That's right.

C101 And she's having her change.   Here I used an expression
                                                she had used before.

M102 Mm-hmm. Because she had B's, B
pluses and B minuses, and C pluses
the first card marking, and Mr. Pap
said he was very proud of Edna. And
Mrs. Simms, the second and third, all
D's, the second marking all D's and two
E's, and the third card marking all D's
and two C's.

C103 So you realize she is slipping.   This may have been a poor
                                                word to use.

M104 She's slipping that's what it is. I wish
you would analyze her and do what

you can to, you know, if she has to go
to a special school, and then whatever   Movement.
I'm supposed to do at home, I'll follow
it right to the letter. You know I . . .

C105   You'll be glad to cooperate.

M106   I certainly would. I took her to the
store with me last night and she had a
jump rope and she was jumping same
as a girl eight years old. She's twelve
and one-half. Most of her girlfriends
who are twelve and one-half haven't
jumped rope in about two years.

C107   What about her friends, does she have   I think this question was use-
close friends?   ful to me.

M108   Yes, she does but she's a person like
this—when she's with her friends and
everything's going along all right, she's
all right. You see what I mean? But
once they disagree, she can turn against
them (*Snap of fingers*) just like that.
That isn't good. You're not suppose
to fly right up and then drop right
down abruptly, it's supposed to be a
gradual fall, or gradual decline, seems
to me. So I talked to her about it, you
know. I said it's just as right for you
to make up with your friends when
you have a misunderstanding as it is
for them to come to you. No one has to
come to you all the time. You have to
come to them. When she has one
friend, she wants to do everything with
that one friend, and then if she has any
kind of altercation with them, she'll
cast them aside, then she'll go back to
this one over here. Then if she falls
out with this friend, then she'll come
back to this one over here. She's done
that ever since she started to school, I
would say about five, you notice things
about children.

C109   So what you're saying is that she doesn't   I thought this was a good
make lasting friendships, she sort of   response.

skips from one to the other. Apparently, she doesn't form any attachments.

M110   I guess not. It seems like when she is getting along with this particular girlfriend, she wants to do everything with them and wear the same type of clothes they wear, or as near alike as possible, you know. You would think everything was just fine. But if anything goes wrong . . . once they reject something she has said, well, she casts them off like you would throw away the Kleenex over there, you know. I would say, "What's wrong with you? Wait a minute now, you stop and think what you're not doing. That girl has a right to her own opinion and to do the way she does." So, all these things, you know.

C111   You feel that she isn't very tolerant. She isn't willing to forgive and isn't willing to understand the other girl.

I think this sums up what she said.

M112   No. No, she isn't. And then when she wants to be tolerant, she can. But she freezes up when I'm talking to her about somethings, and she'll turn her head. I'll say, "Edna, it's impolite when someone is talking to you to turn your head. I don't care if I'm saying something that you dislike, look at me." I said, "See Edna, as long as I'm letting you run the streets, go to this girl's house and that girl's house, I don't mind letting you go. You go swimming or you want to go to the show, whatever it is, 'Give me a dime to go buy ice cream,' that's all right. Then I say, 'Take the trash down, or maybe make the beds that morning,' then it's, 'Aw, shucks!' " I said, "You and I have become arch enemies. That isn't right." So, I say, well, kids go through that stage, some of them anyway. Then some days, Mrs. Simms, she can work all through the house and do everything. Clean out the corridor, sweep the floors, make the beds and, she can do everything real good. Then, if you ask her to do a little something . . .

C113 She seems to go into moods. She's moody.

I think I could have reflected this passage much better.

M114 Yes, I guess so. Well, I would very much like to get her straightened out. I would. Because, basically, like Mrs. Rogers told me at the Detention Home, the girl is a good girl and she wants to obey. But you see, Mrs. Rogers doesn't know all these little troubles that Edna is having now. But I really would like to get her straightened out. I would just hate for her to turn another way because she isn't learning. If it means my mother has to go with someone else, if that will be one of the symptoms to help straighten out Edna, I'm going to go right along with the program. If it means I have to move again into an apartment to myself. If Mother didn't want to leave her furniture, I would be willing to take what few pieces I have. I would be willing to move because I'm going to have to go to the Salvation Army anyway.

Movement here.

I think this is the beginning of her taking *real* action.

C115 So you are willing to do anything that will straighten out Edna as long as you can make arrangements so that your mother can live by herself, or that is, not with you.

Supportive.

M116 Yes, that's right. Yes, and I would even like the authorities to talk to her and let her know that this change is being made to help this child. You see, she raised her children and my father was living. But right now it's hard to reason with her. She's at the age when she, it's hard to reason with her. It's hard. Whatever the outcome, will

She reinforces her own idea.

Movement.

be for Edna and Angie to get them straightened out so they'll be just about normal when they are grown, despite the fact that they were raised in a broken home, I'm going to go along with it. I think I owe them that. I mean I can't buy all the pretty clothes that the other girls wear, but I can get them on a straight footing until they get grown and work, then they can buy the clothes they didn't have when they were growing up, I mean the expensive things. They have nice things.

More movement.

C117   You are looking ahead to the time when they will be independent and if they are adjusted now, they can get a little insight into their problems.

I could do much better here than this.

M118   Yes, that's right. Angie seems to be doing pretty fair now. The House Counselor told me when I called the school that Angie passed. I said, "Angie was worried about going to summer school, what do you think about it? This time I'm not going to do anything that would [Inaudible]." And she said that Angie felt so good after you came to school that Friday. And the first thing she said was, and it struck me so forcibly, that her attitude was so good, because Mr. Pap has said Edna's attitude was so bad.

C119   You can see the contrast.

M120   That's right and so she said, "Let her go to summer school if you can afford it, let her go." Everything's for her. It will put her in a different class, and her marks are good enough for her to advance. And she got achievement slips from her different classes. I'll have to put them in a home. I almost blew my top. That worried strain, you know. I almost went crazy. I almost screamed one day, and my brother said that I should have screamed. I was talking

Very worked up here.

to Miss [Inaudible] and I started crying, and the teacher just shook her
head.

C121   You just got to the limit of your en-   Supportive.
       durance.

M122   I did. She said, "Take them down and
       call me Monday and let me know what
       went on." I couldn't take it. I felt like
       getting on a train and leaving Detroit.
       I couldn't do that.

C123   You realize your responsibilities and   I think this helped her.
       you're trying to do the best you can
       for these girls, alone.

M124   That's right. That's right—alone. And
       then having my mother on top of it.

C125   Do you think you'd like to come back?

M126   Oh yes, I would. I think I would.   Movement.

SECOND INTERVIEW
WITH EDNA'S MOTHER

COUNSELOR'S
COMMENTS

M1   She doesn't mean any harm but, I'm   The tape didn't run at the
       alone there, if I had a husband or some- very first sentence.
       thing like that, you know, where—I
       feel the weight of everybody's problems.
       Then, I have my own problems. I need
       a rest now, see.

C2   She kind of concentrates on you, and   Trying to reflect properly.
       then you have other things . . .

M3   That's right. She has always been a
       perfectionist which—there isn't anything
       wrong in that. But when I've got prob-
       lems, Mrs. Simms, I'll say, "I'll catch
       that up tomorrow." I don't keep a
       nasty, sloppy house, but a lot of little
       detailed things, to her they seem im-
       portant. Well, I feel like I can do them
       another time. Those kind of things
       irritate her because she feels they need   Shows insight.
       to be done and she says she doesn't
       have the physical ability that she used
       to have. Well, she raised a big family
       herself. And a lot of times I don't feel

like hearing that because I've got problems with the kids on me, see.

C4   She wants you to do it right now and   I felt this was a good re-
     you don't feel like it. You're tired.   sponse.

M5   That's right. When the kids come to
     me with their little problems, or when
     they want a dime or a quarter, maybe
     I can't spare it just then, and then she
     comes with her little problem, and
     there I am, see.

C6   You feel that your children, after all,   Supportive.
     come first, and although she is your
     mother, you feel you're doing the best
     you can.

M7   That's true. That's right, and I feel
     that I have other sisters and brothers
     and, they have places and they could
     more or less insist that she stay in order
     to give me a break. Like I was telling
     my sister, the one that used to keep her
     before, "I don't want you to misin-
     terpret things, the situation here at
     the house, I feel bad because the way
     things are going, and I don't want none   Here is where she tries to
     of the kids' uncles and aunts mistreat-   defend girls again.
     ing Angie and Edna because of this
     situation here." A lot of times when a
     person tells a story, when you hear it
     again, it just sounds like something
     else.

C8   You feel torn between wanting to do   Trying to clarify her feelings.
     the right thing by Edna, and your own
     mother. Loving them both.

M9   That's right. That's why I always say,
     "I'd hate to come home, be out to a
     show or to a party, or be just out, and
     come back and a tragedy has taken
     place." Because the children going   Insight here and the need to
     through their phase and she going   change situation.
     through hers, and I would hate to
     come back and find that some trouble
     had happened.

C10 And you would regret it.   Poor reflection.

M11 I certainly would, and I would say if

I had just insisted if some of the kids
would take her. 'Cause like I told them,   Movement.
like Mrs. Tymn, I told her, "It would
be nice of you to send them all letters
telling them of the situation," you
know.

C12 Is that the social worker at the church?

M13 Yes, that's right. So I was telling my
sister that that's what I had suggested   Movement.
Mrs. Willard should do, so she told
everyone in the family, "We're all going to get letters."

C14 She prepared them all for this.

M15 So I said, "That's OK, maybe it's pretty   Movement.
good that I did say it," although I did
ask her to send letters, but I haven't
seen Mrs. Willard. I've got to call her
tomorrow, I was expecting her to come
out to the house on the fourteenth,   She never did come as far as
but she didn't come the fourteenth or   I know. She just talks to Mrs.
fifteenth. So Angie said, "Mother, either   M. on phone and Angie goes
I got my appointment mixed up with   there for an interview.
hers . . ." see Angie's supposed to go
on the twenty-second. "So tomorrow
morning I'm going to get up and call
Mrs. Willard and see when she's coming out."

C16 Perhaps she did get them mixed up.

M17 Yes, just like Edna got hers mixed up
yesterday, see, so they gave her one for
Wednesday. She said, "Mother, if
Daddy takes me down to Harper Hospital for my ear, he's not going to
want to take me over here to the
Clinic." And she said, "I want to stay
away two weeks, so you go down and
ask them to give me an appointment
within two weeks."

C18 It would make it better for her.   Trying to show her I under-
                                                    stood why.

M19 Yeah. She knows her father will start
hollering, "Why is she coming over
here, your mother doesn't do this and

that." So I said, "Don't even tell your father you're going to this clinic. Those people are trying to help you, I'm trying to help you, and I'm even trying to help myself." I said, "Don't tell him nothing that's going to upset him."   Movement.

C20   It would further complicate the problem.   Supportive.

M21   That's right. So Edna said, "Why don't you tell them to give me an appointment within two weeks." She's learning more how to keep little facts to herself.   Movement.

C22   There's only one thing about it—you do know the clinic ends around the middle of August?   Structuring.

M23   Oh, it does?

C24   Yes. It isn't unlimited so you probably would want to keep that in mind.   Structuring.

M25   Yes. Well, if she goes away today, let's see, this is about the nineteenth or the twentieth, well, she would be back before the end.   Movement.

C26   Yes, she would have time. She would have plenty of time.   Supportive.

M27   Mrs. Simms, actually we come down here—I know this records everything we say, doesn't it?

C28   Yes, they're listening to our voices.   Trying to be casual and yet reassuring.

M29   Oh, are they?

C30   People who are learning to be counselors. They are interested more in the —in training.   This is a bad habit of mine. I get mixed up.

M31   Oh, I see. Well do they sum all this up and tell you what to do or what?   I tried not to answer this but she kept pressing and I had to.

C32   As a rule, we feel we can help you best in this Clinic by thinking through your problem and we feel that everyone is a worthwhile person and able in their own way to solve their problems, but it helps to think with them, and we try to do that.

M33	Well, listen, when do you see the people that are listening?	Pressing me.
C34	Well, there are always people there some of the time. It's for training purposes.	
M35	Well, I was wondering, do they sum all this up?	Here again.
C36	It's not personal, it's a matter of training people to become counselors. They are really observing me.	
M37	Oh, is that right? Well, do you talk with them?	She had to know.
C38	Well, sometimes.	I finally answered and think I should have long before this.
M39	You have to in order that they get their training.	
C40	Yes.	
M41	I see because they're going to go out on their own into that field.	Here she accepts it at last.
C42	That's right.	
M43	I often wondered how they did that.	Seems to be satisfied.
C44	Yes, it's rather interesting, don't you think?	
M45	Yes, Edna said, "Mother, I looked through something and I saw someone standing . . ."	Here she keeps on with the questions about mike etc.
C46	Oh, did she?	
M47	She said, "She was standing some place talking and I could see the shadow."	
C48	She giggled. As a rule they don't . . .	She interrupted me and I was glad as she didn't seem upset at the talk of recording.
M49	Well, you know how kids are.	
C50	Well, does it bother you to think about it, at all?	
M51	What, about somebody else looking? No, I just wanted to know after you're down here, like you make several trips, do they take a summary of what you have said and give you some little points to go along with, or just how do they do it?	Here she insists in a pleasant way.

C52   Well, we feel that after you think about your problem, you've thought about, and have concentrated on it with someone to help you concentrate, and then you are able to be more happy with your own decision than you would be with someone else's.

M53   Oh!!

Movement.
I wish you could have seen her expression here. Obviously such a solution had never occurred to her and she liked the idea, although it was new to her.

C54   We feel that what you're told to do sometimes doesn't work out for you as well as what you think up yourself. This is the theory that we . . .

M55   Oh. Well how does this help Edna, the fact that she is so, isn't getting along in school?

C56   Well, it's hard to say. Now there are other things that we do. It's hard always to tell how this helps youngsters. It may help, and it might possibly not. We have, also, tests here available, we do do testing. However, we always let the student pick out the test if he wants such a thing. But even after the test is given, we still feel that people are able to figure out their own course, and that they are happier with it.

I was afraid I'd lose her here.

This surprised her. It was not the thing to say.

M57   Well, see what I want Edna to do before this Clinic is closed, I would like for her to be tested here.

Movement.

C58   You would.

Unnecessary.

M59   I most certainly would. Because I told Mr. Pap that, and also, I don't have my notebook with me, there's someone by the name of, I can't think of the person's name, at the Board of Education, they told me to bring her in and they would give her an individual psychological test.

C60   Perhaps that would be good for you to

do then. As a rule, the way we operate here, we will test the child but . . .

M61 Well, will you tell me the results because . . .

Movement.

C62 It's interpreted to you. It would depend upon what kind of test is given, and we would interpret it to you. We don't solve any problems. As I have said, we feel you will be happier with your own solution.

M63 Well, I would like for her to be tested and would like to know the outcome, and I'll tell you why. So that when I do go down in September to the Board of Education, I'll probably make my appointment for the first week in September for Edna, and I could tell them that she has been coming here all summer and that she was tested, and that will help them . . .

More movement.

C64 Well, what we can do, we can interpret the test to you. Rather, we can say, "Edna is above average, she's average or she's below average."

This is not a sample of my best grammar.

M65 Yes, I do want to know that, and you see, when they test her, they'll put what you say, even if you gave me a letter to take to them, it would be all right, see. That's so that when she starts to school in September, if she has to go to a special class for awhile, I want that done for her.

Movement.

C66 Yes, you're willing to do anything to help her.

M67 Yeah. Yes, I would like to know so if she does have to be put in a special class, she can go in right away, see. She looks forward to coming down here. I can see, actually see her straightening out too, Mrs. Simms. I most certainly can, because the other day I noticed, I asked her to do something and she didn't want to do it. I said, "See Edna, now you're not being fair to me." I said,

"I don't mind you helping the lady with her babies and making a little change." I don't mind because I used to live in the same building with the lady, but I said, "When I ask you to do something, then you frown up, and I said now I'll just do it myself." Edna said, "Oh, Mother, I'll do it." So I can notice a change, see, and she'll be whining, and I'll say, "Now you stop that whining, you don't have to whine. You are too old for that and you're just trying to have your way." She's twelve and one-half and this just doesn't make sense, you know. So I can really see her beginning to improve. All kids have their little habits, like they drop something down or things like that, but her attitude towards me is beginning to change.

Much movement all through here.

C68   Yes. Her thinking through, perhaps.

Maybe this was too interpretative.

M69   That's right. Edna's attitude toward me is beginning to . . .

C70   You can even see this.

Reinforcing and reflecting.

M71   Yes, since she's been coming here. That's the truth.

Movement.

C72   Well, that's good.

Judgmental, I'm afraid.

M73   That's why I don't want her to stop coming here and I didn't want her to tell her father where he would interrupt her from going. She said, "Well, Mother, I'll tell you what." She said, "Cancel my appointment for about two weeks." She looks forward to coming down here, see, and I can truthfully say that the Guidance Clinic is helping her. I can say that because I know last night, I walked out to the store yesterday evening, and I said, "Edna, now watch yourself," I said, "I'm fixing to go out and don't get into anything with your grandmother. Anything she asks you to do, go ahead and do it. It's not

Movement.

going to hurt you." I didn't want the same thing to happen that happened about a month ago or three weeks ago, a little before we moved. So I said, "just watch yourself," before I got ready to leave. My mother got up and I could tell, well, like Angie says, "Mother, when, you leave, Grandmother goes on a war path."

C74   Even Angie realizes . . .   I should have kept still.

M75   Yes. So before I left I walked back in the kitchen and said, "Edna, remember what I said, watch yourself." I said, "Remember you're only holding yourself back." So I can say that Edna has actually made a change since she's been coming here.

C76   So you can see a change that she might   Supportive be developing a little.

M77   That's right. I do want her to continue even when she comes away from visiting with her father. I had thought on my way down here today, well, if she goes swimming and I have to do her hair, I'll have to come home and then   She seems to be in control of I'll call you the night before, and I'll   the situation. keep her that day and then let her go back down there. I'm going to have to do it that way, Mrs. Simms, so he won't interrupt the good that I'm trying to do for her.

C78   He wouldn't like it.

M79   No, he wouldn't. Because when Mr. Pap talked to him and I last December about Edna, all the way back, all he did was accuse me. He said that right in front of Edna, and that keeps her confused. So on my way down, I said, "I'll know what I'll do if Edna goes swimming and wants me to press her hair out, I'll have her come home that night, then I'll make an appointment so that she can be worked in and have her come down here and then she can   Insight.

go on back with him." Because I can see her attitude, I mean I can begin to see a change. I mean it isn't a vast improvement but I can see it changing.

Movement.

C80   Well, of course it's been a long time coming, and perhaps it will be quite awhile, but if you can see some kind of a change . . . Does Edna really want to come of her own accord?

I felt I had to ask this.

M81   She certainly does. She was the one who told me to cancel her appointment for two weeks. She said, "Mother, I'll tell you what, you can tell them that I'll be away with my father for two weeks and I'll come back." I asked her if she had enough car tickets and she said yes, she had enough to get down there one more trip.

Movement on E's part, too.

C82   Is Angie going with him too?

Probably unnecessary.

M83   No, she's in summer school and I told her that I wanted her to go spend a week with him but she said, "Oh, Daddy ain't fair, 'Don't do this,' and I don't want to go." I said, "Well, Angie, it won't hurt you to spend a week if you want to do." So she might change her mind. So I haven't been pushing her, she's been kinda sick. I've got to call the Clinic tomorrow. Every month she has violent, violent, vomiting cramps. I said, "Angie, I can't see you suffering like this anymore." So I'm going to have to make an appointment for her tomorrow, so that she can go to the clinic in the afternoon, and that way she can leave school and go on down to Harper, and I'll meet her over there. She vomits like a dog. The doctor that I had over to the house last month said a lot of it was psychological.

Going on to another new problem.

C84   Having to do with the mind.

I should not have used "mind." It was threatening to her. I realized it at once.

M85   That's what he said.

C86   Perhaps she's worried about something.

M87   Well, that's what he said. Now I used to have vomiting cramps but I was much older than she is now.

C88   You were just like her but older.

M89   That's right, and he asked me that too. So I think Angie better come down here and talk to her and get her straightened out. But you should see, she has to have a bucket by the bed. And this vomiting goes on, off and on, for about five hours.

C90   She certainly menstruated. I know you said Edna hasn't started yet.

    I was sort of talking to myself. Not good.

M91   No, that's right. And that's every month.

C92   She vomits every month.

M93   That's right. Now my older sister used to vomit. I think there was three of us girls that had those type of spells. I don't know if they are hereditary or . . .

C94   Did she ever know that you had them?

M95   Yes, that's where I did wrong. I certainly did.

C96   You think you might have put it in her mind?

    Too judgmental or interpretive.

M97   I think so, Mrs. Simms, since you said it. I remember me saying that now, then all of a sudden she began to have these cramps, vomiting cramps.

C98   Like mother, like daughter, maybe.

    Not a good choice of words. Silence better.

M99   See how the mind can control, isn't that something? Mind over matter. Well that doctor, he was the first doctor that ever offered that solution. He came into the front room and he said, "What seems to be Angie's trouble?" He said, "Is she worried about anything?" That's the first thing he said. So I said, "Well, I don't know. I used to have vomiting cramps but I was

much older." So he said, "There's no
father in the home, is there?" I said,
naturally he had my welfare number,
case number, so he knew. So I said,
"No, divorced." So he said, "Mm-hmm."

Both mother and Edna often
mention lack of father in
home.

C100   So he thought that had something to
do with it.

M101   That's right. So he gave me some pills
to give her to quiet her nerves and that
was all. I just feel like that she should
have maybe some medical treatments
because I had, the doctor told me
that I had an infantile womb. I remember the doctor examining me when
I was about twenty years old and
he said the only way he could make
me stop having those type of cramps,
he cauterized me, a local operation
right in his office.

Going into deeper material.

C102   And yet you had the children, too, and
it worked out all right.

M103   Yes, and he said I never would have any
children until I had that operation,
like a local. But I used to have those
severe vomiting cramps. Maybe I did
sort of put that idea in her mind. I
can't even remember why I began to
have them now, as I look back, because
I didn't have them for a long time.
Then all of a sudden I began to have
vomiting, but I was much older than
she is.

C104   You just remember that you did do it
at one time.

M105   That's the truth. So I said, "I'm still
going to have her go over to the doctor
at Harper Clinic that they go to, and
she's growing quite fast and maybe
they'll give her something to help her
out, some medication." Even sometimes
the thought of taking medicine might
help her so that she doesn't do it.

C106   They'll check her and it will make her
think that she's on the road to recovery.

I tried to say the same thing
in different words.

M107   That's right. Well, I guess that's all   She ended the session herself.
       the trouble I've got today.

C108   Well, you'll ask Mrs. Walton about
       Edna's appointment. See what we can
       do.

M109   All right. Then, I'm going to talk to
       Angie about coming down. Maybe that
       will help her cramps or something. If
       that will help her so she don't have   Movement.
       them, you can, you'll be able to make
       a case record of that.

C110   I doubt if it's me at all. It's just that   Grammar poor.
       it sometimes helps to think about it.

M111   Well that's the first thing that doctor
       said. He said, "Well, what seems to be
       bothering her," and I said I didn't
       know.

C112   He had that on his mind, apparently.

M113   He certainly did.

C114   Well, the mind has quite an influence   Threatening, not good.
       over the body.
       (*Pause*)

M115   Mm-hmm. It's left her so weak.

C116   She's exhausted.

M117   Yes, I'll get her that checkup and
       maybe I'll be able to get her some,
       they'll give her some vitamins. It won't
       hurt her to go in anyway, I know that.   Movement.
       I'll get enough for Edna, too, two bot-
       tles, and that'll make my carfare last.

C118   It should work out all right.   Supportive.

M119   It's time that they need some vitamins   Taking charge of her family.
       again, you know. Now I'll have them
       when the fall starts.

C120   When colds starts . . .   Trying to mention fall sea-
                                                     son in another way.

M121   Yes. Do I have to stay for the hour?

C122   My dear, you do as you like. We do
       whatever you want to do. Would you
       like to see Mrs. Walton now?

M123   Yes, I would.

C124   All right, you're not under any obli-
       gation.

M125   All right then. Well, I'm going to see   Movement.
       if I can get Angie to come down.
C126   All right. Do you want to speak to her
       about that?
M127   Yes.

SUMMARY OF THIRD INTERVIEW WITH MOTHER

The third interview with the parent was seemingly a relaxed, comfortable one for both the mother and me. She was eager to say that both Edna and Angie were improved. She is having Angie see the Church Youth Group social worker and feels that the clinic experience has been "like a father to me and my children." She wants to guard against both girls slipping back into old ways and attitudes, and hopes they can both attend the clinic in the fall.

Foremost in her mind was to ask me if Edna could be tested to show if she needs to be in a special room or school. We looked over the available tests and she seemed to favor the *California Mental Maturity*. I explained that I would try to present the choice of a test to Edna in such a way that she would not feel that it had been forced upon her.

After the interview I hoped I had not led her to feel that I could change Edna's school situation, and I also felt that I frightened her by my explanation that Edna should have a certain freedom in the choice of a test.

FOURTH INTERVIEW WITH EDNA'S MOTHER	COUNSELOR'S COMMENTS

M1   How did her tests come out?

C2   She's uh, uh, she was quite low.

I was extremely awkward here in trying to let the mother know the results showed low ability.

M3   Mm-hmm.

C4   And, uh, now, there's one thing I thought maybe I should say to you. As a beginning, uh, usually, normally we, I would like to interpret it to her first.

Here I felt I must interpret the tests to Edna first, in all fairness.

M5   Oh, is that right?

C6   So, uh, uh, just, in general I think it's better because there is this possibility,

I meant she might discuss the results with the girl before I had a chance to do so.

I'm sure you wouldn't do it, but if you were, uh, oh, to use this in some way . . .

M7   Well, I . . .

C8   It might be best . . .

M9   I understand.

C10 And I think you wouldn't want to do that.

M11 I understand what you mean, mm-hmm.

C12 I mean, if you could, uh, just uh keep it to yourself sort of until she . . .

M13 All right.

C14 Until she comes and I talk with her.

It was near the end of the clinic and I felt impelled to make sure she wouldn't rush discussing the test with Edna.

M15 All right, mm hmm.

C16 Because I think it would be better for her.

M17 Oh, all right, well, I can give you my word of honor . . .

C18 Oh, I'm sure you would.

M19 I won't say anything to her.

C20 I just thought I would mention it.

M21 Mm-hmm, yes.

C22 Because normally in a, in a situation, if we could, if we weren't closing so soon I would really like to talk to her first.

M23 I understand, sure.

C24 I mean, I think you would want to, to think about it.

M25 Yes, I would, mm-hmm, mm-hmm.

She seemed to partially accept my desire to talk with Edna first about the test.

C26 And, you've told me so many times that you do want to do the best you can.

M27 That's right, I do, mm-hmm.

C28 So, I just thought, I hate to spoil it by having you, perhaps, uh, shown concern over it, or worry, or . . .

Clarification.

M29 All right, then . . .

C30 You know.

M31 It works out nice because she, uh, has   Here she finally accepted it.
     gone back down to her father's this
     week . . .

C32 Good.   Judgmental.

M33 So she won't be home until Sunday
     night, so it's working out good.

C34 Well, that's just fine.   Again, judgmental, but I
                                                        think I would still do it
                                                        this way.

M35 Mm-hmm.

C36 Because in a way it would, it'll be just
     so much . . .

M37 And then, if she calls and asks me did
     I go over to this, this center, I'll tell
     her no, I just . . .

C38 Well, you could, I mean . . .

M39 Went downtown.

C40 You don't have to lie about it, uh,
     you can say that I would rather in-
     terpret . . .

M41 Oh, all right, OK.

C42 This to her, and that would really be
     the truth.

M43 All right, then.

C44 You don't have to say I did it 'cause   I should have omitted this
     she . . .   response. I feel I was much
                                                too verbal in this part of
                                                the interview and I had a
                                                hard time convincing the
                                                mother.

M45 OK, then, I'll tell her, then.

C46 You know.

M47 I'll follow this.

C48 Say that I would rather explain it to
     her first . . .

M49 All right, I certainly will.

C50 And, uh, . . .

M51 Mm-hmm.

C52 That, uh, then she can tell you how   I felt the girl would be bet-
     she came out.   ter satisfied if she herself in-
                                              stituted the discussion about
                                              the test results with her
                                              mother.

M53 Mm-hmm.

C54 I do think that, uh, that I will make a report to the school. . . .

> I said this because the mother had expressed the wish to have the girl tested as her prime purpose in sending her to the laboratory.

M55 Mm-hmm.

C56 You see. I'll make a full report to them. I will enclose the test so that they can see how she did.

M57 Mm-hmm.

C58 And, uh, then if you can arrange, if you can talk to Mr. Pap . . .

M59 Yes, Mr. Pap, yes.

C60 I think it would be a good idea if he could arrange for the other test down at the Board of Education. . . .

> Again reinforcing her expressed intention to contact Board in September.

M61 That's right.

C62 Yes, like we talked.

M63 That's right, yes, 'cause I have that, all those notes and, uh, . . .

C64 Mm-hmm.

M65 I'm to call the first of September . . .

C66 Good.

M67 And make this appointment . . .

C68 Mm-hmm.

M69 With this doctor. I can't remember her name. I have it, at the house.

C70 Mm-hmm. ·

M71 And she said that . . .

C72 Mm-hmm.

M73 She would have, uh, she would personally uh, analyze her . . .

C74 Mm-hmm.

M75 Give her that hour.

C76 'Cause this is just one test. . . .

> I wanted to assure her that one could not make a judgment on the basis of one test only.

M77 That's right, mm-hmm.

C78 You know. And, but it is an indication, I think, that, and of course, you said . . .

> Awkward—very poor response. I was trying to prepare her for accepting the idea that Edna might have low ability.

M79 Mm-hmm.

C80 Yourself, that . . .

M81 That's right.

C82 You thought she was . . .   I was leading her here.

M83 That's right.

C84 A, uh, a little behind.

M85 That's right. So, I'm glad that, uh, this   She was beginning to admit
     has showed up because I feel like   what she had not wanted to
     now that, uh, she can be helped . . .   face.

C86 Mm-hmm.

M87 I think.

C88 And as long as you know this . . .   I was trying very hard to
                                                  empathize.

M89 Mm-hmm.

C90 And you're trying to do the best you   Supportive.
     can for her. . . .

M91 I see, and this way by her knowing be-
     fore she goes back to school there's a
     possibility she'll have to have little
     special training, she'll be more ad-
     justed to it.

C92 That's right.   I feel movement here, she is
                                                  making plans.

M93 As I said, because see, she can start
     right into this class, uh, right away
     without going in with one group, her
     normal class, and then being pulled
     away.

C94 It's just the right time of year.

M95 It certainly is.

C96 Uh-huh.

M97 That's true. Well I feel pretty good
     about it, I really do because, uh, I
     want, uh, I don't know, for some rea-
     son I didn't, when Edna was home
     last week . . .

C98 Oh, yeah, this is your handwriting . . .   She had mentioned in a
                                                  previous interview that she
                                                  wanted to show a sample of
                                                  Edna's "improved" handwrit-
                                                  ing.

M99 I could, see this is the letter I got,
     umm. . . .

C100   Mm-hmm.

M101   You can see, July 29th.

C102   Why, I think that's pretty nice hand-writing.

M103   I told my mother, I said, "Now you see, here is Edna puttin' forth a ef-fort. I asked her to write me a letter. And I think she was conscious of try-ing to make it as nice as she possibly could."

C104   She wrote real nice on the test . . .

M105   Well, now that's . . .

C106   And I complimented her on it.   *Supportive and reinforcing.*

M107   Well, that mean now, she has just been doin' that since this summer.

C108   Mm-hmm.

M109   Her writing started to pick up, I think, around, about, a little around May or June.

C110   Mm-hmm. So maybe . . .

M111   So that's her slowness right there.

C112   Just one of them, mm-hmm.

M113   That's right, mm-hmm.

C114   And, maybe if she realizes now that, uh, that this is serious, that for her it has serious implications . . .

M115   Mm-hmm.

C116   Maybe she will be a little better, a little, work a little harder.

M117   That's right.

C118   And all.

M119   That's right.   *She seemed to accept this.*

C120   She may not have been doing as well as she can.

M121   That's right. But I wonder just what, er, um, what, did you find just why she's slow other than just, uh, what do you say, one day you were saying people, they do the best that they can, they go . . .

C122   Everybody has . . .   *I started to say that everyone has his own rate of growth.*

M123   Have a, what did you say, this plateau, and she can't go, uh, above that.

C124 Well, sometimes by a plateau people mean different things. Some people mean that, uh, learning is, uh, a kind of a process where you go along and you make quite a little progress for awhile . . .

M125 Mm-hmm.

C126 And then you come to a period when you can't see that you're getting any place, and neither can anyone else . . .

M127 Mm-hmm.

C128 And so that some educators call it a plateau.

M129 I see.

C130 Sort of a, you know a plateau is a flat . . .

M131 Yes, I see.

C132 Place on a hill.

M133 Mm-hmm.

C134 And, then, after that sometimes motivation, maybe a reason for getting better marks, might then begin to pick her up after while.   Very awkward response.

M135 Mm-hmm.

C136 But, uh, the thing I think we have to always remember is that everybody has just so much ability. I mean, we're all born with, uh, some of us are born, uh, thin and some of us . . .

M137 That's right.

C138 Are born heavy, yes.

M139 That's right.

C140 And so everybody is a little different than everybody else.

M141 Mm-hmm.

C142 And there's, uh, oh, an awful lot of good in everybody and there are things in all of us that have to be corrected. We . . .

M143 That's true.

C144 Don't always do what we should.

M145 That's right.

C146 And so the thing with education, the thing that most teachers, uh, and educators are trying to do is bring out the very best that there is in every child.

M147 Mm-hmm.

C148 And, uh, she may not have had this happen because sometimes the child himself is not very motivated. They, they get discouraged. Say, they, now she, uh, she may have been discouraged in her work. She may have been a little behind and then, maybe a teacher asked, I don't know this because . . .

I was trying to give her insight into what might have happened.

M149 Mm-hmm.

C150 Because I'm not in that situation, but I'm just, I'm a teacher and I know what happens . . . sometimes, uh, the child gets discouraged and then something else happens and they're more discouraged, and then they just think, "Oh, what's the use." You know, they just give up.

C151 And then they get a little nasty to the teacher and they get . . .

M152 That's the bad attitude Edna probably took over.

C153 Sassy. She just might.

M154 That's right, that's right.

C155 And it might have happened to her. She, uh, it seemed to me that she really realizes that she's going to have to work hard.

M156 Mm-hmm.

C157 And I'm hoping that after the summer, after her thinking about this and realizing that you are concerned, as she must know . . . she must know that you're concerned about her, because you've talked to her and the counselor's talked to her.

M158 Yes. Well, she's well aware that, uh, . . .

C159 And, uh . . .

M160 That I'm concerned.

C161 She has a very nice attitude down here.

M162 Mm-hmm.

C163 I just, uh, she's just been as nice as she could be.

M164 Mm-hmm.

C165 And, I think she can be. What I am saying is that from, now I hate to say it from one test, this is an indication to me, though. This is an intelligence test that I gave her.

M166 Mm-hmm.

C167 And it may be that she has a low ability.

I keep referring to the possibility so she will become accustomed to the idea.

M168 Mm-hmm.

C169 And this is something that we all have to accept. I mean, some of us have low, some of us have medium . . .

M170 Medium and high.

C171 Some high.

M172 That's true.

C173 There isn't a thing we can do, except, we can get them in a special, uh, situation where they can get special help. And, very often, these things can be remedied a whole lot. And, uh . . .

M174 I believe that, because that's why I referred you the incident with my brother.

C175 Yes, you've had that . . .

M176 I certainly have.

C177 In your own family.

M178 That's right. And now, he's well off than any of the rest of the kids, and more so. You see that?

C179 See, he's taken advantage of . . .

M180 That's right.

C181 His special training.

M182 It certainly is. Mm-hmm. I can truthfully say this. And he seems well adjusted in his marriage, even with his children. Now isn't that something? And, and I look back now, and he used to cry a lot the same as Edna. You know, cry all the time and, you know, I, I was thinking about that even a month ago when I first start coming here, you know.

C183 And, you think you can see a rela-tion . . .

M184 Sure.

C185 . . . ship between him and . . .

Trying to accurately reflect her thoughts.

M186 I most certainly can. And now he seems more adjusted than some of my brothers. 'Cause I have a brother that's a dentist and he's not as, and he's not as adjusted as this particular boy.

C187 He may have learned at an early age.

M188 I think so. And where the one that's a dentist, by him being the youngest he's spoiled. He's the baby of the family, and by him being the last child, and my father was up in age when he was born, you see, he would cater to him. And this other brother, uh, now, I'm a year older than the one that went to Special Ed. And then there's three children between, uh, myself and the one that's the dentist. You see that?

C189 Mm-hmm.

M190 But the one, he seems more adjusted than half of the children. Because when I was going out, before I started coming here, he says, Ruby, take first things first, and second things second.

M191 You can't handle all of them at one time. I never will forget that. He says, now if you've found that you've gotta move, he says, don't jump and take anything. He said, go ahead and pay the next month's rent, just take your time and find . . .

C192 Mm-hmm.

M193 What you, that's just what he told me.

C194 He just looks at everything in a very calm . . .

M195 Yeah, he said now, now . . .

C196　Way.

M197　Do second thing second. If you think the children will have to have special training and guidance, he said, go on through with it that clinic, 'cause I had, I had talked with Mr. Pap around April about Edna, anyway, see. So I said while they're carrying on, Denny? He said, that's OK. He said, you did right.

C198　Mm-hmm.

M199　He said, now take first things first and second things second and so on.

C200　He certainly is calm . . .

M201　And he was the one that had to have special training.

C202　Mm-hmm.

M203　Well, I know one thing, I'm very happy to know that it, it's been discovered that she will have to have some special . . .

C204　Yes, she will.

M205　And I'm also happy to know that since Edna knows that she's been coming down here she'll be more adjusted for that class.

C206　She's more receptive, probably.

M207　Yes, that's right, mm-hmm.

C208　She, at least she recognizes there is a problem now.

M209　Mm-hmm.

C210　And, uh, because she is calm and she seems willing enough.

M211　Mm-hmm, mm-hmm. It couldn't of happened at a finer time because I think it would, uh, she wouldn't adjust as easy if she had been pulled out of a class, say around October or November.

C212　It's hard when they get all used to everybody.

M213　Yes, so this way she starts out fresh in a class like that . . .

C214　Mm-hmm.

M215   She'll go through those, uh, few weeks
       of becoming adjusted with her teachers
       and those children, and then, uh . . .

C216   Of course, you understand, I don't   Pointing to the reality of the
       know what he'll, uh, do. I mean I have   situation.
       nothing to do with . . .

M217   Mm-hmm.

C218   This school.

M219   I know it, you . . .

C220   But I will make my report. . . .

M221   Mm-hmm.

C222   And then . . .

M223   Well, I told Mr. Pap that I was going
       to work with the clinic all summer
       and that, uh . . .

C224   He probably will expect you, this fall.

M225   Yes he will, I know he will. And I
       think he told me that, I don't know if
       he said they were going to have a class
       right there at school or not.

C226   He did.

M227   It seems like to me he said they were
       getting set up on a program for that.
       And I don't know whether he . . .

C228   Oh, if they did that would be . . .

M229   Was referring to here, about this . . .

C230   Mm-hmm.

M231   Or a special class.

C232   They might because we have one in
       our school. In, in the school . . .

M233   You do?

C234   Where I teach. We have a Special
       Ed. . . .

M235   Mm-hmm.

C236   Oh, a wonderful teacher.

M237   And then they said they had a Special
       Ed. class of, uh, at Angus School, but
       that's an elementary school.

C238   Mm-hmm. Yes, she wants junior high.

M239   Yes, well I hope they will have it, uh,
       you know . . .

C240   Mm-hmm.

M241   Over at Taylor. Well, it doesn't matter

because she has learned how to, uh, go on the bus, anyway, uh. . . .

C242 Yeah, she's coming along pretty well.

M243 So, yeah, here, and then she's going to bus over there to school. So it won't be too, you know, hard for her, you know.

C244 You probably can arrange it.

M245 Yeah, sure because the school gives them tickets and everything, see.

C246 Oh, they do, yes.

M247 She gets a ticket every day to come back the next day.

C248 Mm-hmm. Well, Mr. Pap will probably, uh, know what to do.

M249 Mm-hmm.

C250 Get in touch with him and he'll, he'll probably be expecting you to.

M251 Yes, he will, now, when, now, just like now, when I'll call Mr. Pap the first day of school and tell him that I have, I'm holding Edna out of school until all her tests come . . .

C252 Mm-hmm.

M253 Back and I'll tell him why . . .

C254 Mm-hmm.

M255 That, you know . . .

C256 Mm-hmm.

M257 It won't hurt her to, uh, lay out of school a couple days until they place her because, uh . . .

C258 Or you could see what he suggests.   *I wasn't sure this would be a good procedure.*

M259 Or see what he suggests, that's true.

C260 He may have an idea.

M261 Yeah, that's right, that's certainly right.

M262 Because, uh . . .

C263 Because he knows they're set up and if they're going to have a special room, why, he would know.

M264 He certainly would, yes, 'cause he'd be about the first to know.

C265 Mm-hmm.

M266 Anyway.

C267 Yeah.

M268 I do know that Edna, uh, is going to have to have this, and so, her, this first test indicates it.

C269 Now some . . .

M270 And I'm just as happy about it as I can be because I feel . . .

C271 Mm-hmm.

M272 This way, now she's got a chance.

C273 Mm-hmm. She certainly has. 'Cause you know what happened to your brother.

M274 That's right.

C275 You know what can happen. Uh, some of these, uh, uh, sometimes, uh, the school, I don't know about Murray high schools, are crowded so that some of the children who really should be on this are not able to be put on it . . .

M276 Mm-hmm.

C277 But you have already put in your word . . .

M278 Mm-hmm.

C279 With him and he's already thinking about her because you've discussed her.

M280 I certainly have, and so, uh, I, I when I talked with him, this Dr. something down at the Board of Education, and she told me . . .

C281 Mm-hmm.

M282 She said well you call me the first of September.

C283 Mm-hmm.

M284 And she said I will analyze her, not in a group, but by herself. I said 'cause I have been noticing this for over a year, I said, and Mr. Pap told me at first not to worry too much about it, 'cause he thought Edna might pull up, but I said, but . . .

Summing up.

C285   Mm-hmm.

M286   She hasn't and I said I know . . .

C287   She went on so long with it.

M288   That's right. And I said, now after a year, I said I know something has got to be done.

C289   Mm-hmm.

M290   I said, now some mothers are not concerned, I said, but I am concerned. And, just about all my problems I feel like if I can get her back on the road to learn, or let, even if she has to learn a trade or something like that . . .

C291   Mm-hmm.

M292   Where when she gets grown she can go out in the world and make a living for herself, I had given her one million dollars.

C293   You've given her a . . .

M294   That's right.

C295   Real gift.

M296   That's a gift, that's right, mm-hmm. But just let this go on . . .

C297   Mm-hmm.

M298   I don't think it's right. I just don't.

C299   Mm-hmm.

M300   Because, now, my mother used to take us places, uh, for help for us . . .

C301   Mm-hmm.

M302   Clinics and, there's a place right here in the city.

C303   Mm-hmm.

M304   So, if she could do it, and she had a house full of children, I only have two.

C305   Mm-hmm.

M306   You know what I mean, so I'm not going to just lay back and say, "Oh, what's the use." I'm not going to do it.

Rereading Counselor Responses shows too many mm-hmm's. I did this to avoid stopping her train of thought.

She was very worked up here. Seemed to be moving toward definite action.

C307 Well, that's what mothers are for . . .

M308 That's right.

C309 To help their children.

M310 I've been down to the new Convention Hall, I was trying to get a job down there.

C311 Have you?   Poor response.

M312 Working at nights.

C313 Oh?   Unnecessary, she would have continued anyway.

M314 It was in the cloak room. So the man told me they, well, he said you've been one of the first ones down here. So, I said, "Well I hope you'll call me," I said, "I need something to do, you know."

C315 Mm-hmm. If you can get that, that will really . . .

M316 Yeah, take a lot of . . .

C317 Help.   [C:315 continued]

M318 Pressure off of me. 'Cause, Miss Simms,   [M:316 continued]
      when I get my check, that's, those checks are just for bills. You need something extra to do, you know. I mean, uh, I don't see how some women can just sit back and lay on that little money and just think it's everything, because it's not.

C319 It's hard.   Very poor.

M320 It's, it's for the children, that's what it's for . . .

C321 Mm-hmm.

M322 It's not for the mothers.

C323 When you're raising children you need money.

M324 That's right, see. 'Cause like I was telling my worker the other, uh, about a month or so ago . . .

C325 Mm-hmm.

M326 And, uh, I was telling her that, uh, I just can't make it any more. I said, the children are eating more. I said, I have a daughter five feet eight or nine and eating all the time, . . .

C327 Mm-hmm, she requires . . .

M328 Like I was telling my girlfriend, I said, I had this little dress made, I said, I got the material for about a dollar and something . . .

C329 Very pretty. You did? You had it made?

M330 I had it made.

C331 Why, isn't that wonderful.

M332 And it has an apron, it has a peplum to it. Three pieces.

C333 Why, that's good. And so you can change it.

M334 That's right.

C335 Why, isn't that wonderful? I like to sew too. I think that it's wonderful, but I . . .   I should have refrained from referring to myself here.

M336 I wish I could sew a little too, but . . .

C337 I don't have the time for it. That's right.

M338 I don't have the knack for it, it seems like it. And then I was, I had on a pretty, I should have wore a dress here. I went down to St. Vincent DePaul one Monday.

C339 Mm-hmm.

M340 You should see the pretty shoes I got for seventy-five cents.

C341 Really? And is that fact they have things there?

M342 Yeah.

C343 Oh, that's wonderful.   Not good.

M344 I go, I go there quite a bit and I got the girls, I worked the election the other day and, uh, this lady had been telling me, Miss Reed, you better come and get your clothes before I resell them. So I said, I'm going to work in the election and make some money.

C345 Mm-hmm.

M346 So I went on and picked up the girls some skirts, I said, well, you don't wear these skirts because they're for September.

C347   Mm-hmm.

M348   And one lady was by the house and she
       was admiring a couple of the skirts,
       and I said well, I got those from St.
       Vincent DePaul's.

C349   And, she lets you know so you can get   Reflection—not a question.
       a good selection?

M350   That's right.

C351   That's fine.

M352   And you should see some of Edna's,
       the skirts I've gotten right downtown
       at those places.

C353   So, you're preparing for school al-
       ready?

M354   That's right.

C355   Then, you're all set?

M356   That's right.

C357   Mm-hmm.

M358   Because, you see, since I can't buy, go
       downtown and pay three dollars for
       Angie a skirt, two dollars for Edna a
       skirt, two dollars for a blouse, two
       dollars for a blouse—I can't do it.

C359   You sure can't.

M360   That's what those places are for . . .

C361   Mm-hmm, I know it.   Poor response.

M362   And rich people send those clothes
       down there . . .

C363   Oh, I know some of them are better,   Also judgmental.
       just beautiful.

M364   They certainly are.

C365   Mm-hmm.

M366   That's what those places are for.

C367   She had a beautiful dress on the other
       day when she took her test.

M368   A yellow dress, yes.

C369   Oh, I just loved that . . .

M370   You know, uh . . .

C371   Yellow embroidery.

M372   Yeah, uh, now, uh, a lady gave that
       to my sister . . .

C373   Really?

M374   About two years ago. Angie has worn
       the dress and now Edna's wearing it.

C375   Oh, it's darling.

At the time I thought this talk about Edna's clothes was helping to relax the mother, but now I feel it served no useful purpose. She got off the track.

M376   Isn't that a pretty dress?
C377   It looked like it was a new dress. Isn't it?
M378   Uh-uh, I've washed and ironed that dress so many times.
C379   She looked so nice.
M380   Mm-hmm. Yeah, that's right.
C381   Well, you've got your plans all set.

Here I tried to structure and to lead her back to the subject.

M382   That's right. But you know what, Miss Simms, now I would like to have, uh, is it possible that Angie could be tested before you close? Next week is the last week here, isn't it?
C383   Well, I didn't have Angie, but you could, uh, talk to Mrs. Walton about whoever her counselor is. See, I only know about the ones that I have.

Angie had previously been assigned to another counselor.

M384   I see.
C385   So I didn't have her.
M386   That's right.
C387   But it's possible.
M388   Because I . . .
C389   You can find out.
M390   I would like to have her tested because like I was talking to the . . .
C391   Mm-hmm.
M392   Summer school teacher. I told him that . . .
C393   Mm-hmm.
M394   That, where Edna was coming down here . . .
C395   Mm-hmm.
M396   And I said I wanted Angie to take the right curriculum.
C397   Mm-hmm. Yes.
M398   So she won't take the wrong curriculum.

C399   No, and then be sorry afterwards.

M400   And then be sorry afterwards, see?

C401   Mm-hmm.

M402   So, I'll talk to Mrs. uh, Walton . . .

C403   Walton.

M404   About it. Mm-hmm, mm-hmm.

C405   You can do that.

M406   Mm-hmm.

C407   See if it can be arranged. She makes all the appointments . . .

M408   I see, uh-huh.

C409   And I don't have anything to do with that.

M410   Now, Edna will come back Monday, won't she?

C411   Yes, Edna will come Monday.

M412   But, I'll tell her that I was here and that you said you're going to discuss with her . . .

C413   That I would like to talk with her further.

M414   Yes.

C415   Because we try to, uh, after all, she's a person and . . .

M416   Mm-hmm.

C417   She's getting to be a big girl and we feel that, I mean I think you would . . .   I was very awkward here but I was fearful of hurting the mother's feelings.

M418   Yeah, that's right.

C419   Would agree, it's, uh, it's just that after all, she's the one who did the work on the test . . .

M420   Mm-hmm.

C421   So I would kind of like to explain that to her.

M422   Mm-hmm. So I think she should see you, 'cause I don't know how, I might get excited, or emotional.   Here she accepts the idea fully.

C423   Well, and then you might, you might show this.

M424   That's the truth.

C425   We all get excited.

M426   Mm-hmm.

C427 Sometimes children, uh, take so much from our expression that we don't know . . .

M428 Mm-hmm.

C429 And, uh . . .

M430 Yeah, cause like I told her the other day when she came home, so I said, "Edna, now, how long are you going to be home this time?" She said, "Oh, about, I want to stay." So I said, "I wish you would go back and stay with your father a week or two because I'm trying to get something to do and," uh, I said, "Your grand-

M431 mother's not here." My mother came home, it must have been Monday.

C432 Mm-hmm.

M433 And, uh, I said, uh, "It would give me a little break."

C434 Yes.

M435 I said, "You're getting along all right there aren't you?" She said, "Yes." She helps out with the baby. And uh, so she went back Monday . . .

C436 Mm-hmm.

M437 She went, came here, and then she went.

C438 Yeah. She brought the little boy with her.

M439 Yeah, Larry.

C440 Mm-hmm. Yes, he was so good.

M441 He's a nice . . .

C442 He's a lovely child.   This is the father's little son by the second wife.

M443 He certainly is.

C444 You bet.

M445 He always leave me a note whenever he spends the week or something or the weekend.

C446 I could see what you meant because Edna is so good with him. He just . . .

M447 Mm-hmm.

C448 Loved her. I could see it.

M449 You can see it can't you?

C450 I can.

M451 Uh-huh.

C452 She really knows what to do.

M453 Work with children. She certainly does. So, uh, she said, "Well, all right." She said, "I'll be back Sunday 'cause I got to go, uh, you know, I've got to go back down to the clinic."

C454 Mm-hmm.

M455 So, uh, I was saying now, if I could just, my mother could just stay with somebody else for about six months or a year it would mean so much, you know.

C456 Because she would just give you a little relief for awhile.

M457 That, that's the truth. Miss Simms, you don't know what it would do for me.

Here is the heart of the mother's problem.

C458 Mm-hmm.

M459 Because I know what it did just that one week she was gone, all last week, you know?

C460 Mm-hmm.

M461 And, uh, Angie told my mother, she said, uh, her grandmother said, "Angie why did you leave those pots?" And she said, "Well, Grandmother, I didn't leave the pots," she said, "Mother emptied the pots out last night before she went to bed and I had already washed the things and gone to bed." You can't reason with her sometime. She said, but she has left them.

C462 She just picks at little things.

M463 Yeah, they're just little things, they're minor, you know.

C464 Mm-hmm.

M465 So I said, "Mama," I said, uh, "Angie told you I was the one that emptied out the pots." So she said, "Well, I'm not going to wash any pots, and so and so and so." I said, "Aw, blah," to myself, you know.

C466   Mm-hmm.

M467   I can't let her get me excited no more because I've got to, uh, get those kids, keep these kids . . .

She has begun to have insight into what things irritate her.

C468   You've got to just keep your . . .

M469   That's the truth.

C470   Temper.

M471   Mm-hmm.

C472   And do what you think is best.

M473   That's right. That's absolutely the truth. I'm so glad, and see, right, unconsciously, Miss Simms, I fight all the time to keep her and Edna separated.

C474   Yeah.

M475   Because she's just too hard on that kid.

C476   And this is a strain on you, too.

M477   Yes, it is. It's, it's an awful strain on me, see.

C478   Mm-hmm.

M479   And, and I said to myself, "Yes, I'll let Edna go back there because, uh, Mother's home, you see, and I know the least little thing Edna does is going to get on her nerves. That's going to upset Edna." And, so, uh, Miss Willard told me, Miss Willard is on her vacation, that's Angie's social worker from the Circle, and so, she said as soon as she gets back she's going to come to the house about my mother. I said, "Well I want you to," I said . . .

C480   Mm-hmm.

M481   "Because the children are getting ready to go back to school . . ."

C482   Mm-hmm.

M483   "And I don't want them to have, no, no problems." I said, "Now I've worked hard all summer trying to get these children straightened out," see . . .

C484   Mm-hmm.

M485   And, uh, . . .

C486   You don't want it spoiled.

M487   I, no Ma'am, I don't. So, I'm, uh, when I called her, I think she'll be back on about the 23rd or 4th, I said, "Now, Miss Willard, please send somebody out here to talk to her."

C488   Mm-hmm.

M489   Cause I don't want her tearing out what the clinic has done . . .

C490   Mm-hmm.

M491   And what she's trying to do for Angie, and what you and the clinic has done for Edna.

C492   Mm-hmm.

M493   I don't want that torn down, I just won't have it. I just won't. So, uh, she, uh, she don't mean no harm, but then she doesn't mean well either, 'cause she doesn't know how to agree with you, and you can't even reason with her.

C494   She acts any way she happens to feel, huh?

M495   That's right. Uh-huh, and like Angie said, "Mother," she said, I said, "Angie," I said, "why don't you have some of your girlfriends come over." Uh, she said, "Well, Grandmother, the other day," she said, "the day that you went by Aunt Pat's," my sister was sick one day, and she had me iron for her so she gave me a little tip. So she said, "Mama," she said, "Rita came by and," uh, she said, "I told Rita to watch TV and I'd first get my work done, and that way Rita wouldn't have to talk to me and I could get through quicker." She told the girl, "Angie can't have no company, I guess you better go home." She said, "Mama, the girl wasn't doing anything." Now, those things irk me, see.

C496   Mm-hmm.

M497   Now, here Angie has mapped out the situation. She'll go in the kitchen, scrub her floor, her girlfriend watch TV. Nothing was wrong with that. Angie's doing her work, she's not being occupied trying to entertain her company.

C498   It's just she embarrasses her.

M499   Yeah, see. And, see, I said, "Well, Angie, well, I'm glad you told," I said. "Well, please tell all that to Miss Willard," I said, " 'cause Miss Willard is going to have somebody come out here and talk to her."

C500   Mm-hmm.

M501   And I'm going to have them to come by the house and talk to her every week or every two weeks. I mean that, Miss Simms. I'm not going to have this, all this torn down, I mean it. Now I wish there was some kind of way I could come and let you know just how she's bothering. 'Cause it would help keep me from being all excited . . .

C502   I wish you could.

M503   Because even with me coming here, it has helped me.

She realizes that looking at her problem has made it more bearable.

C504   Mm-hmm.

M505   I don't let things sort of get next to me like I did before I started coming . . .

C506   No, 'cause you can look at it . . .

M507   That's right.

C508   You can look at it a little bit more calmly.

M509   I most certainly can. That's the truth from heaven.

C510   Mm-hmm.

M511   That's the truth. So, uh, I just wish it was so I could come 'cause . . .

C512   This clinic does go on this fall, you see.

M513   Does it?

C514   Yes, of course I won't be here, but . . .

M515   Mm-hmm.

C516   There will be somebody.

M517   Well, I wish you'd let me, I, I certainly will come back . . .

C518   Mm-hmm.

M519   And I'll let you know before I come.

C520   You could let Mr. Pap know because I think they're going to, I know they're going to have a clinic. They told us . . .

M521   Mm-hmm.

C522   That they would.

M523   Well, I would appreciate coming here.

C524   And he would know how to get you in charge.

M525   Well, I can sure, I mean to say, it has helped me and I can see my children, what it is doing to my children, see?

C526   Mm-hmm.

M527   Because I've seen the time I'd flare up in a minute. My mother would excite the children. Now, I say, "Aw, shucks that ain't nothing." I've been sorta halfway getting so I can let it . . .

C528   You can sort of stand off and look at yourself as though you were . . .

M529   Yeah.

C530   Somebody else now.

M531   That's right.

C532   And it doesn't really bother you.

M533   And I don't want to just not come, I want to keep on coming in here because I need somebody, too. To sort of . . .

C534   You need . . .

M535   Understand what I'm going through with. I need somebody to lean on and, because I feel like I've got enough, too much on me to withstand anyway. See?

C536   You're alone with two girls.   Supportive.

M537   That's right.

C538   And it's pretty hard on you.

M539   That's right. It certainly is. So I will, uh . . .

C540   If you can just have somebody to help you think about your problems you can look at it a little better.

M541   That's right, mm-hmm. That's right. And I'll ask Mrs. Willard to have someone to talk to my mother about twice a month.

C542   Mm-hmm.

C543   Did she . . .

M544   Because I want to keep her conscious of, that she's got to watch herself.

C545   Yeah.

M546   I do, I want that, see?

C547   You're all trying and she has to help.

M548   That's right she certainly does, see. Because if she's not made conscious of what she is doing until some one of the other kids take her, she's still there doing damage. And she could be doing it consciously, she could be doing it unconsciously. But if she's made conscious of it then she'll keep herself . . .

C549   She'll try harder.

M550   Mm-hmm.

C551   Yeah. Did she come back to stay or did she go back to your sister?

M552   Uh, no, she came back to stay, uh, let's say, Monday.

C553   Mm-hmm. She didn't stay away very long.

M554   No, barely a week. See? And so, was it last night, or was that yesterday evening, er, uh, just all out of the clear blue sky I said, "Now she won't let Angie reason with her at all, see. She won't let Angie reason with her at all."

C555   Mm-hmm.

M556   So that my best bet is just like I've been coming here, Miss Simms, and Edna's been coming here, and Angie's

been going to see Mrs. Willard. I'm
going to ask them to send somebody
to talk to her.

C557 Mm-hmm.

M558 And all of us will have to try to improve and face our problems, she has
to face hers, too. 'Cause it don't make
sense that your social workers and
teachers are trying to help us and then
she goes scot-free, not made conscious
of what she's doing.

C559 Mm-hmm.

M560 I don't think it's right. I don't.

C561 Well, she's got to help too. Because
it's not one sided.

M562 That's right.

C563 If she could just, uh, live away a little
longer . . .

M564 Yeah. Mm-hmm.

C565 It would help.

M566 So since, until she can live away a little
longer I want somebody to talk to her
every two weeks. I'm going to request
that.

C567 Mm-hmm.

M568 I'll either do that or blow my top, or
walk off from them girls. I just can't
take it any more.

C569 You've withstood all you can stand.   Supportive.

M570 That's right. Right now I wouldn't
even, I wouldn't even try to take a
test or anything right now because I
couldn't pass it. You know what, Miss
Simms, I went downtown the other
day. My girlfriend said Ruby, go, go
down to the employment agency and
take one of those, uh, take one of
those tests. Do you know I passed the
first part of the test, it was like from
A to about L or M . . .

C571 Mm-hmm.

M572 Do you know I flunked on the other
part? You know, the lady looked at
me, she said, "I want you to come

         back when you're not so busy."

C573   Probably upset.

M574   The lady could look at me, I guess.

C575   Sure.

M576   She said, "I want you to come back when you're not so busy." Now isn't that something?

C577   She wants to give you another chance. It is.

M578   Isn't that something. So something said, "Now, get yourself together then you go back."

C579   Go back.

M580   Now, isn't that something? She could look at me and tell. She said, "Now I want you to come back and take the test over when you're not so busy."

C581   Mm-hmm. The way you feel inwardly has a great effect on a test.

M582   That's right, mm-hmm.

C583   You can't do as well as you could.

M584   Now, last week I probably could have passed cause she wasn't home . . .

C585   Mm-hmm.

M586   And, er, uh, no one was at the house every day but Edna and I, Angie was at school, see.

C587   Mm-hmm.

M588   And I could have passed it.

C589   You were calmer then.

M590   That's right. I could have passed that test. So that's what I'm going to ask. I'm going to really request that, er, uh, somebody come out and talk to her every two weeks.

C591   And, maybe if she goes away again for a little time you could go down and try again . . .

M592   I think so too.

C593   While you're all relaxed.

M594   Mm-hmm. So I don't know which one of the other kids will take her for awhile. They're so selfish, most of the kids, excepting me. She's just fallen on me and my younger brother.

C595   Did she get along pretty good in this   Probing.
       place where she was for a week?

M596   Yes, 'cause my sister works at the
       hospital so, and, uh, she lives with
       her daughter and two children, but
       her two children, they were away on
       vacation. So during the day she was
       alone.

C597   Mm-hmm.

M598   See, and then my sister would get
       home, I guess about, uh, 7:00 in the
       evening from the hospital, see.

C599   Mm-hmm.

M600   But she got along all right, see.

C601   Mm-hmm.

M602   But the place is small. It's too bad
       that she can't live with her for awhile.

C603   Mm-hmm.

M604   Or somebody else in the family, see.
       So now, this particular sister, that,
       said she's going to get a bigger place.
       Her husband's job failed on him so
       they've taken a managing job in an
       apartment.

C605   So they wouldn't be able to keep her
       now.

M606   Sure won't. That's why I just told you
       I'm going to ask that they send some-
       body out to talk to her every two
       months.

C607   Mm-hmm. So it looks like you've got
       her again, huh?

M608   Mm-hmm. And, really, I'm, I'm going
       to ask that, because I can't, I can't
       see something building up to help
       children and then it being torn down.

C609   You've gone so far now, you've made
       such an effort . . .

M610   That's right.

C611   That you don't want it spoiled.

M612   No, and I'm not going to have it
       spoiled, either. I'm going to ask that.

C613   You're their mother, after all, and
       you're . . .

M614   Mm-hmm.

C615   The one that's going to have to do it.
M616   Mm-hmm. So, either if Miss Willard's
        hands will be tied towards that, then
        I'll have to ask, tell my social worker
        she'll just have to have somebody come
        up there and talk to her.
C617   Mm-hmm.
M618   I'll say, "Either you do that or I'll,
        these kids can, the ADC can take my
        children because . . ."
        [The rest of the tape is not clear.]

Case Summary and Counselor's Comments

General Case Summary

Edna was referred to the clinic by her high school counselor after he
conferred with her mother regarding Edna's poor attitude and poor
marks. The girl herself perceived no reason for coming except that her
mother wished her to come and had arranged the first appointment.

The first interviews were strained, unfruitful experiences for both
Edna and myself, but, even so, she did relate their family situation with
four females in the same household; grandmother, mother, sister (Angie),
and Edna, the counselee.

She describes the friction and tension between them, portraying the
grandmother as her "arch enemy," as the mother later related, and her
sister, Angie, as a favored child. She told of her father's remarriage and
new family, and of how she once liked to visit there, until recently, when
he always quarreled with her own mother. The essence of her complaints,
though, seemed to be her grandmother who hits her and abuses her
whenever the mother is out of sight.

Edna is not able to verbalize easily and did not fully perceive what the
possibilities of an accepting atmosphere in the counseling situation might
do for her. However, she did finally release much hostility in the subsequent interviews and seemed to have become less of a problem at home
at the summer's end.

Although the case was that of "Edna," it was her mother who really
derived much of the benefit, because she learned to look critically at
their aggravating home situation, to think through possible solutions,
and finally, to take actual steps to have the grandmother live, at least
for a time, with one of her other grown children, so that she could
provide a more favorable home atmosphere for her own two adolescent
daughters.

Another result of the sessions was that the mother began to accept

Edna's academic limitations and was even willing to have her put in a special class for slower learners. At the last session she said both girls were more amenable and that they had had the first peace she had experienced since she and her husband had lived apart. She regarded the clinic as a distinct help and source of guidance and expressed the wish for the girls to continue treatment in the fall.

Edna was given the *California Mental Maturity Test, '57 Short Form, Jr. High Level* at the clinic. Results:

Language Data	Score 12
Non Language Data	Score 15
C.A.	151
M.A.	112
I.Q.	74 = 5th percentile.
Grade Placement	4.1

Counselor's Comments

In this case, the original purpose of the interviews with Edna was to try to evaluate the girl's potentialities. By so doing her mother said she hoped her behavior both at home and at school would be improved. She also felt that perhaps special instruction was indicated. But the end result of the sessions proved more far reaching, and the case resolved itself into two distinct sets of problems. Edna's were the conflict with her grandmother, her jealousy of her sister (although I feel this was minimal and quite a natural state), the lack of, and longing for a father who was never present (he was preoccupied with a second family), and her poor school work, about which she herself had little or no insight. She thought "school was for the bright kids," and didn't understand that while her academic ability was below average she dreamed of reaching the heights (i.e. becoming a doctor).

While trying to get into the girl's frame of reference, I was also counseling the mother, and it was this experience which shed the real light on part of the reason for Edna's behavior. The mother faced the difficulty of having three generations (all female) in one small apartment and Edna's increasingly poor school work and behavior at school and at home. She also faced the conflict between her own mother and her daughter, Edna, which she believed was brought on because her aged mother was not only jealous of the attention she herself paid to Edna, but took out on Edna by physical cruelty what she disliked in Edna's mother. This distraught woman was beset by her own financial insecurity and the responsibility of raising two adolescent girls alone, caused by her broken marriage. She was further troubled by her feeling that Edna wasn't "just right" because she had an inordinate interest in dolls (M78 through M94, Reel 1, Mother), and finally, by Angie's recent illness which she viewed as strangely reminiscent of her own youthful ailment. She feared she herself had transmitted the idea of the illness to Angie by suggestion and by her own attitudes. Underneath all these other troubles was her feeling that Edna might be retarded and should have special help.

This mother came to the first interview intent upon someone "telling her what to do." The idea that she might take actual steps on her own had apparently not occurred to her. She had been talking with Angie's counselor from the Church Youth Service and the case worker had inferred that she would advise her what to do. The mother thus came to the clinic with the hope that we, too, would help her solve her problems.

The tone of the first interview with the mother was one of worry and discouragement. She defined the problem of Edna as one that had grown worse because of the home problem with the grandmother. By the time of this interview I had seen Edna three times and this session helped to shed much light on the case.

As is typical of early adolescents, Edna seemed to have a barrier between her and most adult figures and I had not felt that we had gone very deeply into her background. Although the conflict with the grandmother showed up in the very first interview I wasn't sure the problem was acute. In fact, one of the observers at the laboratory felt that the whole interview was shallow. But it seemed to me that if she was telling the truth about home conditions the deeper material would come out later. I feel that it would have if I could have seen Edna over a longer period of time. Proof of this was in the fourth interview, which was a test situation nearly always producing tension in people, when Edna was more relaxed and talkative than usual. This held over into the fifth interpretive interview when she volunteered that she intended to study harder next year.

The mother's interviews were so inextricably interwoven with Edna's that they scarcely need to be separated in analysis. Of course, they were on completely different levels, and the motivation of the mother led to deeper thinking on her part while Edna came to the laboratory *because her mother had requested it*. The girl never fully perceived the possibilities in a permissive counseling session, while the mother soon grasped the concept of the worthwhile individual who is able to look at himself and his problems, and can take steps to change a given situation. The mother's first interview was a plea for help, against the backdrop of Edna. The second was a frank discussion of her own troubles and showed definite movement wherein she had even made arrangements to *change* a situation which had seemed unalterable. In the third she viewed the clinic as, "A father to my children and a counselor to me." Having taken action, she felt the tension was relieved enough to be able to recount the gains: i.e., she hasn't had to whip anybody; Edna's handwriting has improved; she is ready to accept the idea that Edna may need Special Education.

The fourth interview was a sort of summary on her part of the gains and losses she had made. It was an emotional session, but she seemed to be more ready to proceed with her intention to live alone, in spite of the setbacks which have plagued her. She felt her own mother needed counseling and stated she was no longer willing to have the grandmother constantly with them. Indeed, she seemed more master of the situation, and had moved away entirely from the idea of *asking* for help.

Counselor's Self Evaluation

An attempt to evaluate myself honestly exposes many weaknesses and, I sincerely hope, a few strengths. As I read and reread the typescripts I am dismayed at my frequent, inept replies. Often, I was on the verge of hearing important material when I cut in, usually because the silence became unbearable. This fault was particularly present in the early interviews with the adolescent girl who did not perceive the possibilities of the counseling relationship and, of course, in the first interview with the mother. The first two sessions were quite frightening for both of us for very different reasons: for me, because I had thought we were to use only the client-centered approach and I was not completely comfortable with it just then; for Edna, because she was frightened at the whole situation and was naturally reticent besides. It seemed to me that I tried to be too client-centered in the first interview and that I was superconscious of the observers, to the extent that I could hardly be myself enough to hear what she did say. Then, in the next session, I was too much the other way, asking far too many questions which disturbed and discouraged her, so that she felt she must come up with *something*. I think the change in my approach confused her.

In the case of the mother, I was able to enter her frame of reference more easily, as I am a mother and I sensed her worried state at once. She readily accepted my explanation of the way we work and understood what was possible, so that she very quickly forgot the uniqueness of the situation and became engrossed in a recitation of her problems.

Often, my reflections were quite ungrammatical and incomplete. The first was due partially to my nervousness and the latter because I was preoccupied with what the client was saying and lacked the technique to thoroughly reflect the material in spite of my preoccupation.

Another of my weaknesses is a tendency to sympathize instead of empathize, but I try to remember that sympathy tends to minimize the feeling of the client and defeats the very purpose of the counselor.

It seems to me that I was able to establish early rapport with Edna's mother so that she felt comfortable and sustained during the times she was defining and thinking through her problems. When she first came to the clinic I had wondered if I could explain the self-determination concept convincingly enough so that, in time, she would be able to embrace it. I thought if I could only see her over a long enough period I might be able to help her to feel more adequate in her present situation. I understood her dilemma and tried very hard to enter her frame of reference. A client knows, instinctively, when a counselor is sincerely interested and not merely patronizing. It is an elusive thing—but very real. Personal counseling is an area in which I feel I can do my best work and I am trying to grow with each individual counselee. I like to work with people and find it easy to relate to most individuals.

Finally, I feel that I did bring Edna to some realization that her aspirations may be somewhat higher than her ability, and yet I am sure of one thing: the counselor's perceptions are often very different from the client's, and for me to be very positive about any beneficial impact which these sessions had upon Edna would be presumptuous, indeed. I feel fairly certain, however, that much movement on the part of the mother took place. I believe I provided the atmosphere in which she was able to look hard at her circumstances and to decide upon action which would actually alter those circumstances. In this manner I sincerely hope that home conditions will be made more beneficial for both Edna and Angie. If their mother is free to bring them up as she sees fit, then many of the tensions which may have aggravated Edna's problem will be removed.

If the mother followed her intention to have further testing for Edna and perhaps some type of Special Education also, then more permanent benefit will result, and it is my hope that the clinic visits motivated her to that end.

Case Reviews

Buford Stefflre

In reacting to this case I would like to discuss four matters which seem of special relevance to me. These are (1) the counselor's attitude toward testing, (2) her use of pauses, especially during the first interview, (3) her building and burning of two straw men in her analysis of the case, and (4) the matter of social class as related to counseling effectiveness.

This counselor seems to believe that tests may only be used properly when the client selects the specific instrument to be given. I suppose this attitude is somehow related to a feeling that testing itself is not quite right. Any possibility of being authoritarian is allegedly avoided if the child makes the ultimate test selection. How a dull twelve year old child is in a position to decide whether the *California Test of Mental Maturity, Short Form,* or the *Verbal* section of the *Differential Aptitude Test,* or *Raven's Progressive Matrices,* or some other test is the most useful one, I cannot conceive. In this particular case the counselor has a second difficulty in that she also feels constrained to permit the client's mother to make the test selection. By what legerdemain she was able to have both the mother and the child, neither of whom presumably knew anything about psychometrics, select precisely the same test, we are not told. Certainly this ritualistic maneuver does nothing to indicate that she has a clear conception as to the purpose of testing. It would seem to me reasonable that the client and/or the client's mother, might well be involved in deciding what purpose a test was to serve, but their involvement in the selection of a specific instrument seems to me to be nonsensical.

Furthermore, when the time comes for test interpretation the counselor is neither very clear nor very helpful. She indicates that the score is "low" but what this means to either the child or the mother is difficult to say. Inasmuch as one of the reasons for giving the test was to make some judgment as to whether the child would be placed in a special education class for retarded children, it would have been more meaningful to interpret the test in those terms. I think the counselor would have been justified in saying that this group test indicates that the child was somewhere on the borderline between those who attend special classes and those who are in regular classes. She might have gone on to say that results of the individual test which would help make the final determination might vary a good deal from the group test. (I confess that I do not know the meaning of the designations C and E that the counselor used in talking about the child's previous tests.) I think the low score which the child made must have bothered the counselor considerably more than it did either the child or the mother. In the fourth interview with the mother, (at C114 and C173) the counselor seems to somehow be wishing away the results. At C114 she seems to imply that if the girl would just work harder somehow this disability would disappear. C173 in the fourth interview also suggests that conditions like Edna's are very often remediable. I get the impression that the counselor is not ready to accept the fact that this girl is academically slow. In summary, it seems to me that her treatment of testing was unduly stylized and that her test interpretation is not a meaningful nor realistic one.

A second matter that merits discussion is the many long pauses in the first interview. The counselor seems to be permitting these pauses in the name of "client-centered" technique. It might be interesting to her to read what Bordin has to say about the pause as a creator of ambiguity and its consequent building of anxiety in the client. Does the counselor really want to raise the anxiety level of the child by this device or is she permitting these long pauses simply because she has "learned" that the client must take direction of the interview? In the first interview (at S117) Edna indicates that she feels that she has not done a very good job of filling the time. I would think that the counselor might want to consider the meaning of a pause and recognize that in different contexts it may have different meanings. In some cases certainly it may permit the child to consider and restructure his thoughts, in other cases it may provide such an ambiguous stimulus that the child becomes very anxious, in other cases it may be a way of protecting the counselor from revealing herself to the child, in still other cases it may be a technique by which the counselor punishes the child for being a poor client.

The third element that I want to discuss is the building of two straw men and their subsequent burning by the counselor. In her analysis of the case the counselor says that she felt that she "did bring Edna to some realization that her aspirations may be somewhat higher than her ability." This achievement would seem to be based on a single comment by the girl in the first interview. The counselor asks, (at C17) "What would you like to do?" The client answers, (at S18) "I'd like to be a doctor." This statement is followed by a long long pause, after which the counselor rejects this answer by saying (at C19), "So, you have gone to this school, and you've been somewhat disappointed with it."

I don't think it is Edna who is concerned about being a doctor, it is the counselor who is concerned that the child would give such an "inappropriate" answer. Certainly, C19 is a complete rejection of the girl's expressed desire to be a doctor. I think the rejection had little significance in the interviews, because I think Edna's statement that she wanted to be a doctor had little significance. To claim that as a result of counseling, Edna gave up such unrealistic aspirations is simply to say that it was never brought up again after such an abrupt rejection by the counselor. We really have no evidence as to what Edna would like to do with her life and I am not certain that it is important that we should have, in view of her age and circumstances.

The second straw man that the counselor builds is found in her analysis of the case where she says that she believes that as a result of counseling the mother "is ready to accept the idea that Edna may need special education." I find no evidence that the mother was ever resisting this idea. Inasmuch as the mother had some familiarity with the special education program and some realization that Edna was doing poor work in school, she probably did not have the fear of the labeling involved in special education that the counselor had. As a matter of fact, by her inadequate test interpretation, I think the counselor left Edna's mother with some ideas of special education that are less accurate than those which she started with. The notion that such students are very often helped to remedy their defects, and the notion that perhaps if Edna would just work harder these things would disappear, are not realistic ideas. It is also important that the mother would know that the test result which was characterized by the counselor as "low" was actually very marginal and based on a rather unreliable group test. It would have been more honest to indicate to the mother that this was a very borderline situation and that only the individual testing which would be done later would help in making a decision.

The matter of social class as an element in parent counseling seems to me to be especially important in this case. Research by Hollingshead and Redlich suggests that upper class and middle class clients are more apt to get psychiatric help than are lower class clients because of the availability of the service, and also because the psychiatrist is less able to relate to the lower class client. Perhaps the typical home which is receiving "Aid to Dependent Children," as this one is, has a level of sophistication regarding clinics, outpatient help, counselors, and social workers, such that it may be able to make good use of appropriate services. It may be that the school is the best agency to understand the matriarchal and impoverished home environment of Edna, and help Edna's mother deal with her problems. Certainly the opportunity that Edna's mother had to ventilate some of her feelings and to consider alternative actions was an excellent one. The counseling resembled the case work given by "Family Service Agencies," and if the school is now to play this role we need to make some delineation between those cases which are appropriate for "Family Service Agencies" and those cases which are most appropriately handled by the school counselor. Tentatively, we might say that when the home situation is one which is causing, or is related to school problems such as in the case of Edna, the case might best be handled by the school. When the family difficulties are deeper and relatively unrelated to school problems, then perhaps they should be handled by the "Family Service Agency."

In either event, if the schools move more and more into serving as quasi-therapeutic and quasi-case work agencies, the school counselor acts out a kind of "sibling rivalry" with the social worker, as in the case of this family. The school counselor makes several remarks to the effect that the social worker didn't really follow through on what she said she was going to do, and that the social worker had planned to behave in a very authoritative manner. In truth, we have little real information as to what the social worker planned and what the social worker really did. It would be interesting to talk with the social worker about her ideas as to the role of this counselor and what she did and did not do.

To summarize this case, I would say that the counselor needs to reconsider her use of testing and her use of pauses in her interviewing. It is possible that the counselor will want to revise her method of test selection and be more conscious of the meaning of a pause in a counseling interview. In appraising the case it is not necessary for her to claim credit for Edna's abandonment of the occupational goal of physician, nor the mother's acceptance of special education. On the face of it, it would appear that the mother, particularly, had obtained much benefit merely from being able to discuss her problems with an interested and accepting observer. Finally, I think this case presents us with an interesting problem regarding the relationship of social class to counseling in the school. It may very well be that in those schools which are knowledgeable about their specialized communities, the school counselor will be well equipped to do family counseling. If he is going to accept this job, then our counselor-educator needs to make sure that he has considerable knowledge of social class, so that he can understand the disorganized relationships common in a home like Edna's, and considerable skill in dealing with adults, so that he becomes neither patronizing nor unduly authoritative.

DUGALD ARBUCKLE

It would seem that Edna is a somewhat unwilling client, and shows up primarily because someone told her that she should go to the laboratory. Edna probably expects the usual school adult figure who dominates, who controls, and who directs, and she finds one. When counselors "try" to be client-centered it is always interesting to consider the primary cause of their difficulties. Is it the client or is it their clashing selves?

One cannot be very effective in trying to be what one is not, and this counselor's attitudes, as expressed by some of her comments, contradict somewhat what she sometimes says she is trying to do. The counselor is under pressure, and she is well aware of it, and Edna is not the "easiest" of clients, but one may wonder what would have happened if the counselor had been client-centered in a more philosophical rather than a technical sense. If, at the beginning, instead of soon making it clear that Edna's assumption that the domination and the control by the counselor was correct, the counselor indicated by her behavior that this was not so, what might have happened?

The counselor starts by going along with Edna, but she indicates her position to Edna when, in C17, she diverts her, then, getting no satisfactory reaction, she directs her back again in C19. The counselor could have gone along with Edna in these first few comments with little difficulty, but here, almost right at the beginning, she deliberately directs, and so sets the stage for her increased difficulties later on.

In comments C35 to C41 the counselor diverts, attempts to encourage, probes, and questions. The many long pauses which are not noted in the typescript are invariably broken by the counselor, and by C47 the counselor has pretty well committed herself, and Edna, to her directing and controlling role. Edna's "Yes, Ma'am's" become even more passive.

In C49 the counselor is probably reassuring herself far more than Edna. In C51 and C53 the counselor is operating strictly from her own frame of reference. C53 is so counselor-centered that it does not even elicit a "yes, Ma'am"! C62 and C64 are also good examples of what might be considered by the counselor to be "reflections," but they are pretty much counselor-centered statements, reflecting the counselor's frame of reference.

By C94 the counselor has been trying this and that (eclecticism??), but Edna says, "No." She is leaving it up to the counselor. It is the counselor's business, not hers, and in a way, the counselor indicates that she agrees with this in her comment on C96. The reason she gives for probing might be rationally correct, but one must wonder—why did she want this information? What did she plan to do with it? If she feels, as a result of her probing, that the mother does resent the grandmother more, what will she now do that she might not have done if she didn't know?

One might at least surmise that possibly the major reason why the counselor could not get herself out of a dominating, directing role, was not so much because this was the role that Edna expected (which she probably did), but rather because this is the way the counselor really saw herself. If one believes that the counseling session belongs primarily to the counselor, its direction to be determined by him, then a few "You feel's" and "You think's" will have little effect on either client or counselor.

Thus at the end of this session I have a feeling of some remoteness from Edna, and feel, rather, a struggle going on within the counselor—a struggle which is a central characteristic of counselor education. It would almost seem that the counselor is trying to be what she *may want to be,* but her old self is still dominant, and it wins out in this session. In a way, the session is a good example of the looking at oneself that the student counselor must experience if he is ever to become effective. Edna challenges the weak new version of self, and the stronger, older version of the counselor easily takes over.

Edna—Sessions 2, 3, 4 and 5.   On the basis of these summaries, it would seem that Edna reacted positively to the totality of the counselor. It may be that she pressed the counselor less in these sessions, and the resultant relaxation of the counselor was conveyed to Edna, with beneficial results all around! Again, here, we may see an example of where the counselor is giving an honest try, she is willing to question and to challenge herself, and while she may make mistakes, the brief human relationship that Edna has with this counselor may be the most "Edna-centered" experience that this girl has ever had.

At this point I have not yet listened to or read about Mother. Did the counselor feel any clash here in her somewhat dual relationship with Edna and with her mother? Does this not tend to put the counselor in somewhat of a "referee" relationship *between* two people, rather than being *with* one of them?

Mother—Session 1.   In session 1 Mother sounds like a strong woman and a strong client. She and the counselor appear to relate well, and Mother soon gets going. The counselor's directing self shows itself periodically, particularly at the start, but Mother shoves it aside and continues.

The counselor makes several initial directive stabs, and by C19 and C21 it would almost seem that we have arrived at a "I'll tell you what to do" sort of situation, somewhat as with Edna. But Mother's "All right" in M22 is abrupt, and indicates that the client is not interested in C19 and C21, and she almost brings the counselor back with her. The counselor tries to take over again in C29, and this stops the client. There is a long pause after M30, and the counselor breaks it with her probing question. Soon, however, the client gets going again, and this pattern is repeated several times in this session.

C53 did not sound to me, nor, I think, to Mother, so much a question as a reflection of the client's expressed feelings. The counselor's reaction to C57 indicates where the counselor stands. The comment, ". . . I wanted her to concentrate on her story . . ." indicates fairly clearly that the counselor does not yet trust the client, but she must show her the correct path. Mother, however, is not to be diverted so easily. Throughout this session it almost sounds as if the counselor every now and then is saying, "But don't you think I should tell you where to go and how to do what you're doing . . ." and the client replies, "Now, you're a nice person, and just stay with me, but keep out of the way, and I'll find my own answers. . . ." In C77, for example, it sounds as if the counselor is saying, "You should realize that," but Mother dismisses this easily, then in C79 the counselor makes another, "But after all I'm here too you know" sort of statement, which Mother also dismisses in a pleasant fashion. C83 and C87 are also wonderful examples of counselor responses which would appear to have no other purpose than to bolster the sagging ego of the counselor.

In C105 the counselor reacts to the content of M104, and implies that she will do what is asked in M104. I have a feeling at the end of this session that it was a good one for both Mother and counselor. Possibly both were affected and modified.

Mother—Session 2. The client talks easily in this session, with one or two minor blocks by the counselor, until M27. At this point the counselor gets entangled in an attempt to explain what goes on. It would seem that a very simple answer would have originally sufficed, but the counselor, rather than the client, appears to press the issue. In many client comments there was an expression of uneasiness which was ignored by the counselor as she pressed on with her explanation. In C56 the counselor mentions the fact that tests are available, and thus almost encourages Mother to think of test data as something extrinsic to be used by her to help Edna.

In wondering about the comment after C80 we might ask the counselor why she felt she had to ask this. Was this for Edna, Mother, or counselor? In C126, unless my ears betray me, the counselor says, "All rightie," not, "All right." This is, without doubt, pure bias on my part, but I do wish mature lady counselors would not use this giggling Gertie term!

Mother—Session 3. Mother's statement about the clinic experience being, "like a father to me and my children" probably indicates the basic reason for any good that may come out of this experience. Mother has come in contact with a few people who have a sincere interest in her as a person, people who have some degree of compassion and interest, people who are willing, to some extent, to listen. In this sort of relationship Mother can look at herself and her problems, and ponder over what she might do. This is what she is doing with this counselor.

I have the feeling here that the testing is a hindrance to the development of this positive relationship, but apparently both Mother and counselor are able to move despite this difficulty.

Mother—Session 4. This session starts off in a very awkward way, with the counselor sounding defensive in her explanations to Mother about the problem of Mother, and Edna and the tests. Couldn't this situation have been avoided? Didn't the counselor feel any clash here between her relationship with Edna and her relationship with Mother? The counselor sounds uneasy as she continues to talk about the tests. She overtly is trying to reassure Mother, saying to her, "Don't worry," but she sounds somewhat worried herself. As the counselor continues with comments such as those between C114 and C180, she would appear to be trying to convince herself rather than Mother regarding just what the test data means about Edna. The counselor here sounds somewhat like a worried teacher, and the odd times we hear Mother she sounds quite satisfied and acceptant of the whole thing. It almost sounds as if the counselor is saying, "Maybe you think you're not concerned about this, but I know that you must be. . . ." Finally, around C189, the counselor has reassured herself enough so that she can let Mother go, and Mother gets moving. The counselor rises up again defensively in C216, but subsides quickly. Every now and then the counselor throws in the odd bit of reassurance (C273), but on the whole she stays out of the way for a while and Mother keeps rolling until C329. Here the counselor interjects a personal note, diverts the client, and then, in C381, tries to get her back again. Mother obliges, and keeps going despite one or two mild interruptions, until the end of the session.

This is a good example of a session where the strength of the client shows through. The counselor appeared disturbed and somewhat defensive about material that she herself brought into the session, but as soon as she had settled down, Mother took over. The total basic gestalt of the counselor must have been viewed in a positive way by the client, so that she could move ahead with the counselor, despite the irritants and blocks that were presented.

I have a very deep feeling here of Mother being a very strong woman. She needed less of the counseling than Edna did, and at times the difficulty seems to be that the counselor was unable to be acceptant of the strength of this woman. In the *General Case Summary,* when the counselor says that Mother "was even willing . . ." my feeling was that she was not only willing, but quite able all the time, only the counselor found it hard to believe that this woman really had this strength.

The relationship between client and counselor is not just a relationship between the weak (the client) and the strong (the counselor). People have many different strengths, and these sessions may be a good example of strengths of the counselor affecting the client. In the *Counselor's Self Evaluation,* the counselor takes a perceptive look at herself. She sounds as if she has the basic stuff, and maybe when and if she reads these words, she will have arrived at the point where she doesn't have to tell herself any more that she *must* be client-centered because she *is!*

EDWARD ROEBER

The plot begins with an abortive attempt to counsel Edna. Her counselor made a statement, "It is doubtful if she (Edna) had a well defined purpose in coming." That is perhaps the understatement to end all understatements. As a result of Edna's forced participation, the first contact presents an interesting picture of passive resistance. In C49 the counselor attempts to structure a possible outcome from counseling, hoping that it would overcome obvious resistance expressed in S36 to S48. But, unfortunately, a few responses, C51 (about grandmother), C70 (about mother), and C90 (about father), negate any structuring speech, and must have caused Edna to wonder whose side the counselor is truly on. After the inauspicious beginning, the tempo seems to increase, if we can take the counselor's notes for subsequent contacts at face value. Unfortunately, again, it is impossible to assess a counselor's "success" from his interview notes. (A lack of dates for mother and daughter contacts tend to compound confusion for the reader.) We must assume that interviews with the mother have probably been more productive than any with Edna who "played the game" but with faint heart.

In one manner or another, Edna's mother has located and used many resources in an urban community. Edna, an innocent pawn in the maneuvers of adults who are significant in her life, cannot be held accountable for all her misfortunes. At home, she has been buffeted by three generations of women, a divorce having removed her father from daily influence—although in many ways he still exerts pressure. It is not easily ascertained from the typescript whether the absence of her father from the home is a tragedy or something in Edna's favor. Her mother uses her wits to keep the family at a subsistence level. Between meeting the needs of her children and tolerating a domineering mother, Edna's mother has been caught in a maelstrom of cross currents, unable to reconcile hostilities easily aroused in herself, her mother, her daughters, her brothers and sisters, and her former husband. It is quite understandable that she would seek assistance for Edna—after all, Edna's performance at home and in school is obviously disruptive, and Edna is least able to protect herself. A rejected, irritable grandmother displaces her aggressions upon Edna, the weakest member of the clan. A more talented, older sister has probably used Edna as a foil in fending off grandmother, although the sister is beginning to come to Edna's rescue with increasing frequency. An irritable father, unable to keep steady employment, still has influence upon the girls. To add to Edna's woes, she has been unable to progress steadily in school, probably displacing hostilities aroused at home upon her peers, teachers, and anyone who dares to thwart her.

Edna and her mother were referred to the clinic by some individual at a central office of the board of education. It is a matter of conjecture whether the referral was for testing and/or counseling, or whether it was a way of escaping the persistent inquiries of an "eager" mother. In any case, Mother perceived the clinic as a place where her daughter would be "analyzed" and where she might secure the "proper" prescription;

"proper" presumably referring to a test that would indicate Edna be placed in a special education class. To the counselor's credit, she did not immediately accede to this latter expectation and attempted to counsel Edna and her mother. But eventually a test was administered to Edna, and the case ended on the theme of "everyone living happily ever after." This capsule review of the case is not entirely fair to the counselor who faced difficult odds and, at times, seemed to be an understanding person.

Looking at the several interviews, I see several incidents which, in them, have a lesson for counselors. A few of these incidents are too critical to leave out of this critique.

1. Reading the first interview with Edna raises an important question regarding a counselor's communication of his role to a bewildered, resistant, nonintellectual counselee. The counselor in C49 attempted to give some structure to the contact, but the effort was awkward and Edna's perception of the clinic was not developed at all. The counselor, who is a mother according to her notes, displayed as little understanding as most parents about a child's feelings toward forced counseling. How can a counselor explain or demonstrate his role to another individual, especially to one that is a child? How much freedom of choice can adults tolerate? What if the counselor had asked Edna to explore the possibility of free choice and had been refused? Does a child have a right to such a choice? To compound Edna's confusion about the intent of the counselor, the latter began with, "Tell me something about yourself." This is the last straw. I am now soliciting charter members for the Society to Protect Children from Tell Me Something About Yourself.

2. The counselor, obviously from a middle-class background, made a noble effort in the first two contacts with the mother to show empathy, although there were occasions when her responses reflected sympathy. By the fourth interview, the discussion seemed reminiscent of an "over the back fence" conversation between two women. The degeneration of the contacts raises a question as to how a counselor from a middle-class background can maintain an empathic relationship with a counselee from another stratum of society. To what extent does knowledge about various social strata affect a counselor's performance in counseling individuals? Or, are there other ingredients essential to such empathy?

3. Feeling obligated to give Edna an intelligence test, the counselor permitted Edna's mother to help with the selection of a paper-pencil test. The counselor then "sold" the test idea to Edna. It seems questionable whether Edna or the mother was in a position to choose a test although they might well have something to say about the type of test, i.e., intelligence, achievement, interest, etc. It is, furthermore, of some concern to me that a paper-pencil test was used when obviously Mother, and others, were going to use the test results for some critical decisions upon learning about the test results, viz., Mother's immediate relief and plans

for action in the fourth interview. Why did the counselor avoid the administration of an individual intelligence test, one which might give a more accurate picture of Edna's potentialities? If Edna would be given an individual test later, why bother with a paper-pencil test in the clinic? Why chance distorted perceptions of Edna's level of ability, viz., the discrepancies among intelligence tests and the achievement test administered at Edna's school? If the two tests did not agree, would such a difference affect future perceptions of counseling? Or was the clinic's test used only as a "holding" device?

4.   In the fourth interview with Mother, the counselor blurted out the test results prior to any interpretation to Edna. There then followed an interesting series of responses, C4 to C52, a belated attempt to recognize that perhaps a child has a right to test interpretations prior to his parents. The "pledging to secrecy" ceremony was a travesty on honesty. If the counselor believed sincerely in the basic principle of some privacy for a child, why didn't she apologize to Edna and even the mother for her impulsive behavior. Or was it impulsive? Or, was it another manifestation of sympathy for mother?

Some of my remarks have been highly critical of the counselor's performance. I offer no apology because deficiencies in a counselor's repertoire can diminish his efficiency and jeopardize counseling outcomes. The first two interviews with Edna's mother contain noteworthy examples of acceptance, understanding and communication. On the other hand, their eventual effectiveness was jeopardized by "blind spots" in the counselor's repertoire.

SIGNIFICANT QUESTIONS FOR DISCUSSION

1. Should the counselor have attempted to counsel both Edna and her mother, or should a different counselor work with the mother?

2. Should a school counselor refer a case like this to the school social worker if one is available?

3. The counselor indicates in her comments regarding C49 in the first interview that she didn't do well when she attempted to structure her role. How might the counselor's role be structured to a child like Edna, who comes for counseling because her mother and counselor insist on it, and who, probably, has never had any adult attempt to help her in the way the school counselor hopes?

4. In the second interview with the mother the counselor was trying to explain what counseling was all about at the laboratory. Eventually the mother asked (M55), "Well, how does this help Edna, the fact that she isn't getting along in school?" Would you go along with the counselor's response? If not, what do you feel would have been more appropriate?

5. The cultural background of the client and the mother was quite different from that of the counselor. In what way may this have affected the counseling process?

6. If you had been the counselor in what ways might you have handled the mother and/or daughter differently?

7. If you had a chance to talk with the counselor, what would you have wanted to discuss with her after each interview?

8. Where do the reviewers agree and disagree in their review of *The Case of Edna?* What are your reactions to the reviews?

The Case of Richard

Purpose of the Interviews

Richard was referred by his junior high school counselor who sent a report of his scholastic and emotional adjustment. The counselor wrote the following as reasons for referral: "Extremely poor classroom behavior, citizenship rating D & E. Sometimes is very erratic in his actions. Does not respond to directions given by teacher. Seems to daydream a great deal, and reacts adversely to assigned tasks. Mother requests additional counseling help."

Background Data on the Student

Richard was a fourteen year old Negro boy in the eighth grade who had consistently scored two or three grades lower on standard group achievement tests and was currently doing failing work.

The counselor submitted the following data:

Detroit Group Mental Tests: 1953—C—; 1957—E; 1959—C—.

April 1960 (one year prior to contact) E—, E—, E—.

Iowa Basic Skills 6th Grade—composite score 4.8.

Grade average for the seventh grade: D.

FIRST INTERVIEW	COUNSELOR'S COMMENTS
C1 Make yourself comfortable. Would you like to tell me a little bit about school and the trouble you are having.	Suggestive. I suspect that the use of "trouble" was ill advised.
S2 I don't know what to tell you.	
C3 Uh-huh. You understand the setup here at the Counseling Center.	
S4 Uh-huh.	
C5 Who was it that suggested that you come down?	
S6 My mother.	
C7 She's concerned about how you are doing in school? Is that the reason she suggested it, or what?	

S8 Mm-hmm. She suggested I come down here 'cause I wasn't picking up in Social Studies.

C9 Mm-hmm. Would you like to tell me about that, about the Social Studies? — Probing.

S10 Well, I don't know how to get over some of the work. They are sometimes hard.

C11 Mm-hmm.

S12 That's all I don't know about Social Studies, the work, that's all.

C13 You feel it is the work in Social Studies class that is giving you trouble, is this it? — Restatement.

S14 Mm-hmm, some of it, I know how to do it.

C15 How about your other classes?

S16 They're OK.

C17 You're from Cooper Junior High? — I knew where he was from but hoped to get him talking more about school.

S18 Mm-hmm. What your name anyway?

C19 Mr. Durkheim.

S20 Oh, Mr. Durkheim. My father asked me could I have my period, my forty-five minutes on Saturday?

C21 Ah, yes, I think we could work that out. I have a schedule here we could look at, when you are ready to go, we can see if we can work you in on Saturday. Would it be more convenient for you to come down here on Saturday?

S22 Mm-hmm.

C23 Good.

S24 Were you the one that called me on the phone?

C25 No, that was probably someone else in the office here, but it wasn't me. (Pause) Somebody called you on the phone? — Informational.

S26 Mm-hmm. They said to me when could I get down here, about 3:00? And I said my father doesn't get home until

3:00, so they said could you get in by 5:00, and I said all right. So I was here at 5:00.

C27   Mm-hmm, your father drove you down?

S28   Mm-hmm. Am I going to do any work here?

C29   Well, I was hoping that you would talk to me and tell me what is going on in school and what you are doing.

I am trying to structure the counseling situation.

S30   I take up six subjects.

C31   Mm-hmm.

S32   Swimming—I take up nine. I take Swimming, Gym, Health, Social Studies, English, Math, Science, and Drafting.

S34   Yah, I take nine subjects, but see I have five weeks of Swimming, five weeks of Gym, and five weeks of, ah, we have two weeks of Gym, five weeks of Swimming, and five weeks of Health.

C35   Mm-hmm.

S36   So in these five weeks of school were Health, then my second five weeks were Gym, or Swimming, ah, ah, Swimming, so I got back to Gym, so I got back to Gym for another five weeks, when these is up.

C37   Mm-hmm. How do you like school?

S38   Sometimes I like it, sometimes I don't.

C39   Sometimes you like it, but then there are times when you don't like it.

Restatement.

S40   Mm-hmm. Will there be anybody else down here?

C41   Well, not here really, just me. Just you and I.

S42   What do you do?

C43   Well, I am here really to help you, to help you try and understand yourself better, to understand any trouble that you might be having in school or with your studies.

Informational. I was trying to structure my role.

S44   I'm having trouble in Social Studies.

C45   Mm-hmm.

S46   And a little trouble in Drafting.

C47   You're having a little trouble in draft-   Restatement.
      ing.

S48   Not too much, not as much as I am
      having in Social Studies. The work
      he gives isn't hard but he gives you
      an assignment, several long assign-
      ments, and so he gives you about a day
      and a half to hand things in.

C49   Mm-hmm.

S50   He tells the class we're noisy and he
      keeps you after school. So then he
      picks up the Social Studies work when
      the bell rings and as soon as he walks
      in the door if you don't have your
      book, Social Studies book, out, he gives
      you an E. So I only got one E for not
      taking out my book. So far, every
      other time I took it out, because if
      you don't have it out, he pick up his
      roll book and tells you to stand up, he
      gives you an E and tells you to sit
      down, and if you get so many E's, you
      get one on your card.

C51   I see.

S52   Is this where I'm going to be every
      time someone comes down here, in
      this room?

C53   Mm-hmm.

S54   Same place?
      (*Pause*)

C55   You say that if you don't have your   Returning to a previous area
      book out when the bell rings, he gives of affect.
      you an E in your Social Studies book?
      What do you think about this?

S56   I don't like it. When he comes in, if
      he catch you, he say, "Everybody stand
      up," and then he gives you an E.

C57   Mm-hmm. You don't like the fact that   Restatement.
      he just gives people an E if they don't
      take out their book.

S58   Everybody don't like it.

C59   This is the same teacher that you have, Information seeking.
      is it Drafting and Social Studies?

S60   Uh-huh. I got a different teacher, he
      is my English teacher too.

C61 Your drafting teacher is your English teacher?

S62 Uh-huh. My Drafting teacher is my Drafting teacher, but my Social Studies teacher is my English teacher too, and my Math teacher is my Science teacher too, rather she is. In Gym I got a different teacher, for Swimming I got a different teacher, and for Health I got a different teacher.

C63 Do you get along all right with the other teachers?   Probing.

S64 Mm-hmm, I get along with them but the work is too hard.

C65 You like him all right you just feel that the work in the class is too hard.   Restatement and reflection.

S66 Is somebody over there?

C67 Yes, there are some people that are watching the interview over on the other side of the screen.

S68 How about the last name?

C69 I don't know too much about it. What do you do after school?

S70 Go home, go home, study my lessons and do my homework and this month I must go to a banquet. I'm on a baseball team and we won trophies so we are going to a banquet and get our trophy, too.

C71 You're on a baseball team?

S72 Mm-hmm. Do you know Mr. Kaye?

C73 No, I'm afraid I don't.

S74 Do you know anybody at Cooper?

C75 No. Mr. Kaye is your counselor at Cooper? Is that right?

S76 Mm-hmm. He's the junior high counselor. When I get in the ninth grade, Mr. Lyndon will be my counselor. Mr. Kaye is the teacher but they put him in as assistant counselor.

C77 I see. You will be in the ninth grade next year?

S78 Yeah, I'm in 8B now and in January I will be in 8A, and next year, yeah, next year.

C79	Would you like to tell me something about your plans for the future, do you plan to go to high school?	Probing.
S80	I'm going to Cass.	
C81	Mm-hmm.	
S82	Well, I might be a doctor or a teacher.	
C83	Mm-hmm, but you feel that you would like to go to Cass, though, for high school.	Reflection.
S84	Mm-hmm.	
C85	Mm-hmm.	
S86	When kids come here, what do they do, how old are they?	
C87	Oh, usually people in high school or junior high.	Informational.
S88	What do they do?	
C89	Oh, usually just come here and talk.	
S90	I mean in the part about this here . . . [rest is inaudible]	
C91	Oh, these, the nursery school.	
S92	Oh, for kids.	
C93	For others that come here during the day.	
S94	How old are they, one to four about?	
C95	Mm-hmm.	
S96	Do they have to pay?	
C97	I'm not sure. How did you happen to decide on Cass?	Probing.
S98	Because you got a higher education, higher rating, and everything. It's a good school.	
C99	You feel Cass is a good school and that's why you would like to go there.	Restatement.
S100	Mm-hmm.	
C101	Would you like to tell me some more about the ball team?	He seemed interested in sports so I thought this direction might be rapport building.
S102	Mm-hmm. Well, our team is boys, we have thirteen boys. I was the pitcher and Paul plays first base, Amos plays second base, and Peter played third, and that's all. We have four more games to play so that if we lost even	

one of them we wouldn't be able to
be in the series so if we even beat the
four, and so in the series we would
beat.

C103 Mm-hmm.

S104 [first two sentences inaudible] . . . and
the tickets are about two dollars and
fifty cents for people who want to come
but I got mine free.

C105 Because you're on the team.

S106 Mm-hmm, for a extra child, it's a
dollar.

C107 Mm-hmm.

S108 So I asked my father if he was going,
and he say no that's too much money
for him, and my brother ain't going
because he don't have that much, and
my mother, she say she wants to go
but she ain't got that much for a
ticket.

C109 Mm-hmm.

S110 [first sentence inaudible] . . . and you
can go home and get all you want
free.

C111 Do you have any other plans for after   Probing.
the baseball season is over?

S112 I want to learn how to ice skate. I
know how to roller skate.

C113 Mm-hmm.

S114 I go down to Frank Stevens [rink]
every time I get some money. They go
skating there.

C115 You can go ice skating there?   I knew it wasn't an ice rink,
                                                but felt he might be more
                                                comfortable if I didn't seem
                                                too all-knowing.

S116 No, just roller skating.

C117 Oh, I see.

S118 It's an indoor rink.

C119 I see.

S120 You got to pay to get in there, too. If
you got a skating card it's twenty-five
cents, if you don't, you have to pay
thirty-five cents.

C121   Mm-hmm.

S122   Of course, you got to bring some money because you know you're going to get hungry. You skate there for about five or six hours. They have certain parts for people who don't know how to skate. They have certain hours for them. They got about two or three hours for the kids who can't skate. They get on the floor, and then while the other kids go out and eat. They got hot dog stands and pop stands. But every time when I go skating I get a blister on my foot, right there. So when I get home, I take a scissors and snip it off. It hurts though. I have to put a band aid on it so that the next morning it will be gone. When I first learned how to skate, it was on the figure skates, so my father he bought us some and I learn how to skate, so my mother got me some shoe skates.

C123   Mm-hmm.

S124   I want a pair but they cost too much money. One pair costs about sixteen dollars.

C125   Mm-hmm.

S126   You know those shoe skates, they come up to about there.

C127   Mm-hmm.

S128   Wooden rollers, you know, you can't use them on ice because you'll tear them up, and so they are wooden there.

C129   Mm-hmm.

S130   And last year I got stitches in my finger.

C131   Mm-hmm.

S132   It was this one. I got five stitches put in because I was in, was you know on that big, well you know, that big old blade, so I was sawing, and zip.

C133   Hum?   I was indicating concern.

S134   My finger almost got cut off doing

nothing. So then they sent me down into the clinic so they was, they said to soak it in water, and that got all bloodied up. So he sprayed some stuff on it to stop the blood, and so when I got home he say it would not need no stitches. And so I got home and my mother, she looked at it and, "That is nasty looking," she told my dad. And so he went next door to, she's a registered nurse, and so, yeah, I went next door and she said, "Yeah, I need stitches in it," and so they took me to Receiving [Hospital]. And they stuck me in the hospital for the stitches. First they stuck me in the arm then in the nail. It was there, right there so's they would cure the nerve. Then, about eight weeks again, I broke my ankle on my bike. That was in the summertime. See I was riding my bike and you know they got them bar bells on it, and so I was riding my bike and my foot slipped off the pedal and I hit the ground just like that.

C135 Mm-hmm.

S136 The pedal came up and, soomp. So when I got home I told my mother and she said, "Your ankle isn't broke." So my uncle, he had a cane, and I was hopping around on the cane, and when my father came home, he said can I walk on it, and I said, "Yeah." So he took me down to Receiving and they give me another shot in my arm, then they X-rayed it, and said it was broken.

C137 Mm-hmm.

S138 I missed out a whole week school that time. But when I went back to school, I had so much homework on me I didn't know what to do. I had about six or seven pages to read in Social Studies, about twenty pages of Math, and a lot of Math and a lot of Drafting and Science work. That's a lot of work. And last Saturday, my mother, she had a sty cut off her eye. It was black so she couldn't go to work today.

C139   Mm-hmm.   Understanding.

(*Pause*)

S140   My brother, he goes to Stevens [Elementary]. Before I went to Cooper, I used to go to Patten. I have been going to Cooper for about a year and a half now. They was going to send us to Mitchell, but Mitchell was too crowded so this was the only place.

C141   Mm-hmm.

S142   At first they was against it, so they paid our way over because it was a long ways to walk. So they had more kids around going there, because we ain't got the money to send them. So they paid our bus fare so this is what they gave us, these bus tickets. (*Pulls bus tickets from wallet*) Do you like my wallet?

C143   Mm-hmm.   Interested.

S144   And there is the bus tickets.

C145   Mm-hmm.

S146   A bus ticket and transfer.

C147   Mm-hmm, I see. They just put one of these in the box every day, is that it?

S148   And then you give him that and you get a transfer.

C149   Mm-hmm. I see.   I was trying to show a naive interest in the whole procedure.

S150   They got them marked so a adult can't use them too. And so when I first started going there I didn't like it 'cause I didn't know my way around, the school was too big. At first when I walked in, they sent us to the auditorium, there was about three hundred of us. From all schools, Angell, Marr, and some other schools. So they gave us

groups, 1-2-3-4-5-6. I was picked in group 6. So it took us about three hours to get registered 'cause they had to call off all the names and put them in groups. He called off about thirty names. "All the names called stand up," so they stood up, "and Mr. Burnside, do you see that teacher over there, you all go to that group." He kept on and we did this till we got off.
(*Pause*)
Ah, hey, I want to ask you about something else too. Do you know how many several is?

C151 What do you think?   Probing.

S152 Oh, I don't know, about five or six I guess. It can be any number. More than two because two is a couple. But it can be three, four, or five on up to hundreds. (*Pause*)

C153 So what happened after you got put in groups?

S154 We went down the hall and then a teacher said, "Don't sell your bus tickets, or anything, 'cause high school kids will try and buy them from you. They will try and buy your lunch cards. They will try and buy your lunches and steal things." And then they told all of us to get a combination lock, so I got one for my locker.

C155 Mm-hmm.

S156 Oh yeah, I got my locker for Gym because you got to change clothes and put on your gym shorts.

C157 Mm-hmm.   Understanding.

S158 So if you leave your locker unlocked, and you have some money in there, it won't be there when you get back. So after that we got out. We went back the next day. We didn't hardly do nothing. We just stood around and talked. And filled out cards. The next day we came back and started going

to our classes and have work. The
next week we started having homework. First we were getting out at 2:30
for about half a semester and then the
next semester we got out at 2:15. So
that's what time we have been getting
out. We have been getting out at 2:15
and you can get home about 2:30
'cause we have buses running one behind the other.

C159   Mm-hmm.

S160   See, they got about ten buses because
the high school and the junior high
kids come, so when one bus gets loaded,
they go there, another one be right
behind it so you can get home in a
hurry, if you get on the first bus. But
if you don't it take long, and if it is
a new bus line you better not get on
a new bus, because you won't stop
until it is packed and crowded, and
then when you ring the bell you can't
get off. He stops, and if he don't see
nobody, he keeps going. You get on
one of them old buses and if it is a new
bus behind, they will wait. You got a
whole bus to yourself almost. And then
the first day I started there I didn't
know how to get over there, so my
mother, she gave me a lot of money,
and plus bus tickets, not these, you
know the kind. She gave me two of
them to get home and back. And I
said, "I don't want them," so I walked
and spent the money. I told her I spent
the money 'cause I got hungry, so I
walked with some of my friends. And
then they gave us bus tickets to get
back on, but I still didn't know my way
so I kept on walking until I knew the
way. So now I know the way. 'Cause
it's right across the street from the
McGraff Police Station and Fire Department.

(Pause)

S160 And then, when they have fights in
there, they be bloody fights, 'cause I
can remember one time there was these
two boys fighting. So this one boy, he
had his cane, beating this other boy in
the head real hard. So then the other
boy took out his knife there, he stuck
him right in the shoulder, so he
dropped his cane and started hollering.
And you know the police station is
right across the street, so here come the
police and they grabbed him and took
him away. And then one time they had
the whole police over there because
the kids, they was about twenty kids
from the East Side and they was coming over to gang up on Cooper. So
about twenty boys came out there and
there was a big fight. Everybody ran on
the bus because the police was hitting
everybody with them sticks and black
jacks, those high school kids especially.
They was in the fight trying to break
it up because you know when they
come over to break it up, peoples trying to knock them down, and they get
out of the way, so they grab, and just
grab them. There was a lot of them,
a lot of policemans, and then they
have a bus detective too. And they
sneak on and get us. You will be riding there, they look you straight at
you, and then if you do something
they throw you off the bus, if the
bus driver sees you. But then in the
morning you got to catch the bus on
the corner every time they run. Sometimes they run poorer because they
don't have time to get you if they go
fast, because the other way they get
you home on time. If you wait on
time they get you to school in about
a half an hour, but if you don't they

are slow that there is no telling what time. The Clairpointe bus gets you there on time. Do you know a boy named Hubert Robinson? That's my dad's first cousin. He lives right over there in the first housing project. (*Pause*)

S160 When I left home today I asked my mother what was you all going to do, and she said, "I was going to talk." And I said, "What about?" And she said, "About anything at all you want to talk about." And I said, "I don't know what to talk about." I still can't see there's anything to talk about. I got another brother, too. He's over there. He must be outside playing with my cousin. Then when we started on our way coming over here, we almost got lost because we didn't have that map 'cause we came up the Expressway. And I told him it was a big parking lot and then a small one, so we walked down to the small parking lot around the corner and them came on down, and then building of 101, ah, 901. I went to Mr. Kaye today, so he gave me a map showing me. So you can get the Western bus without a transfer and get here but from where I live I got to catch a transfer, and these bus tickets in my pocket, you can use them only on school days.

C161 Would you like to tell me something else about your other classes? (*Pause*)

S162 Mm-hmm. I'll tell you something about English. Well, every day we got to come in and first we copy our spelling words, get the dictionary and look up the words, and find out what the meaning is, and get the meaning and write it down, and catch a sentence. And then they say, "John went blank to the store." So you got to fill the word that fits in and we got twenty spelling words.

C163   Mm-hmm.   Understanding.

S164   And then you got twenty answers, and then if the class is noisy, she make you write fifty times. She make you write a long sentence. Like here's a one of them, "I will not be naughty anymore so I can go to assemblies, and I will not get any more E's on my tests." And you write this fifty times and when you write it fifty times, you get pretty tired, too. Because that is about three lines and you got to write it fifty times

C165   Mm-hmm.   Understanding.

S166   You get tired.

C167   Mm-hmm.

S168   From now on when I come here, is this what we're going to be doing?

C169   Well, pretty much.

S170   I haven't got much stuff to tell you. Then, what will we do? I might run out of stuff then I can't come up here every day with something new.

C171   Mm-hmm.

S172   In about a week's time, there ought to be something exciting. The *Detroit Press* bought the *Detroit Globe*.

C173   Mm hmm.

S174   So, the boys that delivered the *Detroit Globe* will deliver the *Detroit Press*. It will be the *Detroit Press and Globe*. Our teacher said he likes the *Detroit Globe* better because it got better comics.

C175   Mm-hmm.   Understanding.

S176   I like the *Globe* better because I can't understand the *Press's* writing.

C177   But you can understand the writing in   Reflection.
the *Globe*.

S178   Um-hmm.

S179   I don't like the *Detroit Gazette* too much 'cause their writing's all slanted.

They make the a's like this sometime, like a capital A; I can't even understand it.

C180 You feel you can't understand the writing in the *Gazette?*   Restatement.

S181 'Cause when they see the *Detroit Gazette* the d's and g's are all made funny. Who do you think will win the election, Kennedy or Nixon?

C182 What do you think?

S183 Kennedy.

C184 Mm-hmm.

S185 And too, in school, we voted on the ballot machine. So our teacher, he showed us one model of it. He showed us one board and the board was was something like that, so he showed us a lot of candidates and everything. So when I got into the booth the screen paper was about this big. I couldn't understand anything so I found the Democratic lever and just pulled it. Then after that we only had a half hour in there so I just pulled the Democratic lever. I was almost confused in there. I know you are supposed to pull something so I pull the red handle so I looked on it and it said Democratic, Democratic, so I pulled it straight Democratic. So I tried to start looking for some levers and when I started looking the time was up. When the time was up, the girl went just like that on the curtains, and the time was up. You can't stay in there too long or they might come in after you. I thought it was just a little machine but it is a big, although when I voted at Pattenville they gave us them paper ballots. Did Detroit ever have to use them paper ballots?

C186 I think they did.   Information and support.

S187 I have to have a pencil and have to use, and put it in front. It takes a long

time to do but now they announce the
new president about 3:00 in the morning.

C188   Mm-hmm.

S189   On Channel 4 they say it will be the
quickest. On Channel 4, 'cause every
time you vote for somebody, the vot-
ing machine register your number in
there somewhere. Like if Kennedy has
four hundred and Nixon has about
three hundred, then if you vote, it is
three hundred and one, or something
like that. Are you going to stay up and
see who the new President will be?

C190   What about you?   Probing.

S191   No, I'm going to go to bed as soon as
I get home, then get up about 12:00.
But I don't think I will make it. I
couldn't go back to sleep 'cause there
will be them kids, and I'll hear them
out there playing football and I'll have
to get up and play football with them.
So I guess I won't see it.

C192   You won't be able to watch it because   Restatement.
the kids will be outside playing foot-
ball, and you'll have to get up to go
and play football with them.

S193   It seems like we ought to be in school
longer than 2:30; 'cause in the elementary school the classes are thirty minutes long but ours are forty-five. Of
course you have to eat, and it will be
about 7:30 or 8:00, then you go to
school about 8:00 and do all your
work. But I have five minutes between
classes, and you can go to the store if
you make it back in time, but you
won't be back in time from school,
from across the street.

C194   Mm-hmm.

S195   If you jay walk the police will get you.
If you are a chicken. Do you know they
made up that law you can't ride a bike
unless you got a license on it. So they

gave me a ticket. It wasn't much. It was just a warning. If you get caught it will be something though.

C196   Mm-hmm.   Understanding.

S197   A policeman he will do nothing. This man, he said you know there is people that are parking, and them policeman will try and come up and will sell him a ticket to something, and he will see him again parking. I was tying up traffic too, but the policeman don't do nothing. I got back in front of a car and go.

C198   Mm-hmm.

S199   Now if you would have been on the curb and you would have told a man to come out, and a policeman would have been coming along, he will give you a ticket as long as you are on.

C200   Mm-hmm.   Understanding.

C200   And you feel a policeman will do any-   Reflection.
       thing to sell something.
       (*Knock on door*)

C201   Yes.
       (*Five minutes*)

C202   Thank you. Go ahead.

S203   I forgot. Then when I went down to get my license I thought you would have to take your bike, but you got to take your bike because he had to place my ticket plus one dollar. And then he said I don't need the dollar, but he isn't worried about the dollar. But if your bike is stolen, you go to him. You come to him to look for it and if you don't have a license on it, but if somebody is going to steal the bike all they have to do, if they want, is to cut the thing off, and the policeman won't know a thing.

C204   Mm-hmm.

S205   And they claim if you lost your bike they will get you another one. Will they?

C206	What do you think?	Probing.
S207	I don't know. You know my brother? Somebody stole his bike but there wasn't no license on it.	
C208	Mm-hmm.	
S209	When we get through, can we go in the other room and look through here?	
C210	Oh, I think we could if you would like to.	Information and support.
S211	Is that tape recorder in there too? Are you going to play it over?	
C212	Not now, maybe some other time. (*Pause*)	
C212	Is there anything else you would like to talk about before we stop today?	
S213	Nothing. I'm just about talked out. Is that a big tape recorder in there?	
C214	Not very.	Informational.
S215	Is it a small one about that big, or something like that?	
C216	Well, why don't we stop for today then? Would you like to come back on Saturday?	Termination.
S217	Mm-hmm.	
C218	OK.	Indicating approval.

**TWELFTH
INTERVIEW**

**COUNSELOR'S
COMMENTS**

S1	Did you find a picture of yourself yet?	
C2	No, but I'll look again and maybe on Friday when you come, I'll have one. I'm sorry we'll have so little time today, but I have another commitment and I'll have to get away.	Informational and supportive (client was 45 minutes late).
S3	I've got another one that I'll bring next time if you want me to.	
C4	If you'd like to, sure.	Reassuring.
S5	This one is when I'm about a year old. (*Pause*) My mother said this one is when I was two weeks old.	
C6	Oh, I see. You were a little fella then, weren't you?	I just liked the picture.

S7   How . . . a, were you waiting long for me?

C8   Since about 3:30.

S9   Wow. . . . (*Pause*) When I got through talkin' to you, do you think it took me a long time to get down here.

C10 What do you think?

S11 Huh? It's slow on buses. I wanted to get here in a hurry, but today I couldn't get there real quick.

C12 Well, I knew you do the best you can. (*Pause*)   Reassuring.

S13 When I, a, I mean, do you want me to come again this week?

C14 How about Friday?

S15 Huh . . . Friday? Yeah.

C16 OK.

S17 I'll come next Friday.

C18 That will be about ten to five, or five o'clock. Will that be all right?   Structuring.

S19 OK.

C20 I'll see you for a whole hour on Friday, since we don't have much time today.

S21 You should have some pictures of yourself at home!

C22 Um, could be; I'll see if I can find some.   Reassuring.

S23 Do you wish you had a camera?

C24 Um, how about you?

S25 I do sometimes. When you was a baby, did you want to be a boy or a girl?

C26 (*Pause*) Um, I think I wanted to be a boy, how about you?   Information, then probing.

C27 Do you think sometime when babies are small they want to be . . .   I was impatient to pursue this area.

S28 No, nobody want to be a baby. (*Pause*)

S29 When you called me, you thought I wasn't coming?

C30 You'd forgotten about it?   Focusing back to client.

S31 I thought it was a quarter after four, it was quarter to four wasn't it? So next Saturday, i come at 5:00.

C32 Friday of this week.

S33 We'll start at 5:00 and be out about quarter after six.

C34 About six, or a few minutes after.

S35 I had to come today, 'cause Mr. Kaye, he give me my bus ticket.

C36 Um, you were talking to Mr. Kaye today?

S37 Huh? Did you talk to him today?

C38 No, I just talked to him once. I called him last week. I'd never talked to him before. He said you were getting along real well. I haven't talked to him since then.

S39 Have you ever saw him? Do you think he has a nice voice?

C40 Um, what do you think?

S41 Has anybody ever saw him here?

C42 I think Mr. Wilson has.

S43 The other class you have to go to, is it a grownup class?

C44 Oh, this isn't a class, it's another appointment.

S45 Oh, another student?

C46 No, a doctor's appointment.

S47 Are you a doctor?

> This is a fairly typical example of the client's lack of organization.

C48 No, I have to go to a doctor.

S49 Oh, what for?

C50 A tooth fixed.

S51 Do you have a bad tooth, do you have to have it pulled?

C52 I hope not. Just filled.

> Informational.

S53 It hurts when they fill it. You have to kill the nerve when you fill it.

C54 It has a temporary filling now.

S55 I mean when you had the temporary filling in it, did they have to do. Did he give you a shot to kill the nerve?

C56 He went ahead and drilled it then.

S57 He drilled it? With what?

C58 A drill like dentists use.

> Informational.

S59 Oh, what did he put in it, sort of a gold stuff?

C60 No, it's more of a plastic.

> Informational.

S61   You going to have a lot of pain to-
       night, ain't you?

C62   Maybe.

S63   Do you think if you have enough pain
       you will go back to him?

C64   Um, would you?   Refocusing.

S65   Yeah.

C66   If it was painful, you'd go back and   I was trying to get the client
       see him again?   to talking about himself.

S67   Where is your car parked at today?

C68   Over on First Street.

S69   Can you park in the parking lot?

C70   It's in a lot.

S71   It is. . . . Which way do you go to
       the dentist? That way?

C72   No, north.   Informational.

S73   Oh, What is your dentist's name?

C74   In the Fiske Building.   This seems to be the most
                                                   effective way to end such a
                                                   question barrage. As in pre-
                                                   vious interviews with this
                                                   client, my apparent misun-
                                                   derstanding of one of his
                                                   questions, helps him refocus
                                                   on himself.

S75   Oh, mine is Dr. Johnson.

C76   Um-hum, do you like your dentist?   Probing, since he is again
                                                   talking about himself.

S77   No, he can put you to sleep, too. It
       costs you more if he puts you to sleep,
       don't it. [Next sentence is inaudible.]

C78   You say you don't get put to sleep you   Restatement.
       just get stuck with a needle?

S79   Do it hurt you. Take, if he be stitchin'
       the nerve, what would you do?

C80   What would you do?   Probing.

S81   I'd take it out of my mouth.

C82   Take the needle out of your mouth?   Restatement.

S83   It don't hurt if they stitch you down,
       it's when they stitch you up, it hurts
       like that.
       (Pause)
       Do you dread going to the dentist?

C84   No, not really.

S85   How did you get that rotten tooth?
Eatin' candy?

C86   No, I think a piece broke off.   Informational.

S87   Did you eat that piece of candy I give
you?

C88   Um-hum.
(Pause)
Did you eat yours too?   Refocusing.

S89   Yeah, I ate mine after I left.
(Pause)
Do you like getting shots?

C90   How about you?   Probing or refocusing.

S91   When you have to get a shot, what
would you rather have, a shot from
your dentist or a shot from a doctor?

C92   How about you?   Probing or refocusing.

S93   Shot from a dentist. When they give
you a cold shot, they got that white
medicine in there. They stick it in
slow and it take its time goin' in too.

S94   Do you want a shot from a dentist or a
doctor?

C95   You don't like to get shots from the   Restatement of his first re-
doctor?   mark.

S96   A regular shot is OK, but a cold shot,
no! Too much white medicine in that
cold shot for me.

C97   Um-hum.   Support.

S98   When I had pneumonia I had to keep
getting them every day. I caught it
when I was seven years old. I had
penicillin every day.

C99   You had penicillin every day?

S100   Yeah, my brother too. He bigger than
me, but when the doctor give him a
shot, he started hollering. It took a
doctor and some nurses to hold him.

C101   They held you down too?   I didn't really think they did,
but was trying to return to
him, feeling he was really
ready to talk about himself.

S102   No, they ain't supposed to hold you
when they give you shots. Have you
ever been in the hospital?

C103 Um-hum.

S104 For what?

C105 Sinus trouble.   Information.

S106 Oh, you mean up here?

C107 Um-hum.

S108 Any other time?

C109 No.   Information.

S110 Did you get shots too, in the arm or
      in the hip?

C111 The hip.   Information.

S112 (*Laughs*) Who give you your shot?

C113 Nurses.   A falsehood which I felt
                                              might bring some affect. (The
                                              client's father is a hospital
                                              orderly and mother is a
                                              nurse's aid.)

S114 Nurses? I'm scared of nurses. Do you
      like a lady to give you a shot, or a
      man?

C115 What do you think?

S116 A man. I don't want no lady looking
      at me.

C117 You'd rather have a man give you   I was avoiding the trouble-
      shots?   some area for the moment.

S118 Did you have a lady or a man?

C119 It was a nurse.   I thought of remaining silent
                                              here, but was afraid the
                                              thread might be lost if I
                                              did.

S120 What would you rather have, a doctor
      or a nurse?

C121 I'd just as soon have a nurse, how about An attempt to rearouse the
      you?   reaction in S116.

S122 It's just a shot, shots the same no mat- Obviously the client rejected
      ter who gives it to you. It's still a shot. this.
      (*Pause*)

C123 But you wouldn't want a lady looking   A final push to recapture
      at you?   S116.

S124 (*Client shakes his head but doesn't
      reply.*)

C125 Is there anything else you'd like to   (*A knock indicating time was
      talk about before we stop today?   up.*)

S126 I guess that's it.

C127 Let's stop here then. I'll see you on
      Friday.

EIGHTEENTH INTERVIEW	COUNSELOR'S COMMENTS

S1   Mr. Durkheim, how come you smoke cigars?

C2   I don't all the time, but I do kind of like them.

S3   Huh?

C4   I don't all the time, but I do kind of like them.

S5   Which is the strongest, that or cigarettes?

C6   Well, this is a real mild cigar. With cigarettes, you smoke a lot of them; whereas with cigars you smoke one, and you're satisfied for a while.

S7   Three cigars will last you as long as a pack of cigarettes will.

C8   Just about. Yeah.

S9   What kind of cigarettes do you smoke?

C10   Salem.

S11   What kind of cigar is that, Robert Burns?

C12   No, William Penn.

S13   How long had you been smokin' that one?

> This sudden interest in my smoking is rather typical of this client's extremely high distractability.

C14   About a half hour. About three minutes after three; this lasts a half hour.

S15   I saw you come in.

C16   Oh, did you. I didn't see you. Where were you?

S17   I was hangin' my coat up. You was walking right across there.

C18   I saw your coat, so I knew you were here; but I didn't know where you were. I had a phone call to make anyway.
(Pause)

> Client often arrived early and wandered around the building, running the elevators, etc.

S19   Have you got on anything new today?

> This had become a ritual. The client would look at my clothes to see if I was wearing something new.

C20 I think you have seen all of this stuff before.

C21 How about you?

S22 Huh?

He wasn't quite ready to talk about himself.

S23 You might not have seen this shirt before; I am not sure whether you have or not.

S24 Have you seen this shirt before?

C25 You have worn that before, haven't you?

S26 It isn't mine.

C27 Oh, I see.

S28 You see how big it is?

C29 It isn't too big. I would have thought it was yours. Sleeves are not long for you. Whose is it?

C29 and 31—Client is envious of his brother's size. I was trying to be supportive.

S30 My brother's. He is bigger than I am. See, he weighs more than I am. He is fatter.

C31 He couldn't be too much taller than you. It fits you pretty well.
(*Pause*)

S32 You got a hair cut?

C33 Not yet, no.

S34 You haven't. Can I see how the back of your head looks again?

C35 It's a little long. It's shaggy. I like it a little shorter than this.

S36 You do? When you get it cut are you going to get it cut in the back? Not in front?

C37 A little off the front, yeah. Flatter on the top too.

S38 What if they took too much off?

C39 I would be in a bad shape then.

S40 Suppose they flattened it that much?

He indicated a one-fourth inch length.

C41 I had it that short one time.

S42 Side burns off? What did it look like?

C43 It was pretty short. I was in the Army then, so I had to wear a hat anyway and it didn't show too much.

S44 You ever been bald?

C45   No, but it was pretty close; it was only that long.

S46   All over?

C47   It was all shaved off on the sides.

S48   (*Laughs*) Clean on the sides?

C49   Just my white head, you know?

S50   (*Laughs*) Anyone make fun of you?

C51   No, they all had haircuts like that. I had a brush cut when I went in so it didn't bother me too much. But a lot of guys had long hair, and they looked scalped.

S52   The side of your head was just like your face?

C53   Just about.

S54   Was it bad?

C55   It looked real white. The rest of my face was kind of suntanned. It looked real white.

S56   You were scalped then?

> This Army theme need never have been started but the client seemed to really enjoy the prospect of my shaved head. His hair was always close cropped.

S57   What did the girls say?

C58   There weren't any girls around.

S59   I mean when you went to take some out.

C60   Then I was in basic training. By the time I saw girls again it was grown back in.

S61   You stayed in the Army two years? How come you came out, because you were in college? They couldn't keep you no longer could they?

C62   They only keep you for two years, twenty-one months.
      (*Pause*)

S63   What was the highest thing you ever got to be?

C64   A sergeant.

S65   First time. (*Pause*) You had to come over a lot of people, didn't you?

C66   No. I really didn't have any command

responsibilities. I was an instructor in the cooking school.

S67   Oh, you cooked.

C68   No, I just taught them how to cook.

S69   Oh, you know how to cook.

C70   Little bit.
     (*Pause*)

S71   In the Army, what did you have to do to be an M.P. or a three-star general?

C72   Well, to be an M.P. you had to be in police work before the service. Of course, it took a long time to work up to be a general.

S73   What do M.P.'s do, they bosses everybody doesn't they?

C74   Huh?

S75   Get in there and straighten up your bunks and everything? You just can't be an M.P. in two years can you?

C76   Oh, yeah, if you have been a policeman before you've been in the service, you can be one. You can be an M.P. right away. You have to go to police school. They send you to school to be an M.P.

I think this information-giving was unnecessary.

S77   Oh, I have a cousin that's an M.P.

C78   Uh-huh.

S79   He was my dad-daddy's cousin.

C80   Uh-huh.
     (*Pause*)

S81   Watch any TV this week?

This was a standard question too.

C82   Yeh, ah, let's see. I watched the story of Will Rogers on Tuesday night.

S83   That's all?

C84   Uh-huh.

S85   What was it about?

C86   About Will Rogers.

S87   What was he doin'?

C88   Umm, riding a horse, swinging a rope; part of it.

S89   Sunday night?

C90   No, it was Tuesday night.

S91   I didn't see it.

C92   Bob Hope narrated it.

S93   Oh, Bob Hope?

C94   Uh-huh.

C95   He wasn't in it. He just narrated it. It was his voice, while the movie was going on.

S96   Oh! You goin' watch TV tonight?

C97   I might.

S98   When was the last time you been to a show?

C99   Umm, I haven't been to the show for a while.

S100 You haven't.

C101 How about you?

S102 I'm suppose to go this Friday. This Friday, or Thursday, or something. Know what's playing? You'll never guess. A knockout, this one's got a knockout in it.

C103 Oh what, the Patterson fight?

S104 Yeh, that's it.

C105 I was thinking of a real movie first.

S106 You were?

C107 Uh-huh. Is there a movie on with it?

S108 Uh-huh. *City Beneath the Sea*. Did you see the previews of it? Did you see them on TV? Did you see the round where they knocked him out? It was on TV and they was talkin' to him in his dressing room. It was on the sports edition. You listened to it didn't you? Who did you want to win, Ingemar?

C109 No, I wanted Patterson to win it.

I really had no preference but knew Patterson was his favorite.

S110 You did?

C111 It was a good fight.

S112 In the first round I thought Patterson was goin' get knocked out.

C113 That would have been something. (*Pause*)

S114 Did you know how much it cost to go down to the Fox and see that fight?

C115 How much?

S116 I don't know, the cheapest seat was three dollars and something. Up close it was about twelve something. Do you ever play baseball?

C117 Not very often, no.

S118 Did you play your last year in college?

C119 No.

S120 You didn't?

S121 Mr. Durkheim when you go to get in Wayne here, and they give you an exam, is it hard?

C122 It isn't hard; no, not really.

> I probably should have communicated to him how subjective this answer was.

S123 Did you have to take it?

C124 Uh-huh.

S125 Suppose you was a straight A student, would you have to take it then?

C126 I don't think so. I think if you have got a B average or better, you don't have to, as I remember.

S127 Did you have about a C average?

C128 I had below a B average, yeah.

S129 What was some of the questions on the test?

C130 Umm, I don't remember, it was a long time ago.

S131 Suppose you flunked it, what would happen then?

C132 They might not have let me in. What do you think I would have done then?

S133 You would have took it over, could you? First, when you took it, don't they give you a little booklet to take it with?

C134 Uh-huh.

S135 Was there questions?

C136 Uh-huh, that's right.

S137 Was some of the problems arithmetic problems? They time you on it? How long did it take you to take it? How many days?

C138 No, it was all at once. It just took a couple of hours, I think. It took three hours or so.

(Pause)

S139 When do you want to get married, when you get about thirty something? *The client had never discussed marriage before.*

C140 Yeah.

S141 About thirty-one?

C142 Uh-huh.

S143 You don't want to get married, not when you in your twenties, do you?

C144 No, not particularly.

S145 Why not?

C146 Huh, what do you think?

S147 Huh, I don't know. You got a job, you got a car, you got a steady job. You can't get laid off, can you?

C148 Uh-huh.

S149 You got a lifetime job, don't you? Got everything you want, don't you?

C150 Pretty much.

S151 What do you want most now?

C152 What do you think?

S153 I'm gonna ask you. What do you want most now? A lady that would marry you? And you wanted to marry her? Wow! Or a new car. Wow!

C154 What do you think?

S155 I don't know.

C156 Guess.

S157 A house?

C158 Yeah, I think so. How about you?

S159 Yeah.

C160 You'd rather have the house?

S161 Yeah. A lady can't keep you warm, but a house can, can't it? *He may have wanted (or expected) me to deny this, but I remained silent.*

(Pause)

S162 What size shoes do you wear?

C163 Size eight.

S164 Uh-huh, eight? Boy, you have little feet. Guess what size this is?

C165 Seven and a half?

S166 I told you haven't I?

C167 I think so.

S168 Guess what size shirt this is?

C169 Umm, medium.

S170 No, what size: two, four, six, eight, ten, twelve, fourteen, sixteen, eighteen, twenty.

C171 Fourteen.

S172 No-o-o-o. Fourteen would be about here on me.

C173 It must be a sixteen then.

S174 It's chubby.

C175 It isn't that big for you, I don't think so.

S176 Look at this.

C177 Umm, yeah a little bit.

S178 They out there playing baseball now aren't they?

He seemed more disorientated than ever, following the pause after 161.

C179 Who?

S180 The college people.

C181 Outside the building you mean.

S182 On the playground.
(*Pause*)

S183 Mr. Durkheim, do you have to go to work tomorrow?

C184 No, I'm off all next week.

S185 This is just like school, huh. Secretaries off too?

C186 No, they're working.
(*Pause*)

S187 Which do you like best, to stay at home or go to work?

C188 How about you?

S189 I like to go to school best. Nothing to do at home sometimes. If I was a man, I would like to stay at home.

C190 You'd rather stay home than go to work?

S191 Yeah. If I could, uh-huh.

C192 How come?

S193 Well, if I had a car and everything, I would go ridin' around. Go places, go downtown, go to the show.

S194 Mr. Durkheim, I'm gonna ask you this, would you go give up, and would you go and sell one pint of blood? Just answer the question, tell me.

C195 Oh, I might. Uh-huh.

S196 You would? After you sold it would you walk downtown? Catch a bus?

C197 I'd catch a bus.

S198 Would you go to the show?

C199 I might.

S200 Would you spend all your money on popcorn and candy? (*Laughs*)

C201 How about you?

S202 I'm askin' you, would you?

C203 No, I don't think so.

S204 Uh huh, I didn't think you would.

C205 What do you think I'd do with the money?

S206 Mum, probably go to the store and spend a dollar on hot dogs or something. You could save the rest, put it in your wallet so you have some change.

S207 I think you get twenty-five dollars for the pint. My cousin, he's a man, he went downtown and he walked, him and his friend, they went and sold their blood. They went downtown and blew it on popcorn, peanuts, and candy. They stayed down all night almost. Then they went back and sold some more. I wouldn't do that would you?

C208 Why not?

S209 You would?

C210 Why not, why wouldn't you?

S211 That's stupid. That's just like throwing twenty-five dollars away.

C212 You feel that spending it on popcorn   Restatement. and peanuts is just like throwing it away?

S213 If you spend too much of it, I do.
(*Pause*)
[Richard starts talking about Banlon sweaters while asking Mr. Durkheim about the shirt he is wearing. He is also interested in the price, and Mr. Durkheim replies.]

C214 About the same I guess, about four dollars.

S215   How much is Banlon sweaters? See if we look at the ones, you know, umm at Harry Suffrins, it will cost you fourteen something.

C216   Umm.
        (Pause)

S217   When do you want me to come on down?

C218   Next week's vacation, so why don't you come Thursday of the following week. How would that be? I'll get the date for you and write it down. That be all right?

S219   You mean after I'm back to school, you mean that Thursday?
        (Pause)

S220   Mr. Durkheim, do you have a graduation picture of yourself?

C221   I think so.

S222   Will you bring it?

C223   I think I've got a graduation picture.

S224   Have you found one of them baby pictures?

Richard had suggested I bring a baby picture like the one he brought earlier.

C225   No, I haven't found one of them yet. I have a graduation picture that I can bring you.
        (Pause)

S226   Can you tell if the tape recorder is on?

C227   No.

S228   When it's off, do you still hear that hum?

C229   No, that's the switchboard in the other room. I think that hums all the time. Whether it's on or not.

C230   If you had your choice between the three, you'd choose the house, huh?

The hour was nearly over and I thought he might be willing to return to the house discussion.

S231   How old were you when you finished school. Sixteen?

The client would have no part of this and began talking about me again.

C232   Seventeen.

S233   How many years did you have to go to college?

C234   You've asked me that before.

S235   Four?

C236   You've asked me that before.

S237   Two?

C238   Don't you remember asking me that
       before, the last time you came?

S239   Un-un . . . [no]

S240   Do you have homework every night?

C241   Just about.

S242   It's hard. You've been teaching two
       years haven't you?

C243   No, this is my first year.

S244   This is the first year you've been teach-
       ing? (*Taps table*)
       (*Pause*)

S245   When you were young, did you ever
       think when you got up to twelve
       years old you'd want a brother or sis-
       ter?

C246   Not particularly.

S247   You happy by yourself?

C248   Uh-huh.

S249   You get your own bedroom?

C250   Uh-huh.

S251   When you were goin' to college did
       you ever get into any fights?

C252   No, not in college.

S253   How about here at Wayne?

C254   No, not here.

S255   What would they do if you got in a
       fight?

C256   What do you think?

S257   Kick you out?

C258   They might.
       (*Pause*)

S259   Do I have all my fingers?   He was playing the game of
                                              clasping his hand and hiding
                                              one finger.

C260   No, there is one missing.

S261   Where did you see that?

C262   It's on the side.

S263   Which one is it? There aren't five . . .
       see.

C264   That's what I meant. The next one is
       missing.

S265 This one?

C266 The one before that.

S267 There is one missing.
      (*Pause*)

C268 You're not getting a new suit for Easter,
      huh?

S269 When you were about seventeen, or   He just isn't ready to talk
      when you were about fifteen or sixteen,   about himself.
      how big a knife did you carry?

C270 I didn't carry a knife.

S271 What did you fight with, your fists?
      How many did you win and lose?

C272 I don't know, it's been a long time ago.
      I lost a couple of fights.

S273 Did you run home crying? Did they
      make you bleed?

C274 I had a bloody nose a couple of times.

S275 When they knocked you down, did you   His preoccupation with vio-
      get up quick? How did the fight stop?   lence seems directed at me
                                                 now.

C276 Usually they'd get broken up.

S277 When you were beatin' somebody, you
      were mad then. You didn't want it
      broke up then, did you?

C278 What do you think? Don't you think   This suggestion that people
      when you get mad in a fight you kind   sometimes want external con-
      of want the fight broken up?   trols seemed to escape him.

S279 No, not if you're beatin' somebody.

C280 So if you're winning, you wouldn't   Restatement.
      want the fight broken up?
      [The next few lines are inaudible]
      (*The client is writing me a note*)

S281 Here you read this.

C282 Oh, OK. . . . Where did you get this?

S283 From the teacher.   He was referring to a stolen
                                                 pencil rather than the note.

C284 What are you going to do with it?

S285 I don't know.
      [The client continually tapped on the
      table and kicked it, which makes the
      tape inaudible at this point.]
      (*The client is showing me the contents*

*of his wallet. I'm reading the Cub
Scout card, etc. to him.*)

S286   If you don't look at this, I'm going to
       tear it up.

C287   What do you think it means?
       (*Long pause*)
       (*Knock on the door.*)

C288   We shall vote, huh?

S289   (*Laughs*) Uh-huh.

C290   Why don't we stop here for today.

S291   OK.

Case Summary

Richard impressed me as an extremely hyperactive boy, given to prolonged outbursts of scratching, squirming, and general restlessness. He just couldn't sit still. He also seemed rather small for his age, and he bit his fingernails.

The first five interviews progressed in much the same fashion, with the client apparently incapable of focusing on himself and my continuing to probe about with little success.

In the sixth interview, I administered the *Mooney Problem Checklist* and Richard checked all but a few items. This, along with my growing awareness that probing seemed to be doing little for the relationship, seemed to be the turning point in his counseling. The next two interviews were filled with long pauses as I refused to probe or question the client. Toward the end of each interview he hesitantly, and then with growing confidence, began asking me personal questions.

Even though this was obviously still a form of resistance, I felt encouraged since now he was able to stop generalizing and begin to talk about specific people and situations. Also, it was clear that this interest in his counselor indicated that a real relationship was developing.

In the ninth and tenth interviews, I began to use the phrase "how about you" in response to many of his questions (after answering the first few) with very encouraging results.

After this interview I phoned his school counselor and learned that Richard's citizenship and attention span had improved remarkably.

Encouraged, I remained even more silent during interview eleven and witnessed a surprising lack of restlessness and new composure coming over Richard. He also seemed to be talking more and more about his feelings particularly his concern over a lack of close friends.

Richard was confused about the time of his twelfth appointment, and when he didn't show up on time, (he had been coming fifteen and twenty minutes early) I called him at home. He explained his misunderstanding of the time and I suggested another appointment later in the week. He sounded so disappointed and eager to come, however, that I suggested that we could still meet for twenty minutes or so if he wanted to make the trip.

The somewhat greater period of resistance at the start of this session might be partly a result of an unconsciously perceived rejection on my part (although the first half of most recent sessions had been spent pretty much in this manner) or it may just have been a final reaction to the more dynamic material he was about to uncover. He had never before talked about sex differences, or any feeling toward women. Also, his showing me the baby picture, the suggestion that he would bring one taken when he is a year old, and the talk of his own body, suggested to me that he might at last be trying to look at himself.

In the thirteenth, fourteenth, and fifteenth interviews Richard talked more about school, (the semester was ending and he was concerned about the future) and this led to a discussion of his future plans. His usual pattern of questioning me about my development and school history continued, but he seemed more able to verbalize his attitudes also.

In the sixteenth interview I first raised the question of termination and was totally unprepared for the reaction I received. He became quite angry and asked if I didn't understand that he enjoyed coming to see me and wanted to continue as long as he could. I quickly assured him that he could continue coming until the school year ended. He seemed relieved but was never quite as relaxed after this discussion, almost as if he constantly anticipated the ending of the relationship.

The seventeenth interview was almost entirely devoted to a discussion of sports with particular emphasis on violence and bloodshed. When I suggested to the client near the end of the hour that he seemed to enjoy the thought of violence, he replied that he did as long as it wasn't happening to him.

In the eighteenth interview (which is reproduced here) Richard seemed ill at ease and displayed much of the nervous activity of the first sessions.

The nineteenth interview which was the last appointment he kept at the lab was not recorded, due to last minute technical problems. Its content was much the same as the last few sessions with no new patterns of behavior.

Richard was scheduled for a final hour the week after the nineteenth interview and he knew this was to be his last appointment. He phoned me at the scheduled conference time and without giving any specific reason for cancelling, simply stated that he preferred to say goodbye over the phone. He asked for my home number so that he might call me during the summer, and I gave it to him. This was how the case terminated.

In a follow-up phone call to his school counselor after the semester ended, it was reported that "Richard's grades had improved markedly" during the year he had been coming to the lab. Even more rewarding than this, however, was the report that his behavior and classroom deportment were much better also.

Self Evaluation

It has been nearly a year since I last saw Richard, and a good deal has happened to change my perception of counseling and the counseling process.

I came to counseling from Clinical Psychology, having spent the two years prior to the lab experience working as a Psychodiagnostician and intake worker at a large metropolitan psychiatric clinic. During this time I had become quite attracted to the psychoanalytic approach to personality theory and was eager to apply these principles whenever I could. At the time I enrolled for the practicum I was also teaching an introductory psychology course which, in combination with the afore-mentioned psychoanalytic interest, left me with an almost overpowering desire to dissect and study my counseling client's personality.

Richard was my first client and the questions I asked at our first sessions were of the type I had used when taking social histories at the clinic. Gradually as I worked with him I became aware of my client as a boy who was unhappy and needed help. Slowly my desire to probe and study gave way to a wish to really listen to what he was trying to communicate.

I am afraid that I was never totally successful at doing this and that even after the change of format that occurred after our fifth interview I never quite fully accepted the client's self-worth.

I used to grow impatient with his question barrages and annoyed with the way he was controlling me and the interview. My reference to termination in the sixteenth interview followed a lengthy interrogation period by the client and was clearly a hostile retort on my part to such treatment. This difficulty in relating to young people may have been a function of my lack of teaching, or previous counseling experience, and was probably compounded by the fact that the client was a Negro. This case did help me to learn to be more accepting of young people, a facility which has been most helpful in the counseling I have done in the year since termination. I regard the case of Richard as a personally rewarding learning experience and an important step in my growth as a counselor.

Case Review

DUGALD ARBUCKLE

Section 1. As I listen to the tape, it appears that Richard is an "un-motivated" client, who knows little about counselors or what to expect from them. This poses an interesting question. If Richard has been referred to the laboratory by a school counselor, just how did this counselor conceive of his function? Could not the school counselor have worked with Richard? At least Richard should have some understanding about counselors. He appears to have none.

In the first few minutes the counselor tends to talk rather rapidly, and soon indicates that he is counselor-centered rather than client-centered. C37 is a needless interruption, and in C69 the counselor invites Richard to change the subject. Thus at the very beginning, Richard is getting the impression of the counselor as a person who dominates and controls. Richard does talk, and express feelings, but the counselor would appear to be operating from his own frame of reference, and very rarely indicates a sensitive awareness of what Richard may be trying to communicate.

In C115 the counselor indicates the first of several times when he is deliberately dishonest. This might, at least, be considered as a question-able means of establishing a positive relationship with a child. The counselor is being dishonest to himself and to the client. Again, in C149, the counselor should not have to show a "naive interest." If the counselor is actually disinterested, he might be more effective if he were to honestly express this feeling.

Despite interruptions and distractions, and a lack of sensitivity by the counselor, Richard does talk fairly easily. But he keeps getting pulled back and directed by the counselor, as in C161. Richard's S166 was *very* expressive. The "You" was personal, and Richard actually sounded tired. The counselor again missed the feeling expressed, and in S168 Richard changes the topic. The counselor is operating almost entirely from his own frame of reference, and at times seems almost oblivious to what Richard is saying to him. He is setting the stage for the difficulties that he gets into later on. In this first session the counselor either dominates Richard, or lets Richard dominate him. In C202 the "Go ahead" was a sharp command, and Richard's reaction was natural.

Richard may have benefitted some from the fact that he was at least able to talk, but in this entire session there appeared to be little in the way of a real understanding of Richard by the counselor, and Richard's attempts to communicate were rebuffed again and again. There was no counselor reaction to client feelings, and the closest the counselor could come to this was his rather demanding and ineffective "What do you think?" which became even more ineffective when it was used in later sessions.

Session 12. The counselor soon becomes trapped in a question and answer period, and he almost seems relieved to answer the client's questions, with an ineffective and periodic "What do you think?" Richard's questions were certainly more than just questions, but the counselor seems to be unaware of this, and simply reacts to the questions as questions. Richard becomes the interviewer, asking many personal questions of the counselor, and he has a most willing "client" who appears happy to answer any and all questions!

Periodically the counselor indicates in his comments that he was trying to get the client to talk about himself, but he seems unaware of his own apparent eagerness to talk about himself to Richard. As long as Richard has a counselor who is willing to tell all to him, why should he talk about himself? In the feeble attempts where the counselor "tries" to get back to Richard, as in C90, Richard understandably pays no attention. S93 was another example of an expression of much feeling by Richard, but missed by the counselor.

In C101 and C113 the counselor again uses a highly questionable "technique" in being deliberately dishonest. Counselor honesty and an empathic relationship would seem to go together, and the deliberate dishonesty of the counselor is likely to be at least one of the causes of his difficulty.

This could have been, and may actually have been, a significant interview, with Richard's late appearance, but nowhere in the session did the counselor give any indication of an acceptance and an understanding of Richard's feelings—of what he was really trying to communicate. Richard was pushing the counselor around during the entire session, possibly liking it, but the counselor appeared to be unaware of the dynamics of the session and went along, almost in a rote manner, as the answer man in a question and answer period.

Session 18. The extent to which the client controls the counselor, after eighteen sessions, is quite amazing. This has become the pattern, and there would seem to be no doubt that Richard receives some form of satisfaction from this pushing around of the counselor. It possibly relieves his need to exert pressure elsewhere, but it is doubtful if it results in positive growth for the client. I have a feeling here that the counselor has almost surrendered his own integrity, and is, in a way, trying to appease the client. Many times the counselor actually sounds as if he enjoys answering the personal questions that Richard directs at him. In C76 it is intriguing, after the reams of information that have been supplied by the counselor to Richard, to see the necessity of the counselor commenting, "this information-giving."

So many of the questions in this session are loaded with information about Richard, but nowhere does the counselor come back to what Richard *is telling*. He always answers what he thinks Richard is *asking*. S149 is fairly typical of these comments, but the counselor takes it as a straight question, and gives a straight answer. Again in S194, we hear the demanding, "Just answer the question, tell me," and the counselor can see nothing in this but a question. In C201 we see a good example of client domination and counselor withdrawal. The counselor asks, "How about you," but the client will not answer, but when the client asks, in S202, "Would you?" the counselor answers immediately! After being completely dominated and controlled by the client, the counselor, in reply to S217, "When do you want me to come down," indicates when "he" wants the client to come down!

An interesting point here, too, seems to be the almost complete counselor unawareness of what is going on. When the counselor comments, after S269, that, "He just isn't ready to talk about himself," he does not seem to be aware of his role in making it almost impossible for Richard to talk, at least directly, about himself. These sessions are good examples of what is meant, to me at least, by the term counselor-centered. In S273, S275, S277, for example, the counselor is so self-centered that he cannot really hear Richard, so that all he does is give a personal answer as if Richard was asking the time of the day.

Case Summary

It would seem from this summary that the counselor did not hear either Richard or himself in quite the same way in the three sessions that we have reviewed that I did as I listened to the tapes.

Self-Evaluation

This gives some reason for the pattern of counselor behavior, although by Session 18 I could hear little indication of the counselor listening or understanding, although, of course, the counselor may have been trying to listen and to understand.

To what extent has the counselor now moved from his own self concern so that he does not have to "try" to listen to the client, so that he can easily and comfortably operate within the client's frame of reference, and so that he has no need to deliberately concoct falsehoods in order to build a relationship with the client?

Edward Roeber

According to the counselor's interview notes, the most productive counseling took place during interviews which were not reported in type-script form. This is almost always the case. The counselor's notes also revealed a steady improvement in Richard's classroom behavior and even school achievement, both of which were more or less attributed to the counseling. Except for an adult-child relationship, one not ordinarily associated with counseling, the counselor's techniques and methodology could hardly account for any improvement. Long, uncomfortable pauses, as well as responses which generally reflected little understanding of Richard's predicament, were so frequent that any "success" could only be caused by a relationship and/or conditions apart from the counseling situation. In many ways, the counselor seemed to play the role of "big brother." With increasing frequency he answered questions or parried them with, "What do you think about it?" In his responses he tried to please Richard, viz., XVIII-C109, "No, I wanted Patterson to win," when the counselor actually had little preference, and Patterson was obviously Richard's preference. This type of verbal interaction might have been even more effective had it taken place on a playground, or sitting on a cracker barrel. If there were any significant changes in Richard's behavior and achievement, it was probably due to an adult who took time to be "big brother," or to be a model that was superior, even with all the counselor's intolerance, to any within Richard's range of experience.

Even though I might like to conclude this review at this point with the generalization that the interviews can hardly be classified as counseling, I feel certain other features of the case carry with them critical lessons for a counselor.

1. The nature of a referral made to a counselor as well as the latter's repertoire for handling a referral is directly related to counseling out-comes. Richard was referred to the clinic by his mother and school coun-selor who were presumably concerned about Richard's behavior and per-formance in school. Although no genius, Richard nevertheless must have wondered what was going to happen to him at the clinic:

> I-S28, "Am I going to do any work here?" I-S40, "Will there be anyone else down here?" I-S42, "What do you do?" I-S52, "Is this where I'm going to be every time someone comes down here, in this room?" I-S86, "When kids come here, what do they do, how old are they?"

In his haste to get to the problem, the counselor indicated little or no empathy for Richard's bewilderment. Without knowing how Richard felt about the idea of coming to the clinic, and specifically the manner in which Richard was probably scheduled by mother without his consent, the counselor launched into, "Would you tell me a little bit about school and the trouble you are having." As mentioned previously, Richard sought clarification but received very little assistance. Richard, therefore, controlled the interviews and turned them into his purpose, a big brother relationship. Recognizing that the referral was probably a poor one, there is still no excuse for a counselor who ignores sensitive areas associated with referrals, good or bad. It is also necessary to recognize the difficulties which may be encountered in structuring the goals of counseling to a junior high school student who has not read the counseling textbook. Meaningful communication in lay language then becomes a major asset to any counselor's repertoire.

2. Continually during the preparation of counselors, emphasis is placed upon good listening and upon productive uses of pauses. The counselor in *The Case of Richard* must have slept through this particular lesson—seldom have I seen pauses used so inexpertly, they almost became depressive. Richard, though, had considerable patience and tolerance—more than the counselor. Certainly the latter exhibited little sensitivity to Richard's discomfort.

3. Counseling is directly dependent upon the quality of the relationship between a counselor and a counselee. Other person-to-person relationships also have their unique qualities and may serve useful purposes. *The Case of Richard* illustrates a noncounseling, person-to-person relationship which had special significance for Richard. Although the counselor's behavior was not a credit to the profession, from Richard's point of view it was probably superior to that of other adults—at least the counselor had the stamina to stay with Richard for eighteen sessions. Perhaps an important hypothesis can be drawn from the case, i.e., a person-to-person relationship, including a counseling relationship, can at times be more potent than techniques or problem solving per se.

In conclusion, the counselor rationalized his behavior in terms of previous preparation in clinical psychology and his work experience. It is difficult to accept this defense—clinical preparation and work, *ipso facto,* do not lead to a cold, calculating approach to other members of the human race. Instead the lack of sensitivity to others' feelings and the art of communicating can certainly be associated with a counselor's personal characteristics. I see little recognition of this hypothesis by the counselor.

BUFORD STEFFLRE

Of the five cases in this book, I find this one the most difficult to conceptualize. The counselor, in his comments and analysis, sounds like a sensible and literate man, and his nineteen hours with the distractible and hebephrenic-like Richard must have given him a new depth in his understanding of the trials of Job. Whether his time was well spent is a more difficult problem to answer.

The case illustrates the difficulties of doing evaluation in counseling. Richard behaves badly in the classroom and gets poor marks. He talks to a counselor nineteen times. Richard then behaves better and his marks improve. Is the talking related to the improvement causally or only temporally? Obviously we don't know (1) if his behavior really changed, (2) if only his teacher's perception of his behavior changed, or (3) if his teachers' system of marking changed. We would be helped in understanding this case by having much more information about Richard's physical development during this six months (if that is how long it took him to have nineteen interviews), his home situation, and his total life space.

Certainly there is no internal evidence in the typescript to suggest any great changes in Richard. We are told of a fine interview (#11) during which he was composed and talked about his feelings but unfortunately the interview was apparently not recorded. We are left, then, with the school counselor's report that "remarkable changes" occurred in Richard and presumably we are under an unspoken obligation to relate the improvement to the nineteen interviews. (I'll try but I remain skeptical about the relationship and about my ability to discover the crucial elements in *The Case of Richard*.)

What are these nineteen conversations between Richard and the Counselor? If the three which are reported are representative of the total, they are not "counseling" according to any standard definition. I cannot believe that this is a "relationship in which one person endeavors to help another to understand and solve his adjustment problems." Do they illustrate "catharsis"? The word typically implies emotionally laden material not found in this case. Are they even "interviews"? Not if we agree with Bingham, that interviews are "conversations with a purpose," for I see no purpose in them. They have elements of "play therapy" with Richard supplying the riddles (first interview), games (twelfth interview), and toys, in the form of the contents of his wallet (eighteenth interview) —but they lack the focus and interpretive purpose characteristic of play therapy.

Is the "success" of *The Case of Richard* explainable by the concept of extinction? Perhaps Richard's anxiety in school leads to aimless talking which leads to punishment which leads to anxiety which leads to more "misbehavior." If so, the nineteen sessions may have permitted him to break the circuit by engaging in much unpunished behavior of the kind which was previously reinforced. (Granted such an explanation is tenuous and farfetched—but I don't have to believe it, just present it!)

I suppose the most salable explanation would be one which hypothesizes a supporting relationship between the counselor and Richard of such a nature that Richard first changed his views of himself and then changed his behavior so that it was more in line with his new views of his worth. If this is the explanation we are to use, what was the source of the support Richard found in the relationship? First, the counselor remained physically present while permitting Richard to control the conversation for nineteen hours—no mean feat! Second, with a few exceptions (eighteenth interview C234), the counselor successfully concealed his annoyance with Richard's ramblings. Third, Richard obviously liked the counselor and must have been gratified, if not by a return of his affection, at least by the absence of overt rejection.

If these interviews do not embody all we would like, what do we propose as more suitable treatment for Richard? First, a thorough health check would have made the counseling approach to his distractibility more defensible. Next a school that could not be characterized by remarks such as those at S50, 60, 162, and 164 in the first interview would help all the Richards in their confusion. Finally, a patient, interested adult, of the kind embodied in this counselor, placed somewhere in Richard's life, perhaps as a coach, a neighbor, a teacher, or a playground director, might help his situation.

To the counselor it remains but to say that if he wishes to counsel it will probably be necessary for him to recognize and use the relationship between the client and the counselor. In the first interview, at S40, 52, and 86 to 96, Richard seems to be trying to talk about his relationship to the counselor, who does not permit him to do so. Throughout the other two interviews, by his request for a picture, his concern for the counselor's clothes, and his gift of candy, and particularly by his poignant remark at S245 in the eighteenth interview, he is trying to explore the relationship with the counselor but the counselor will have none of it. Before relationship therapy can be therapy it must admit and explore the relationship. I wonder if the counselor's avoidance is a deliberate effort to keep the interviews casual or is it a way to keep from exposing himself as a person. In either event he succeeds wonderfully well, but at the expense of trading nineteen counseling sessions for nineteen conversations in search of a purpose.

In summary, I fail to see pattern or form in these talks. If the counselor worked from a theoretical base I do not discover it. His patience, however, is monumental and this may have been a rare commodity in Richard's life. In future cases the counselor may want to distinguish between catharsis and talk, between physical and psychological relationship, between listening and receiving, and between reports of change in the client and evidence of the worth of counseling. The fine case analysis suggests that these and other subtler distinctions are well within the possible responses of this counselor.

SIGNIFICANT QUESTIONS FOR DISCUSSION

1. In what ways does this case point up the distinction between conversation and counseling?

2. The counselor who made the referral was questioned after the tenth interview as to Richard's status in school. His response was, "Whatever you're doing keep it up. He's no longer getting into trouble." All three reviewers agreed that there is no evidence of real counseling taking place. What might account for the changed behavior if the relationship defies our concepts of being a helping one?

3. In the counselor's self-evaluation he indicates that he was "impatient with his barrage of questions and annoyed with the way he was controlling me and the interview." Can a school counselor feel this way about a client and still develop a positive relationship with him?

4. If you had been the counselor in what ways might you have handled the client differently?

5. If you had a chance to talk with the counselor, what would you have wanted to discuss with him after each interview?

6. Where do the reviewers agree and disagree in their review of *The Case of Richard?* What are your reactions to the reviews?

SUGGESTIONS FOR DISCUSSION

III

ASSESSING
COMPETENCY

Reactions to the Reviews

Dugald Arbuckle

As I read, for the first time, the reactions of my counseling educator colleagues to Carl, Jack, Jane, Edna and Richard, and to their counselors, several thoughts come to mind.

1. The reviewers, as well as the counselors and the clients, have their own particular set of glasses, rose tinted or otherwise, and they see the counselors and the clients from their own particular frame of reference. This suggests that if the student counselors discussed in this book were to have as their practicum adviser one of the reviewers instead of another, they would not necessarily hear the same thing regarding their effectiveness as a counselor. The counselor of Carl, for example, might have had the following said to him:

From Arbuckle: You start off very dominant, but appear to become more acceptant of the client, who seems to make real progress. You tend to be too concerned with techniques and methodology.

From Stefflre: Your third interview was good, but the last was not very good. You were not "close" to the client.

From Roeber: By interview three you were doing pretty well, but you withdrew too much in the last interview—you became a silent partner. You follow the words but not the melody.

From Dugan and Blocher: You made excellent use of techniques, and created a warm positive relationship. In the last interview Carl was able to talk more positively about himself. You need to accept more responsibility.

Jack's counselor might hear the following:

From Arbuckle: You have difficulty accepting Jack, and insist on dominating and controlling him. You tend to be too "technique" centered. You are not too aware of "self" as yet, but you show high promise of self-understanding.

From Stefflre: You follow the "party line," but you are on your way to becoming a competent counselor—and a free person.

From Roeber: You are too "methodology" centered. You did not establish too much in the way of a positive relationship with Jack.

From Dugan and Blocher: You were too "technique" centered. There appeared to be little or no communication with Jack. You appear to have no goals.

Jane's counselor might hear:

From Arbuckle: You understand intellectually, but did not appear to get close, and to empathize with Jane. You stressed the intellectual content rather than the feelings, which were more apparent on the tape than in the typescript.

From Stefflre: You did little more than respond with restatement of content. You were skilled in omission, and you appeared to avoid areas where you felt uncomfortable. I have respect for your analytic ability.

From Roeber: You appear to be dedicated to a client-centered methodology. You have more than the ordinary talent for counseling.

2. The differing frames of reference also show up in the degree to which the reviewers stress different aspects of the sessions. There is a difference on the stress of the relationship of cultural and environmental factors to the client (with Stefflre probably putting most stress on this), on the degree of the analysis of the client (with Arbuckle possibly putting the least stress on this), and on the extent to which there are better and different ways of making more effective use of tests in counseling (with Roeber probably stressing this the most).

3. These differences tend to show the necessity of the counselor educator being stable enough so that he is capable of being content with the student counselor learning from him, rather than becoming a carbon copy of him. This also means that the student counselor must,

at least by the time of counseling practicum, have developed a strong enough self-concept so that he is willing and able to learn from the counselor educator, but he has no need to copy him.

4. These reviews suggest that counselor educators must be very wary of their particular version of counselor adequacy. The student counselor who is not willing to accept the counselor educators' version of counselor effectiveness, may be closer to "right" rather than "wrong." Possibly the best way out of this dilemma is to make sure that the adequacy of a student counselor is always the cumulative version of several counselor educators who have had contact with him, and that he is never left to the mercy of one counselor educator and his particular set of biases. I have a hunch that the reviewers in this book, despite their apparent differences, could easily come to some common agreement on each of the student counselors. It is equally obvious, on the other hand, that if the evaluation of the student counselor was solely dependent on one of these counselor educators, it would differ from one to the other.

Edward Roeber

For the five practicum cases, reviewers identified and described many questionable counselor behaviors. To list again all of the counselors' deeds and misdeeds, most of them regularly committed in a practicum, would be an anticlimax to a series of interesting reviews. Instead I prefer to react to four sets of stimuli, two of them furnished by specific statements of reviewers, and two of them reactions to the five cases as a whole.

Although I do not wish to champion the performance of *all* school counselors, I take exception to Dr. Stefflre's statement in *The Case of Carl* (p. 68), "Taken as a whole, this is better counseling than Carl would get in ninety-five per cent of our schools or training laboratories." In *The Case of Carl* you will recall that the counselor withdrew from active participation in the final interview, and Carl was obliged to carry on a monologue. Such counselor behavior is so inadequate that Stefflre's indictment is unjustly severe. It gives little credit to those school counselors who are performing acceptably. I cannot believe that ninety-five per cent of the school counselors perform so miserably as Carl's counselor. At least before accepting this statistic, I would like to examine the data which Stefflre used to derive his generalization.

Also in *The Case of Carl,* I take exception to Dr. Arbuckle's comment (p. 62), "Many of the comments that follow seem to illustrate the difficulty of trying to combine a counseling function with an information giving function." (He further implies that information should be dispensed by a secretary, or by written word, or by someone other than a counselor.) This dichotomy between counseling and information giving is, of course, characteristic of a client-centered point of view. It is simple to defend such a position because, by definition, information giving is excluded from the counseling function. I question the exclusion of information giving from the counseling function and believe that school counselors can use information during a counseling interview without playing the role of God, a teacher, or an autocrat. Not all maturation processes of students are consummated through self-discovery. In most cases, students lack experiences from which to develop necessary self-perceptions, and information is one form of experience. A skillful school counselor is able to use various forms of information as a vehicle for assisting students to higher levels of self-understanding. Generally speaking, it is not merely a case of giving information to someone but rather one of eliciting reactions so that the information is actually used to explore attitudes, values, and other facets of affective and cognitive behavior. Furthermore, I question Arbuckle's generalization when the rationale for it is always based upon counselors who are obviously unfamiliar with the information they are attempting to use and have not developed sufficient skills for using the information. It would make as much sense as condemning client-centered counseling because a group of practicum counselors, such as those in this series of cases, was unable to use effectively and consistently a client-centered methodology.

Turning now to the five cases as a group, I feel somewhat uneasy about them, and especially so if anyone assumes that they are typical of a school counselor's ideal caseload. After reviewing the five cases, I wondered why they all had a focus upon family and other interpersonal relationships. It seems to me that a practicum counselor on his way to becoming a school counselor might develop "tunnel vision" if he were only exposed to this set of counseling cases. Counseling situations which could involve more than seventy-five per cent of a student body do not depend upon long-term series of contacts with "therapy" overtones. Instead there may be two or three contacts throughout a school year with many students, the nature of these contacts would be as surely counseling as those represented by these cases. Certainly, the latter type of interviews may not contain materials which have as much intrinsic interest for a case-book as those of Jane, Carl, or Jack; but these interviews may have as much, if not more, impact upon a larger number of students who can also be assisted to higher levels of planning, development, and adjustment. Inadvertently, many circumstances dictate the case material in a casebook, and yet the content of such a book may lead to erroneous conclusions regarding the work of a school counselor. I guess my major concern is that a prospective school counselor who reads these cases does not assume that this type of "problem" counseling represents the highest priority for his future workload.

A final observation is warranted from a study of the case reviews. Again and again reviewers emphasize the personal development which a practicum counselor must undertake if he is to become a proficient, independently functioning counselor. These cases demonstrate rather dramatically the individual differences which exist among counselors as they interact with counselees. They also show in what ways each counselor, if he is to attain an acceptable level of proficiency in helping relationships, must understand himself, must conceptualize all his learnings, and must develop a personal philosophy and theory of counseling. It is equally obvious that a summer practicum, or even a one-semester practicum, may not be long enough for a typical practicum counselor to initiate some personal plan of action toward the mastery of the aforesaid developmental tasks. Counseling practicums, although becoming more common each year in programs of counselor preparation, are unrealistically too short in duration for the typical practicum counselor. It seems that the length of a practicum, on the other hand, must eventually depend upon the length of time it takes for a given practicum counselor to attain an acceptable proficiency level and must lead to an endorsement only when a counselor demonstrates this level of proficiency.

Buford Stefflre

As I read the comments of the four reviewers I am reminded of the folk tale of the blind men who met an elephant. The first blind man touched the elephant's tail and went away telling people that an elephant was like a rope. The second blind man touched a leg and believed for the rest of his life that an elephant was like a tree. The third, who touched the side, thought the elephant was like a house. And the fourth, who touched an ear, thought the elephant like a fan. In the present context it is left for the reader to put the elephant back together and see that he is more than any one reviewer believed him to be. For myself, I sometimes found it very difficult to believe that the other reviewers had met the same elephant that I had.

At this point it seems only fair that someone now publish a book built around the reactions of these five counselors to the work of the reviewers. Perhaps they could visit our classes and then write up their reactions to what they saw. They could question our theoretical orientation to teaching, our techniques, and make kindly, but slighting, remarks about our naïveté, authoritarianism, and lack of central purpose. Obviously, their reactions would need to be documented by reference to a typescript of the class sessions, thereby making their criticism "objective." In short, I am feeling somewhat guilty as I read the almost uniformly critical and negative reactions that I had to the work of these student counselors.

In spite of these twinges of guilt, I believe that I would hold to my original judgment in most of the cases and in most details. This perseverance means either that I am excessively rigid or that my original reactions were excessively shrewd and penetrating. The one change that I might make would be in *The Case of Jack* where it now seems to me that perhaps I was unduly impressed by the counselor's energy and activity and insufficiently critical of his lack of a consistent theoretical orientation. Random activity may be better used to get a cat, than a counselor, out of a box.

As I look at the completed product it now seems to me that it might have been a mistake that three of the cases were of both low ability and presumably of minority group membership—Carl, Edna, and Richard. At the same time it was probably also a mistake, because it gave a somewhat unbalanced picture of school counseling, to have three of the clients involuntary referrals—Jack, Edna, and Richard.

I am not now as convinced of the teaching value of these exercises as I was when I undertook my part in the project. I fear that the student of counseling may find these diverse reactions and, at least my own, too frequent concern with minutiae to be confusing and distracting rather than clarifying. Perhaps illustrations of "better" cases would have served the pedagogic purpose more successfully.

Finally, I would say that the exercise of writing these reviews has been interesting and helpful to me and the pleasure of reading them, as they were done by the other reviewers, has resulted in profit and pleasure and possibly even some insight into my reasons for my reactions.

William Evraiff

That the reviewers knew nothing about the five counselors might not affect their reviews, but would it affect supervision? It is quite probable that the counselor educators would differ considerably in the manner in which they approached an actual supervisory situation with any one of the practicum counselors.

The counselors who handled the cases in this book were of varying professional backgrounds. Carl's counselor was an advanced graduate student with three years of teaching experience in a junior high school, but no previous counseling experience. Jane was counseled by a young woman with just one year of teaching experience in a junior high school; this was her first case. Jack's counselor had been a high school counselor for several years and had had about eight years of teaching experience. The counselor who worked with Edna and her mother was in her early fifties and had several years of teaching and counseling experience in junior high school. Richard's counselor was a young man who had no public school teaching or counseling experience, but he brought with him a good background in clinical psychology.

Practicum experiences are intended to give student counselors an opportunity to apply the information from their counseling courses and to develop counseling skill by working with real clients under supervision. The author, in working with student counselors in a practicum, encourages them to develop their own counseling approach, but it is evident that many students tend to adopt what they believe to be their supervisor's bias. This is clearly demonstrated in *The Case of Edna* where the counselor in her self-evaluation indicates her fright at the thought that she *had* to be client-centered. She expressed this fear to her supervisor in the statement, "Oh, I thought we had to do it a certain way at the lab, not like the way I'd do it on the job." Although it is easy to pick out weaknesses in their counseling procedures, most clearly seen in their use of test materials, these five counselors constitute a better than average group of students in a practicum experience.

No counselor-educator or school counselor could help being intrigued by the diversity among the reviewers in their reactions to each case. For example, what makes it possible for Arbuckle and Dugan, who hold opposite theoretical views, to have positive feelings about the fourth interview in *The Case of Carl*, while Roeber and Stefflre had negative reactions? Or consider *The Case of Jane*. Roeber comments that, "There is a dedicated commitment by the counselor to a client-centered methodology," and, "On the whole, the counselor indicated more than ordinary talent for counseling." Arbuckle, however, states, "In these three sessions the counselor was with Jane, but usually only in words, not in feeling; she understood intellectually, but she did not empathize." With whom does one agree? What brings about this difference in perception regarding counselor skill? These are challenging questions that remain unanswered, but ones which should stimulate a good deal of discussion among all professional people interested in school counseling.

The variation in the reviews might create an initial impression that there is a real conflict among those who have different counseling points of view. The author prefers to believe that in a series of counseling contacts the reviewers would be able to agree among themselves as to the competency of a particular counselor. But, as Arbuckle points out, we might want to be sure that a student "is never left to the mercy of one counselor-educator and his particular set of biases."

This book might legitimately be subtitled, "Helping Counselor-Educators Grow Professionally," and counselor-educators would be the first to acknowledge the need for continued professional growth. It seems apparent that we would benefit by meeting in postdoctoral seminars to discuss material similar to that contained in this book. Perhaps too many of us in counseling have become Don Quixote's, and are tilting at windmills on such matters as counseling methods. Perhaps, instead, we should come to grips with the difficulties of helping school counselors function professionally in the realities of their complicated world, the school setting.

Competency, Educators, and the Counselor's Self-Concept

"In order for a person to be fully functioning, when he looks at his self, as he must, he must see that it is enough—enough to perform the task at hand. He must see in his experiential background some history of success."[1]

The counselor's self-concept has particular relevance at three times in his career: at the time of his application for admission to a counselor education program; while a graduate student studying to be a counselor; and, finally, while functioning as a counselor on a real job.

There are few, if any, counselor-educators who would claim that their selection process succeeds in admitting only candidates who possess a high degree of psychological maturity. Many factors must be considered in the problem of admissions. What motivates a teacher's desire to become a counselor? How many are seeking to fulfill personal needs? Has the teacher had a "history of success" or is it occasionally the reverse? How often do teachers retire from the classroom because they think counseling will be easier? How many teachers view counseling as offering prestige, higher salaries, or a step towards becoming an administrator? It is quite probable that there is a combination of motivational factors which combine to produce aspiring school counselors. To uncover these factors, let alone assign hierarchical value to them, seems impossible as well as of doubtful value. We would still be left with the question, can this person become a competent counselor?

The school counselor begins his professional education with a self-concept, subject to the same anxieties experienced by clients approaching the counseling situation. The concept of anxiety cannot be adequately conveyed to a counselor if it remains an academic issue divorced from the reality of the counselor's perceptions, feelings, and impulses.

The initial difficulty in counseling, experienced by many graduate students, probably stems from unclear concepts of counseling and counselors. Eventually, each student counselor begins to develop a clear image of the kind of counselor he wants to become. This image permeates the counseling sessions and influences the counseling process. It thus affects the counselor's procedures, the client's perception of the counselor, and the kind of relationship that is eventually established. Each counselor needs to have counseling experiences compatible with his self-image if he is going to be at ease with himself and grow towards increasing competence. But, a counselor who devotes his energies to the pursuit

[1] Earl C. Kelley, "The Fully Functioning Self," *Perceiving, Behaving, Becoming: A New Focus for Education*, ASCD 1962 Yearbook. Washington, D.C.: The Association for Supervision and Curriculum Development, a department of the National Education Association, 1962, p. 10.

of an idealized and unrealistic self may be unable to discover and develop real strengths. The process of understanding others, and helping others to understand themselves, requires real self-understanding on the part of the counselor. If a helping relationship is the kind created by a person who is psychologically mature, the degree to which a counselor can create relationships which facilitate the growth of students is a measure of the growth the counselor has achieved in himself.[2]

Can an individual studying counseling dare to reveal his real perceptions, attitudes, values and beliefs while he is himself engaged in the learning process? To what extent is a counselor's picture of himself as a counselor influenced or distorted by instructors? Is the counselor, as a student, free to develop his own image of a counselor, or must he be bound by the image projected by the professional figures in his life? As was pointed out earlier, the counselor's ability to function is affected by the expectations of those with whom he works in his school. In the same sense his ability to grow in understanding and competency will be somewhat determined by his instructors.

There are many teachers in counselor-education who feel, quite strongly, that they can help a counselor become more competent only if they themselves can create understanding, accepting, and permissive relationships with their students. They are undoubtedly influenced by the belief that students can examine their feelings and conflicts only when they feel they are understood, and feel free from the threat of external evaluation. The difficulty in accomplishing this has been illustrated in striking fashion by Carl Rogers.

> "For myself I find it easier to feel this kind of understanding, and to communicate it, to individual clients than to students in a class or staff members in a group in which I am involved. There is a strong temptation to set students straight, or to point out to a staff member the errors in his thinking. Yet when I can permit myself to understand in these situations, it is mutually rewarding." And later, "Can I free him from the threat of external evaluation? In almost every phase of our lives—at home, at school, at work—we find ourselves under the rewards and punishments of external judgments. 'That's good'; 'That's naughty.' 'That's worth an A'; 'that's a failure.' 'That's good counseling'; 'that's poor counseling.' Such judgments are a part of our lives from infancy to old age. I believe they have a certain social usefulness to institutions and organizations such as schools and professions. Like everyone else I find myself all too often making such evaluations. But, in my experience, they do not make for personal growth and hence I do not believe that they are a part of a helping relationship. Curiously enough a positive evaluation is as threatening in the long run as a negative one, since to inform someone that he is good implies that you also have the right to tell him he is bad. So I have come

2 Carl Rogers, "The Characteristics of a Helping Relationship," *The Personnel and Guidance Journal.* Washington, D.C.: A.P.G.A., Sept. 1958, Vol. XXXVII, No. 1, pp. 13-14.

to feel that the more I can keep a relationship free of judgment and evaluation, the more this will permit the other person to reach the point where he recognizes that the locus of evaluation, the center of responsibility, lies within himself. The meaning and value of his experience is in the last analysis something which is up to him, and no amount of external judgment can alter this. So I should like to work toward a relationship in which I am not, even in my own feelings, evaluating him. This I believe can set him free to be a self-responsible person."[3]

Why does Rogers find it difficult to promote this kind of growth with students in his classes? Is there a thin line of distinction between helping people grow personally and professionally? The counselor's first obligation is to the client. Is the counselor-educator's obligation primarily to the student counselor, or to the future clients who may or may not be helped by the student counselor? That this presents a conflict is a gross understatement. There are few counselor-educators, if any, who approach their evaluation and recommendation of student counselors with the feeling that their judgment is infallible. The fact that the counselor-educator can never totally remove himself from the role of professional evaluator is bound to influence the perception the student counselor has of him. If the student's graduate advisor or supervisor can't function as an accepting, non-threatening adult, who can? Perhaps it must be someone else on the staff: a counselor in the counseling center, or an advanced graduate student assigned to help beginners. At any rate, it must be someone who will not use the relationship judgmentally, and who will not rate the student as being a good, mediocre, or poor counselor.

What happens to the school counselor once he leaves the security of the counseling laboratory and the theoretical influences of the university? What will the counselor do if the realities of the job don't seem to permit him to function in a manner that gives him satisfaction. Will he change the experiences that are making him dissatisfied, will he distort the experiences so that he can once more be comfortable with himself as a counselor, or will he revise the image he had of himself as a student counselor? What he does may be a reflection of the way in which he learned to handle the anxieties and hostilities that have arisen at other crucial points in his life. (In some cases it becomes necessary for even the most psychologically mature counselor to get a new job in a different school system or become a counselor-educator.)

We have learned a great deal about the many facets of the counseling process, and can study techniques quite accurately. We are also in agreement on the need to develop healthy relationships and the need to help the student move toward mature and responsible self-direction. Although there has been much concern with counselor-education, we still do not know a great deal about helping people become "good" counselors. We

3 Ibid., pp. 13-14.

attempt to impart understandings and skills to those already in the program with academic ability, sensitivity potential, and some degree of inner security. The counseling profession is moving toward a recognition that the encounter with self-acceptance and self-understanding must take place in the life of the counselor as well as in that of the client. Each counselor needs, ultimately, to be his own evaluator. This is particularly true in the counseling function because what goes on in the privacy of the school counselor's office cannot be assessed accurately by others. Only the counselor's alter ego furnishes the motivating drive towards becoming and remaining a professionally qualified counselor.